The

ROBIN WOOD TAROT:

The Book

Bright Blessings!

R. Wood

BY ROBIN WOOD

#104/500

The Robin Wood Tarot: The Book

A Livingtree Book / July 1998

All rights reserved

Copyright © 1998 by Robin Wood

Library of Congress Catalog Card Number: 98-091568

ISBN: 0-9652984-1-8

Book Design by Robin Wood

Cover © Robin Wood 1998

Tarot Cards © Robin Wood 1991

Chapter Heading Illustrations © Robin Wood 1998

Fonts: Adobe Garamond Book, Bold, and Italic; Adobe Caslon Expert Regular

No part of this book may be reproduced or transmitted in any form or by any means,
electronic or mechanical, including photocopying, recording, or by any information storage
and retrieval system, without permission in writing from the publisher.

We are dedicated to reducing waste of all kinds.
Because of this, we don't permit our covers to be "stripped" for returns,
but instead require that the entire book be returned, so we can resell it. Thank you.

For information contact:

Robin Wood
3319 Greenfield #102
Dearborn, MI 48120

or visit our website at:

http://www.robinwood.com

Table of Contents

This book is dedicated to the unknown people who first developed the Tarot, to all those who helped me, and put up with me, and fed me, and posed for me while I was making the Robin Wood Tarot, and to everyone who bought one of the decks, and enjoyed the cards.
Thank you all. I owe you more than I can say.

Special thanks to the folk at Dragonspawn Crafthall, whose fine jewelry work inspired the leafy vines on the front cover.
I owe you guys!

But most of all, Thanks to my wonderful husband, Michael Short, without whose hours of patient work, loving care, and rummaging for ISBN programs on the Internet, this book would not have been possible.
I love you!

Forward

All Right.
You Win.*

*This footnote doesn't count against the "four word" word count,** but may serve to explain. You see, for many years now (ever since the Robin Wood Tarot came out,) people have been asking me for a book explaining all of the symbolism for each card. For just as many years, I have been trying to get someone else to write this book, or waiting for people to stop asking me, or just plain putting it off. Now, however, I am writing it. So all those people who have been after me for so long finally win.

**Footnote to the footnote (is that allowed?) Why not take the term *four word* literally? Writing as Haiku, only different!

Chapter 1
This Book

Almost twenty years ago, I became interested in the study of the Tarot, and began my journey along that path.

This book is my way of sharing that journey with you, because so many people have asked me to help them with their own exploration of the Tarot.

Here, I will share with you what I have discovered about the origins of these cards, and how they evolved into the tool that we have today. I will also give you the history of my own deck, the Robin Wood Tarot; why I decided to make it, and what happened after that decision was made.

I'll discuss the "language" of the Tarot, the symbols and colors that are common to many decks, and the patterns that I saw emerging from them, and so used in my own. To put it as simply as possible, my interpretations of the various common symbols.

There will be a section where I explore how the Tarot works; both the reasons that I have heard from various people, and the reason that I have found for myself.

The bulk of this book will be given to a detailed discussion of why I choose the particular symbols that appear on each card; what I was thinking at the time, and what those symbols mean to me.

I'll also teach you how to go about reading the cards, the way I teach it to my students. These are the methods that I recommend, including preparing yourself and the space that you will be using.

Finally, I'll speak briefly about "spreads," the patterns in which the cards are laid out. I'm not going to go into exhaustive detail there, though, because the book quickly became far larger than I had anticipated. Instead, there will be a companion workbook to this book, covering all the information I have collected about various spreads, and so on. I'm sorry to have to do it that way, but economics being what they are, I didn't feel that there was a better choice.

Throughout this book, I will emphasize the secret of reading the Tarot. It's simply this. Trust your own instincts!

When you lay out the cards, in whatever pattern you choose to use, you will get an immediate, visceral response to them. Use it.

The cards work beautifully as a gateway to open your own awareness of what is happening at a very subtle level, and to allow you to pick up information from things you are not even aware of intellectually.

I advise you to allow this to happen. Don't hinder the process by looking everything up in a book (not even this one!) The meanings in the books are sometimes contradictory, sometimes confusing, and sometimes they will feel odd to you. The meanings in your heart, when you look at the cards actually spread out before you, are far more likely to be accurate.

This is because the meanings of every card depend on the other cards in the spread with them. Since it's impossible to give all the combinations of cards in a book, it's just skipped altogether. This isn't accurate, but it's the best compromise possible under the circumstances. But don't be fooled! The meanings given in isolation are not the actual, only, totally accurate meanings of the card.

I've been teaching people in workshops and gatherings all over the country to read by tossing the book, and letting the cards speak to them, for many years now. And a few people are made nervous by this approach. They have asked me if just looking at the cards doesn't unbalance the meanings. If a card never looks to a Reader as if it means what it's "supposed" to mean, then isn't that concept missing from the deck?

I don't think so. In my experience, a reader who cannot see the traditional meaning in one card will find that very meaning in another. So my advice is not to worry about it. It all comes out in the wash.

But, and I cannot emphasize this point enough, that is my opinion. In fact, nearly everything in this book is my opinion. It's not gospel, it's not the one right way, and just because it's true for me doesn't necessarily mean that it will be true for you!

We are individuals, and we each bring our own unique perspective to everything we do.

The only things in this book that I will tell you without any room for disagreement are absolutely true are the things about me. Where I was, what I was doing, my reasoning behind things, and so on. I know these things, and that's that! But those are the only things I do know, with absolute certainty.

Even the "facts" given in the chapter about the History of the Tarot may be faulty. I'm depending on other people for research here, because my publisher (who is me) won't fly me to Paris to look things up for myself. And if I did get there it would do me little good, because my French is virtually non-existent!

So you can see that I'm not about to argue with you about the meanings behind the more esoteric things in this book. I think that the color yellow represents joy and vitality, for instance. If you think of a yellow traffic light when you see this color, and for you it means "proceed with caution," then that is what it means when you are reading the cards!

Do you see?

This whole business of reading the Tarot is a partnership between the person who designed the deck, and the one who is reading. I put certain symbols there, but you are the one who has to interpret them. I did my best to make them as clear as I could; but they are, when you get down to it, those symbols that had meaning for me, that evoked the response I needed to each of the cards in the deck.

That is why it's so important that you pick a deck that feels "right" to you, that uses the symbols that you are comfortable with. And if that isn't mine, that's

OK too! I mean, sure, I'd like everyone to have a copy of my deck. Who wouldn't? But I long ago got over the feeling that everyone has to agree with me, or my opinions are valueless.

A lot of people have written to me, and told me how much they enjoy my deck and how well it works for them. And that makes me very happy. But people, it's not the only deck out there, by a long shot.

And even if it's the one you like best, and I have to assume that you like something about it, or you wouldn't be reading this book, I'll bet that the interpretations that I give to some of the cards are different than the ones you use.

And that's fine!

Remember that as you read this book. If something that I say just doesn't fit in with your world view, then don't get upset. We can agree to disagree. It's like the story of the Blind Men and the Elephant. (Which is in Appendix A, in case you aren't familiar with the story.)

I'll listen to your view, and you listen to mine, and perhaps we can triangulate, and compare, and between them we might actually get a better picture of the shape of the whole animal!

That being said, let's begin our exploration of the Tarot in general, and my own deck in particular.

Chapter 2
The True History
of the Tarot

The true history of the tarot can be told in a single sentence.
No one knows, and does it really make any difference?

Chapter 3
History Theories

While I was doing the research for this chapter, I found so many conflicting theories, and refutations of those theories, that I was left with the feeling that, in an attempt to make the whole thing even more mystical and magical than it already is, someone had been fudging.

But as I dug deeper, a picture began to emerge, mainly because several of the most recent authors knew who had been doing the obfuscation, and weren't afraid to expose the guilty parties.

Now, I'm assuming that their research was correct. I don't have the budget to go to France (where most of it seems to have happened) to check it out myself.

But here is what I've found, and the names of those who provided the various bits of information.

Playing cards seem to have appeared sometime in the fourteenth century.

Barbara G. Walker, in *The Secrets of the Tarot*,* states that "Tarot cards were the ancestors of modern playing cards" as if it were a fact, and goes on to assure us that the Trumps were suppressed by the Church; but she gives no evidence to support this.

Sally Gearhart and Susan Rennie, in *A Feminist Tarot*,** tell us that the earliest deck still in existence is composed of 17 cards, now in the possession of the Bibliotheque National in Paris, that belonged to Charles VI of France. They note that the court treasurer showed payment to an artist named Jacquemin Gringoneur for 3 packs of these cards in 1392. (They don't, however, tell us how much he was paid.) I find this amusing for a couple of reasons. The first is that Charles VI of France was also known as Charles the Mad, and the Grolier encyclopedia says that his bouts of insanity began in 1392. The second is that according to Walker the cards were banned in Paris in 1397, only 5 years later. (Since we still have them, the king must have been allowed to keep his deck.)

Ronald Decker, Thierry Depaulis & Michael Dummett, in *A Wicked Pack of Cards*,*** on the other hand, say that the proof of payment and the existence of the Charles VI deck as proof of a fourteenth century date for Tarot cards was "propagated in 1842 by the French antiquarian M.C. Leber." They point out that the payment did happen, and that there is a deck, which was in the collection of Roger de Gaignières in France by 1698 at the latest; but there is no evidence that the cards are Gringonneur's, or that Gringonneur's cards were Tarot cards, which

---

* *The Secrets of the Tarot Origins, History, and Symbolism* by Barbara Walker ©1984. Published by Harper & Row. ISBN 0-06-250927-6

** *A Feminist Tarot* by Sally Gearhart and Susan Rennie ©1981. Published by Alyson Publications, Inc., Boston. ISBN 0 932870 56 2

*** *A Wicked Pack of Cards* Ronald Decker, Thierry DePaulis & Michael Dummett © 1996. Published by St. Martin's Press, NY NY. ISBN: 0-312-16294-4

they say were not generally known in France before the Sixteenth century. They point out, as well, that this was first noted by W.A. Chatto in 1848, and again by R. Merlin in 1869. Using the normal scholarly method of dating artwork by costume, artistic style and close similarity of design with other work, whose dates are known, (in this case a deck made for Ercole I d'Este, Duke of Ferrara or his predecessor Borso d'Este,) the "Charles VI" tarots are now commonly identified as having been painted by a Ferrarese artist in about 1480.

Anthony Lewis, in *Tarot Plain and Simple*,* says the first mention of the Tarot is when King Alfonse XI of Leon and Castile issued a proclamation banning its use in 1332. By the end of that century, says Walker, lots of places had banned them, starting with Florence in 1376 followed by Germany in 1378, Marseilles in 1381, and so on. (I have been unable to verify any of that; but then, I don't have a law library or anything of the sort handy, and I couldn't find the information on the internet.)

In fact, most of the authors that I examined who placed the date of the earliest decks sometime in the 1300s, seem to use as evidence the banning of decks. But Cynthia Giles, in *The Tarot: History, Mystery and Lore*** states that these bannings may have been based more in economics than in morality. She says that in 1441 the Magistracy of Venice banned the importation of cards to protect its own cardmaking industry, and by 1464 England had done the same. But, as she also points out, we don't know what proportion of those cards banned had trumps. She also states that there was a four suited deck before there were trumps, and says that in 1377 a Swiss monk mentioned a four suited deck, but made no mention of trumps.

Decker et al state that all of these were regular playing cards, which they say "reached Europe from the Islamic world in the second half of the XIV century in a form with fifty-two cards, consisting of four suits of ten numeral cards and three court cards each." They further state that the suit signs used on the Tarot cards were those used on normal Italian cards until the end of the fifteenth century. The suits that we have now in English speaking countries are actually a French design that employed stencils, and therefore was easier (and cheaper) to make than the previous ones, which needed woodcuts. It was a marketing coup that occurred in about 1470, they tell us. They go on to say these suit signs are by no means the universal ones we tend to think they are.

They place the date of the earliest deck of Tarot cards as 1450, and base this on a letter, written by Duke Francesco Sforza to his treasurer, asking that a Tarot pack be sent to him, or, if one couldn't be found, "an ordinary deck of playing cards."

They further state that all fifteenth century references specifically to the Tarot (as opposed to cards) are from Italy, and that is where they were invented. From

---

* *Tarot Plain and Simple* by Anthony Lewis © 1996. Published by Llewellyn Publications, St. Paul. ISBN 1-56718-400-6

** *The Tarot: History, Mystery and Lore* by Cynthia Giles ©1992. Paragon House. ISBN 1-55778-312-8

there they spread to France and Switzerland, due, they are sure, to the wars. And from there, I presume, to the rest of Europe.

Both Decker et al and Giles say that the Trumps appeared in the fifteenth century.

The evidence is overwhelming that, whenever and wherever the Tarot was invented, it was mostly used in a family of games known collectively as Trionfi, Tarocchi, Tarrock, Triumphs, or Trumps. (A set of rules for one variation of this game is given in Appendix D.)

Decker et al say that the game originated among the upper classes, and was picked up by the lower ones. As evidence they state that the earliest painted decks that survive are older than the oldest printed decks, which would have been used by the masses.

Giles quotes Robert V. O'Neill, from his book *Tarot Symbolism*, which I was unable to get, who uses very well reasoned arguments to show that it went the other way 'round. He points out that the hand-painted decks of the nobility were much more likely to be saved than the cheap woodcut ones of the peasants. He also observes that the printed decks we do have have "more interesting symbolism than the painted ones." By which he means that the painted ones seem to be toned down, as if to suit the delicate sensibilities of ladies. He also says that there is not a single Devil or Tower card left among the 7 partial decks derived from one Bonifacio Bembo (an early Tarot artist, who, according to Giles, was working sometime after 1440, and painted several decks known as the Visconti decks) and that the odds "of losing these cards by chance among the surviving decks is twelve in 10,000." He argues that they weren't lost, they were never made, because they weren't considered suitable for Royal Ladies.

No matter which way it went, we know that these games became immensely popular, and were played by all social classes all over Europe for centuries.

The only actual evidence that I could find that they were used for anything other than games comes from Decker et al, who say that in Italy, in the seventeenth century, they were being used in "a curious minor verse form known as tarocchi appropriati. The poet selected twenty-two people from some group…and assigned one of the trumps (including the … Fool) to each of them." Then each would be described using a verse which included the name of the Trump card. But this was neither esoteric nor divinatory. They also describe several other games which use the names of the cards, or verses printed on them, for amusement. And they mention two Discorsi (orations) from the sixteenth century which attempt to find meanings in the cards; but they state that the "proposed interpretations" were neither plausible nor esoteric.

None of the other authors had any evidence that the cards were used for anything except playing one form or another of Tarocchi, if you discount the few who still hold to the idea that they came from Egypt with the Gypsies, and they used them as we do.

And I think that's safe to discount, since the Gypsies didn't come from Egypt, but from India, (where, according to the *Grolier Multimedia Encyclopedia,* they were know as Dom,) arriving in Europe, according to Giles, in 1411. Giles (among others) also points out that when the Romany people tell fortunes, they generally engage in palmistry. When they do use cards (and she says there is no evidence that they ever did before the 18th century) they used, and still use, an ordinary deck. (And, in fact, I can add here from my own experience that the only person I know who was taught to read cards by her mother, who was taught by *her* mother, and down through the generations, was taught to use a regular deck, not a Tarot deck.)

Decker et al write that the whole Gypsy connection was first explored (as opposed to mentioned; de Geblein mentioned it in the eighteenth century) by a writer named Boiteau d'Ambly in *Les Cartes à jouer et la cartomancie* (Playing Cards and Cartomancy) published in Paris in 1854. Interestingly, he asserted that the cards came from India, not from Egypt. He also thought that they were unknown in the Islamic world. So he arrived at the conclusion that they skipped it by coming into Europe with the Gypsies, who came from India.

The problems with this theory, they point out, is that cards were known in the Islamic world, and that the Gypsies first came to Europe in 1417, (six years later than the date given by Giles. The Encyclopedia simply says "early fifteenth century.") reaching Italy in 1422 and not arriving in France until 1427. This was before the Tarot, but not before playing cards in general, which they say were known in Catalonia by 1370. So Gypsies cannot have brought them. (Unless, of course, they shipped them on ahead.)

While we are talking about the Gypsies, the Gypsy theory seems to have been fixed by a book called *Les Rômes: Histoire vraie des vrais bohémiens* (The Romanies: The True History of the Gypsies) published in Paris in 1857 and written by Jean-Alexandre Vaillant. But, according to Decker et al, he made most of it up. They also seem to think that it wasn't really his fault, and tell us that he was suffering from a kind of intellectual split personality. In this book, he not only says the Tarot was used by Gypsies, and had been from antiquity, but according to Decker et al, he also says that the Gypsies are responsible for everything else; from civilization itself, to the cults of Diana and Apollo, to a myth of Isa-Kris'ten, "a sun god introduced in India in the eleventh century B.C., [who] gave rise to the myth of Jesus Christ." He seems, at the least, to have been very confused.

But Eliphas Lévi (of whom we will learn more later,) believed him, and that clinched it, because, as we shall see, lots of people based their work on his.

In fact, Giles (among others) points out that although much was written about esoterica, including alchemy, astrology, natural magic, and so on all through this period, there is no mention at all about the Tarot.

(Decker et al think that's why the Gypsy theory holds so much attraction for occultists; if it were true, it's evidence that the Tarot was always used in an esoteric manner, and fills "the void created by the absence of any mention [of such use] before 1781.")

However, there is plenty that we know about the games, and about the designs on the cards themselves.

At the earliest stage, most of my sources agree, there were no numbers on the trumps. Players were expected to memorize their rank, much, I suppose, as they were expected to memorize the rank of the people all around them. There was also some diversion in exactly what pictures appeared, and what they were called. The Magician, for instance, was often called The Mountebank, the Hermit is sometimes The Hunchback and appears with an hourglass, and so on.

Eventually they were given numbers, but according to all the authors who had anything to say about the matter, these did not always agree.

Decker et al also give an interesting history of cards as a whole, stating that the suit signs that we see now on Tarot cards (Cups, Coins or Pentacles, Swords, and Batons or Wands) came from the Islamic suits of Cups, Coins, Swords, and Polo-Sticks. The Polo-Sticks changed, because Polo wasn't played in Europe at the time. They further state that the Italian suits remained Cups, Coins, Swords and Batons for a long time, while other countries experimented with other suits.

And, they tell us, the extra court-card in the Tarot deck (as opposed to the ordinary deck) is not the Knight, but the Queen! They explain that in ordinary Italian and Spanish packs the three court cards are the King, the Knight, and the Jack. They hypothesize that the Queen comes from early decks which had six court figures, like one painted in Milan in around 1441, where each rank had both male and female. If the Dame and Maid were dropped, that leaves the four we are used to.

If the Tarot did, indeed, originate in Italy, as they contend, this would make sense, and would also mean that the only cards added to the then normal deck were the Trumps themselves. The rest of the deck was left unchanged.

So, we have a set of cards that were used to play a family of games that became extremely popular. Decker et al state that they were eventually played all over Europe, with the exception of Britain and the Iberian peninsula. The heyday of the games, they tell us, was the century between 1750 and 1850.

However, even during that time, other forms of entertainment, newer and therefore more fashionable, had edged the Tarot into obscurity in some places. One of these places appears to have been Paris, where the game was considered obsolete by the middle of the eighteenth century.

So, let us look at Paris in the 1770s.

It was a time when Secret Societies were all the rage. Freemasonry, which had begun in England on June 24, 1717, according to the Encyclopedia, had spread into Paris.

Hermeticism, based on the writings of Greek scholars living in Egypt between 50 and 300 CE was also widespread. Hermetic literature, according to Howard Batchelor, writing for The New Grolier Multimedia Encyclopedia, was written in Greek and Latin, and concerned philosophical, theological and occult topics. These essays were all attributed to Hermes Trismegistos, which means "Thrice-Great Hermes," and is the name the Greeks gave to the Egyptian god Thoth, who was "patron of the literary arts and originator of all mystical wisdom." They dealt with everything from alchemy and astrology to divine revelation, and the idea that humanity could be redeemed through the knowledge of God.

According to Giles, this literature is mainly written as dialogs with Hermes. When it was discovered in the Renaissance, it was all taken literally. So by the 18th century, it was firmly established in occult circles that anything wonderful and magical was obviously Egyptian.

At this time, as well, the Rosetta Stone had yet to be found (that happened in August 1779, when some of Napoleon's soldiers stumbled across it while conducting "engineering works" at Fort Julien, some 35 miles east of Alexandria) let alone deciphered (which was done by Jean Francois Champollion in 1822.) So it was still widely believed, according to several sources, that the hieroglyphics held all the wisdom of the ages, which had been lost with the library at Alexandria.

Occult scholars at the time assumed that everything written in this wonderful, magical, indecipherable script had to be lost knowledge from Hermes Trismegistos himself. And therefore, since the hieroglyphics were pictures, anything magical that was in a picture script was known as "hieroglyphics."

Into this milieu came a Swiss Protestant pastor named Antoine Court de Gébelin in 1762. His father, Antoine Court, had been a prominent French Protestant pastor, who had fled the Protestant Persecutions in France in 1729, and moved to Switzerland. Richard Roberts, in *The Original Tarot and You** says that Court de Gébelin was born in 1728. But Decker et al say that there is some doubt about this date.

In any case, he joined the Freemason's Lodge of Les Amis Réunis when he got to Paris, eventually joining and becoming the secretary of the Lodge of Les Neuf Soeurs (the very same one that Voltaire and Benjamin Franklin belonged to) in 1778. In 1780 he left it to found the Société Apollonienne, where he was President, and which eventually became the Musée de Paris, which, Decker et al tell us, was not "a museum in our sense, but a center for lectures, readings, and

* *The Original Tarot and You* by Richard Roberts © 1971,1987. Vernal Equinox Press, San Anselmo, CA. ISBN 0-942380-06-1

STEVE,

ITS ALL SET —

Leave A Msg if
you have Any
problems.

767-0969 — Home

1889 here

SOFTWARE

□ □ □ □ □

CONSORTIUM

Windows & Relational Database Experts

Development, Integration & Solutions

Sheldon Shulman
Senior Systems Engineer

100 West Road
Suite 300
Towson, MD 21204

(410) 583-9393
Fax (410) 583-5335
102135,554@compuserve.com

discussions." He retained his membership in Les Amis Réunis, and, they say, was one of seven twelfth degree masons in that lodge by 1783.

All of which shows that he was very active in the occult, mystical circles in Paris at that time.

He was also a writer and sold books by subscription, which was a common practice then. One of these was a many volumed work, never completed, called *Monde Primitif* (The Primitive World.) In it, according to Decker et al, he hypothesized a golden age, before there was such a thing as cultural diversity, when the original civilization flourished, and all men had a common language, common customs, common culture, and common religion. He further stated that by an etymological study of known languages he could reconstruct that common language, along with the primitive, 16 letter alphabet. Most of the books, they tell us, are concerned with these deductions. If you are interested, Decker et al have several in their book.

The important thing about it here, though, is that sometime between 1773, when de Gébelin published the outline for these books, and 1778 when he wrote about the Tarot, he was invited to a dinner party in Paris. There, according to his own essay as quoted by Decker et al, "We found [our hostess] occupied in playing this game with some other people. We play a game which you surely do not know. - That may be; what is it?- The game of Tarots. - I have had occasion to see it when I was very young, but I have no idea of it. - It is a rhapsody of the most bizarre, the most extravagant figures ... I scrutinize them, and suddenly I recognize the allegory: everyone abandons the game and comes to look at this marvellous pack of cards in which I have perceived what they have never seen. Each one shows me another of the cards: in a quarter of an hour the pack has been run through, explained, declared Egyptian; and since this is in no way the product of our imagination, but the effect of the deliberate and perceptible connections of this pack with everything that is known of Egyptian ideas, we promised ourselves one day to make it known to the public."

This essay was published, according to Decker et al, in Volume IV of his *Monde Primitif* in 1776. Giles says he wrote a history of the Tarot in a book called *Le Jeu des Cartes* in 1781. He seems to have written about the Tarot quite a bit, and what he wrote was widely disseminated among the mystical, esoteric, occult thinkers of the day.

He went on to "intuit" lots of other things about the deck, such as the word TARO being composed of the Egyptian words 'Tar' meaning 'road' and 'Ros or Rog' meaning 'royal.' And remember, he did this before the Rosetta Stone. Unfortunately, it turns out that there were no such words. He also states that the Tarot is actually an Egyptian book, the last remnant of the magnificent libraries of Egypt, and explains that it was written on plates, in spite of the fact that the Egyptians used scrolls.

Interestingly enough, another writer in Paris at the around the same time also thought the cards were Egyptian in origin. His essay appears in one of de Gébelin's volumes, and is signed M. le C. de M.***, which Decker et al suppose means Louis-Raphaël-Lucrèce de Fayolle, comte de Mellet. They state their reasons for this identification, but I don't have room for them here. In any case, his essay seems to pre-date de Geblin's, since it never refers once to that one, which would be unthinkable in society at that time. His conclusions differ from de Geblin's in a number of particulars; most notably, his is the first published account to assume that the Tarot is The Book of Thoth. He arrives at this hypothesis by breaking the word Tarot into 'T,' a definite article, and 'Rosh,' which means Thoth. Obviously, he concludes, the whole thing is descended from Hermes Trismegistus.

And so the idea of the Tarot as Egyptian still lingers. In fact, several of the authors that I examined still have this down as fact, and list de Gébelin as their authority. This, I assume, is because, as Decker et al say, most occult writers simply quote other occult writers, without examining the facts themselves. Much as I am doing now, I'm afraid!

So, now the idea of the Tarot as Egyptian is firmly established in the esoteric community in Paris. But it's still considered collected wisdom. How did it come to be used for divination?

To answer that question, we have to turn to another player in this drama, one Jean-Baptiste Alliette, better known as Etteilla. According to several of my sources, he was a professional cartomancer working in Paris, who, Decker et al say, had published a book about Fortune Telling using an "ordinary French pack of 32 cards, supplemented by one other" in Amsterdam in 1770. It was called *Etteilla, ou maniére de se récréer avec un jeu de cartes* (Etteilla, or a way to entertain oneself with a pack of cards.)

Now, he was not the first to use cards for divination. Decker et al state that a 62 card Tarocco bolognese, which "differed greatly" from the Tarot de Marseilles, which had become the standardized deck, was used to tell fortunes in Bologna as early as the middle of the eighteenth century. In fact, they quote a "single loose manuscript sheet giving cartomantic interpretations of 35 cards of the Tarocco bolognese [which] was discovered by Franco Pratesi in the Library of the University of Bologna." They also state that there exists a double-headed Tarocco bolognese pack from the 1820s, where all the divinatory meanings are written by hand at each end of every card. And they cite some evidence that cartomancy was being used in Russia in the eighteenth century, as well.

In any case, it seems that it was Etteilla who, (besides apparently coining the term Carotonomancy, later shortened to Cartomancy) popularized the Tarot as a divinatory system, as all the sources who mention him at all seem to agree.

He published a number of books dealing with the subject, as well as whole-heartedly embracing the Egyptian origin of the deck. In fact, he went so far as to intuit that the "vile cardmakers" had gotten the numbering all wrong, and made several other mistakes in the deck, and claimed to "rectify" the cards by going back to what he was sure was the "original Egyptian" order and motifs.

He also added a few other things to the lore of the Tarot. It was his contention (supported, as far as we know, only by his own intuition) that the Book of Thoth, as it was known, was designed by seventeen magi led by Hermes Trismegistus in the 171st year after the Flood. He also divined that the first copy was inscribed on "leaves of gold," which were arranged in a fire temple at Memphis. He even went so far as to explain exactly how they were so arranged!

He went on to print his interpretations of the cards, and to form a society called the *Société des Interprètes du Livre de Thot* (Society to Interpret the Book of Thoth,) which seems to have helped defray the costs of printing. (Reproductions of his deck, by the way, are still available if you are interested, under the title Grand Etteilla Egyptian Gypsies Tarot. Amazon.com lists it as out of print, but you may still be able to find it.)

Etteilla, too, according to Decker et al, was the first to try to marry the Tarot to the wider occult traditions of the time, including astrology.

He was followed by a number of students and disciples, who kept his traditions and theories alive until they were discovered by a man called Eliphas Lévi Zahed, or simply Eliphas Lévi, who was born Alphonse Louis Constant in 1810. A failed Catholic Priest, he became interested in the occult in 1852, and it quickly absorbed all his energy.

He believed that the Jews were the source of all magical teachings, which is why he changed his name, but he seems to have had no problem combining that belief with Hermetic writings and philosophy.

In fact, he excelled in combining all the known occult systems, creating a synthesis from them which forms the basis of Western Magical Tradition to this day. (We won't call this "mushing them all up together." That would be rude.) Actually this process, according to Decker et al, had begun far earlier, in the Renaissance. But by the middle of the nineteenth century, High Magic was failing in Europe. Cartomancy and other forms of divination prospered, and people still wanted talismans and spells, but, they say, the occult sciences that "offered a conception of the working of the cosmos appeared at last to have withered."

Lévi revivified it.

In the process, according to several sources, he returned the Tarot to a form based on the Tarot de Marseille, (he seems to have despised Etteilla) and he also revived the idea that de Mellet had; that the twenty-two trumps corresponded with the twenty-two letters of the Hebrew alphabet. So he drew correspondences, and attached the Cabala to the Tarot.

Decker et al point out that if Etteilla was wrong in ascribing the cards to the Hermetic literature, which didn't show up in Europe until several decades after the

Tarot, then Lévi was even more wrong in assigning them Cabalistic significance, since the Cabala was not translated for the Christian public until 1486.

They say that Lévi's claim that the Tarot "was known to all nations of the ancient world" is "preposterous," and point out that it couldn't have been invented by both the Jews and the Egyptians. This, however, doesn't seem to have bothered Lévi himself in the slightest. He held, in fact, that the Tarot and the Cabala were indissolubly linked, and understanding one was impossible without the other.

There is lots more written about Lévi, if you care to look it up. But for now, it seems that he was the one who linked the Cabala and the Tarot firmly together, and also the one who established the Tarot as part of the Occult tradition.

Meanwhile, contemporary with Lévi, there was another writer living and working in Paris. (In fact, they knew each other.) His name was Jean-Baptiste Pitois, but he was better known by one of his pseudonyms, Paul Christian. Decker et al say outright that he was a charlatan, and (in a phrase I just love) that he "made use of two daring devices: the spurious quotation, and the circumstantial historical narrative made up out of whole cloth."

He also used a host of other pen names, including, they assert, A. Frédéric de la Grange, under which name he wrote a book called *Le Grand Livre du Destin* (The Big Book of Fate) wherein he described a totally spurious history of cartomancy beginning in the courts of Henri II, and continuing through a detailed story about Louis XIV consulting a famous cartomancer, Marie Ambruget. He goes on to tell about a tailor named Fiasson, a cartomancer who was visited by the duc d'Orléans, incognito. This is told as a long quotation from the *Memoirs of the comte e Nocé*, published at the Hague in 1733.

The story, about Fiasson being visited by the duc along with two companions, and how their fates, as told by Fiasson, came true has been quoted many times.

The only problem is that it all seems to have been a work of fiction. Decker et al tell us that there appears to have never been any such book as the *Mémoires;* and the rest of it is also entirely fake.

Unless they are also making use of the "bold literary device," I am inclined to believe Decker et al. They have, after all, five and a half pages of bibliography, in nine point type, including de la Grange's book. If there had been a book called *Mémoires* by the comte e Nocé, I think they would have found it.

Hortensius Flamel, who wrote *Le Livre rouge* (The Red Book) in 1841 and *Le Livre d'or* (The Golden Book) in 1842 appears to have been another name used by Pitois. That being the case, everything in them is suspect. What makes it worse is that he seems to have periodically put a bit of truth into these works of pseudo-history. Decker et al, for instance, assure us that the quotations from Charles Fourier, who made talismans, are accurate, or at least actually exist.

But when dealing with an author who is known to take delight in fooling his audience, as Pitois seems to have done, it's best to look elsewhere for the truth.

This is really sad, because, as Paul Christian, Pitois contributed a lot of things to the mythos of the Tarot.

For instance, Susan Gerulskis-Estes, in *The Book of the Tarot** in her chapter Origin of the Tarot states that the "twenty-two pictures of the Major Arcana were painted on the walls of an Egyptian initiation chamber located in the lower chambers of the Sphinx. In order to be initiated into the order of Hermes-Thoth, the neophyte was taken through the gallery by a member of the order who would explain the symbolic meaning of the twenty-two pictures." She appears to be quoting from de Gébelin here, and states that he wrote in 1392 that the Tarot was actually a book saved from the destruction of a temple in Egypt by fire.

Since he was born over 300 years after that date, we'll assume it was a simple error on her part.

But the story about the temple is pure fiction, and was devised by Paul Christian, who, by the way, consistently referred to Hermes Trismegistus as Hermes-Thoth.

This one, so Decker et al tell us, comes from his *Histoire de la magie, du monde surnatural et de la fatalité à travers les temps et les peuples,* (History of magic, the supernatural world and prophecy covering the passage of time and the people) published in 1869, and translated into English in 1952.

Unfortunately, it became required reading among students of the occult.

There, in Book II, Decker et al say, he put "the … most impudent [piece] of invention" in the whole *Histoire*. It is an account of the Egyptian mysteries, including a very detailed description of the initiation sequence given above, reputed to have been quoted from a manuscript left by "Iamblichus, who lived in the first half of the fourth century A.D." complete with a footnote reference to a bilingual edition of *On the Mysteries* in Greek and Latin published in Oxford in 1678.

As usual, he mixed a tiny dab of truth in with his fiction. There is indeed such a treatise, Decker et al point out; but it has nothing at all like this initiation in it. The trickiest bit is that he never mentions the word "Tarot" at all; so a reader who knew about the Tarot, confronted with what they could only assume was a translation from an ancient manuscript about an initiation into Hermetic mysteries, would instantly recognize it, and not know that Christian knew all about the Tarot, too! This would have the result of adding a large flavor of authenticity to the entire account. And that must have tickled Pitois pink.

He also goes on, in this book, to make up things about many other branches of the occult; but since we are only dealing with the Tarot here, we won't go there.

Decker et al also say that Pitois AKA Paul Christian invented the name "Arcana," which became divided into the Major Arcana and Minor Arcana.

---

* *The Book of the Tarot* by Susan Gerulskis-Estes © 1981 by Morgan & Morgan, Inc., Morgan & Morgan, Inc. Publishers, Dobbs Ferry, NY ISBN 0-87100-172-1

Lévi died in 1875, and Christian in 1877. After their deaths, there was, as Decker et al say, "a lull, lasting about a decade, in magical activity and the production of books on magic."

But, of course, that didn't last. By the late 1880's, secret societies were active again, and the occult and spiritualist movements were beginning to flower.

In 1888, Stanislas de Guaita (and others) founded the Ordere Kabbalistique de la Rose-Croix (Cabalistic Order of the Rosy Cross.) This became, so Decker et al tell us, the "embodiment of Rosicrucianism in France." He went on to meet Oswald Wirth, a Swiss freemason who practiced hypnotic healing, and introduce him to occultism. Together, these two men designed a set of Trumps, now called Major Arcana, based on Lévi's work, and published in 1889. These, according to Decker et al, were "the first published set of occult Tarot cards" not deriving from Etteilla. From the descriptions, they were the true forerunners of the cards we use today.

In that same year Dr. Gérard-Anaclet-Vincent Encausse, also known as Papus, and also a Rosicrucian, brought out *Le Tarot des Bohémiens* (The Tarot of the Gypsies.) This book was a "systematic interpretation" of the Tarot, and used the Tarot de Marseille "discreetly embellished with Hebrew letters" (as Decker et al put it) and Wirth's new deck as illustrations. He also uses the terms "Minor Arcana" and "Major Arcana," but seems to have relied heavily on the work of those who went before him, who, as we have seen, ranged from confused to outright lying; however, now his book added substance to theirs.

The last important phase in the history of our Tarot takes place in England.

The Order of the Golden Dawn was founded in Britain in 1888. Gearhart et al tell us that it lasted only 15 years, but its influence was far reaching, and, indeed, is felt even today.

One of its founders, MacGregor Mathers, and his wife Monia, were very interested in the Tarot, and conducted what Gearhart et al call "deep research and study" into it. This, I think, can only mean that they studied everything that had been written about it at the time. And, it seems, among the things they studied were Paul Christian's writings.

In any case, they seem to have taken the idea of an initiation into Hermetic Mysteries using the Tarot as a focus very much to heart. Giles says that they used the cards in their initiations. And, it seems, all the members who reached a certain level were expected to design their own decks.

Among the members of the Order were A.E. Waite, Paul Foster Case, and Alestier Crowley. Does this begin to ring a bell? They were responsible for the Rider-Waite deck, the BOTA deck, and the Thoth deck, respectively. All of them were trying to reconstruct the "true" deck, according to Gearhart et al. (I also find it interesting that all of them turned to women to actually draw the decks they envisioned. The Waite deck was drawn by Pamela Coleman-Smith, the BOTA by Jessie Burns Parke, and the Thoth by Frieda Harris.)

It's possible that all of these, (and the Rider-Waite and BOTA are quite similar,) are descendants of the deck used by the Order. They always said that they had access to a secret oral tradition, which lent their deck "its special puissance" according to Gearhart et al.

In any case, it's certain that these three have influenced all subsequent "traditional" decks!

And that brings us up to the present. Today there is a huge body of written work, with more being published every day. Unfortunately, a lot of it still uses the stories written by de Gébelin, Etteilla, Lévi, Christian and so on. In fact, these have entered deeply into the things "everyone knows" about the Tarot, since many of us are forced to rely on the writings of others. But more scholarly, well researched material is also appearing. This chapter would have been impossible only a few years ago, since the books that I used to find out about the earlier stories had yet to be written. And I only glossed over the details; if you are interested, I strongly suggest that you check these books out for yourself; especially if you can read French, and can get to Paris!

There is also a virtual explosion of divinatory decks, some of which have very little to do with the Tarot, and don't include suits, or court cards, or any such thing.

Mine is a "traditional" deck, in which I kept not only the Major and Minor Arcana, but also the suits, the numbers, the court cards; the whole structure of the deck, in fact. I didn't want to change that. I wanted to change the symbols. And I did; but that is a whole 'nother chapter.

I think it's safe to say that whether the original Tarot, used for games in the fifteenth century, had occult significance or not, it surely has now. We have stuffed it full of significance, every one of us who has designed a deck with that in mind.

And if it's true that the occult use of the Tarot is relatively recent, well, I guess that doesn't bother me either. Everything had to be developed sometime!

But, when you get right down to it, even if the whole thing was an Italian invention in the fifteenth century, there are still a lot of questions about the beginning. Questions like; What was going on in the minds of the original inventors? Did they know how esoteric some of these symbols were? How long were the cards in a particular family or group before they were published?

And the only real answer still has to be: no one knows, and does it really make any difference?

Chapter 4
History of the
Robin Wood Tarot

And so we come to the history of my own deck, which I know very well.
I became interested in the Tarot in 1979.

At that time, I had just begun my spiritual journey after 25 years of dutifully believing what I was told to believe.

I won't tell you how that happened, because it would take too long and would probably bore you to tears. (Or, worse yet, to closing this book!)

Suffice it to say that I found out about Wicca, and it felt like coming home. But I didn't know much, and didn't really have anyone to teach me. (Does this sound familiar to any of you? I thought it might.)

So I kind of cast wildly about, and decided that Wicca was occult type stuff, and occult type people read Tarot cards, don't they? So I decided to learn to read them.

Now remember, this is in the late seventies. There was not nearly the wealth of decks and books and stuff that there is now. It was still almost twenty years before the year 2000, and the spirituality that always accompanies large round numbers in the Julian calendar was only beginning to begin. (Ever notice how many people are afraid of big round numbers?)

I bought a Rider-Waite deck, and *Mastering the Tarot* by Eden Gray, and started to learn.

I wrote down every reading that I did, and all of my interpretations of the cards (right out of the little book that comes with the deck, with some elaboration from the bigger book) and what actually happened that could be correlated to the readings. (By the way, I recommend this method to anyone who is trying to learn any system of divination.)

As I did so, I slowly began to see patterns emerging. Some of them were what I expected from the books, and some were not. It's been eighteen years now, and I've moved over a dozen times, so I can't give you any actual examples; but I began to think that reversing cards just made everything more jumbled for me. I couldn't remember which ones meant the reverse of the thing the card said, and which ones just meant that the effect was lessened. And the more I decided that I didn't like to use reversed meanings, the less they showed up! I was still shuffling the deck normally, but all the cards were beginning to show up top side up.

About this time I realized that I could get books to feed my growing hunger for knowledge about spiritual things. I was too poor to buy any, but the library had a whole section about the occult.

One of the books I checked out about the Tarot told me a number of important things. First, it said that you should create a sacred space to work in before you begin to read. I did that and the clarity of my readings improved. Secondly, it said the important thing was figuring out how to ask questions. Boy, is that ever true! And the third thing it said was that everyone reads in his or her own style; some use reversed cards, and some don't, and there are literally hundreds of ways to lay the cards out.

I wish I could remember the name of that book, or the author. I owe her a lot. She gave me permission to leave the path that others had blazed, and follow my own.

So I continued to read and study. And eventually I found friends I could talk to about these things.

Now, during this time I had married a man who was in the Army. In 1980 we were exiled, I mean sent, to Okinawa, Japan. We were there from July of 1980 to December of 1982.

There weren't many books about the Tarot, or Wicca, or anything occult in the base library at Tori Station. Since all the reading I had been able to do was from the library, this effectively cut off my source of new information.

There was nowhere to learn more, except to turn to the cards themselves. So that's what I did. I started at the beginning of the deck, with card 0 of the Major Arcana,* (The Fool) and spent time studying and meditating on each card.

As I did so, the patterns that I had begun to notice in the States became clearer, and I began to recognize the symbols in the cards without having to refer to the books at all. Pretty simple stuff, at first, but we all have to begin somewhere.

I realized that the Ace of each suite was about the beginning, which I knew; but I noticed that it also contained the seed of the whole suite, like a pea contains a plant in miniature. All the twos were about balance in some way, and so on.

I also found common symbols throughout. Mountains always stood for enlightenment, rivers for the mystery of the female side of things, etc.

And I noticed that a whole lot of the symbology was Judeo-Christian, and the cards were not very well drawn. Besides which, the colors were funky and depressing.

In short, I began to realize that although there were things about the Rider-Waite deck that I liked, there were also things I did not.

To the best of my knowledge, there were no Tarot decks for sale on Okinawa at that time. At least, if there were I never saw any. And I was pretty sure that if I searched until I found one, it would just be the Rider-Waite again, anyway. I didn't know if there *were* any decks that had the Pagan/Wiccan/Nature bias that I wanted. But I knew that I could draw, and I knew what I wanted on the cards; so the obvious thing to do was to begin to draw my own deck, and that's what I did.*

Being an orderly sort, I started at the beginning, with the Fool (as I had when I first began to look at the deck,) and thought and meditated about what the card *should* have, as opposed to what it had in the Rider-Waite deck. I'll tell you what I decided in the chapter on the Major Arcana. For now, it's enough to tell you that I

---

*The Tarot is divided into two parts, the Major and Minor Arcana. The Major Arcana is composed of the named cards, or Trump cards, ranging from 0, the Fool, to 21, the World. The Minor Arcana is composed of four suites of cards, with each suite containing four Court Cards (King, Queen, Knight and Page) and 10 cards numbered from 1 to 10. There will more about this when we get a bit farther along.

drew the symbols that would remind me of what the card meant. I made for myself a picture that evoked the exact visceral response that I thought the Fool should elicit, and tucked pictorial reminders of every meaning or correspondence I thought it needed inside the design.

As soon as I had the sketch the way I wanted it, I realized that I would have to put it on something. But art supplies in Japan are different than they are in the States, and I didn't know what sort of media to use.

I was puzzling over this, when I went to check my mail, and there in the box was a catalog that an occult mail order company just happened to send me for no adequately explored reason. This was really strange, because I had had absolutely no contact with any such company at all ever! The only things I had purchased that could be construed as occult had come from a book store in the States, where (if I recall correctly) I had paid cash, and avoided their mailing list. But here was this catalog, fortuitously appearing in my mail; so I used it.

I ordered a set of blank Tarot Cards, just the same size and with the same pattern on the back as the Rider Waite deck I was so used to.

And when they came, I painted a tiny miniature oil painting of the Fool I had designed on the first one.

Of course, I wanted to share this with my friends back home; but there was no way to show them the finished card, so I sent them bad xerox copies of the sketches. By that time, I had four or five finished. (It took a while for the blank cards to arrive in the mail.)

And while I waited for a response from them, I painted the Magician, and the High Priestess, and the Lovers on the cards. (I'm no longer sure why I skipped ahead to the Lovers, but I did for some reason. I know, because I still have the painted cards, and those are the ones I have.)

About the time that I finished the Lovers, a letter came back from the States. My friends were very enthusiastic. In fact, they told me that they liked them so much that they each needed to have a set of these for themselves. And one of my friends threatened me with bodily harm if I didn't make this possible!

I knew that I would not be able to afford color separations for the things. And I decided that giving everyone 78 photos of my cards would be too expensive too. So I re-drew them, using pen and ink. I figured that the line drawings would be easy enough to reproduce, and they could all color their own decks.

During the next year or so, while we were still in Okinawa, I designed the entire Major Arcana, and drew them in pen and ink, sending the xerox copies

---

*I had actually sent a couple of cards of a proposed deck to Llewellyn a few years before, when I had just begun to study all of this. I no longer remember why I did it – I didn't really know anything about Tarot at the time, and I didn't work for Llewellyn (or any other publisher) yet. But I drew designs for The Lovers, the Ace of Wands, and the 6 of Pentacles just the same. They weren't very good, or very well thought out. In fact, they bear not the slightest resemblance to the cards that would eventually form the Robin Wood Tarot. But I thought I'd mention them anyway, in the interest of being as complete as possible here. If you want to see them, check Appendix E.

back to my friends in the states, and getting really involved and interested in the whole process.

Then we came back to the US, and suddenly my life, which had been composed mostly of free time, became very, very busy. I started working for gaming companies, and found that I no longer had much time to do anything just because I wanted to do it.

I did finish the Court Cards of the Minor Arcana, mostly because several of my friends and I had begun an artist's consortium, and were making T-Shirts for a company that we called Dreams from Home. The person who ran the company, who is also a dear friend, thought that pictures of the Tarot would sell well and wanted the Court Cards to fill out the roster; so I did them. But although I continued to study, and plan what I wanted to put on "my" cards, I didn't do any more drawing.

Years went by. I started working for Llewellyn in 1985, and established a very good relationship with Terry Buske, who was the Art Director there.

During that time, a rumor began to circulate among all of the artists at Science Fiction Conventions that Stuart Kaplan, from US Games, was collecting the decks that folks had made themselves for a new volume of his *Encyclopedia of the Tarot*. Like all the rest of us who had drawn part or all of a deck, I sent mine in. (At the time it existed only as a coloring book.) If you are interested, and you look it up, you'll find that ancient and early rendition in the *Encyclopedia of the Tarot, Vol. 2*.*

At some point during this time, my friends and I decided to print the cards as cards. So I took the designs I had done, and began to color them. I hadn't gotten very far when we decided that the format I was using was going to be too small. (The cards I had finished were the size of the Rider-Waite deck.) So I started again, from the Fool, at twice the proposed card size.

Some of the cards were redesigned as this process went on.

But after I had done a dozen or so, we realized that we would not be able to afford the color separations after all. So I sold the large ones I had finished at science fiction convention art shows, and went back to doing other stuff.

Then, in 1987, I began to work with Anne McCaffrey on a book of portraits of the characters she had written about in her Dragonriders series. This became *The People of Pern*.** It was a huge project, and it took virtually every moment for the better part of a year to complete.

I'm glossing over my life here, of course. I'm not mentioning my good friends next door, or my amazin' room mate, or any of the others who were there for me

* *The Encyclopedia of Tarot, Vol. II* © 1988 by Stuart R. Kaplan. US Games Systems, New York, NY. ISBN 0-91386-636-9
** *The People of Pern* by Robin Wood ©1988 by Robin Wood and Anne McCaffrey. The Donning Company/Publishers Norfolk VA. ISBN 0-89865-635-4. If you are interested, I think it's still available from the Science Fiction Bookclub.

when I needed them, because I don't want to "out" them.* But it was a difficult year, and without their help I'm not sure how I would have made it. (You guys know who you are. Thanks. Love you.)

The important part is that by the end of 1988 I had grown a lot, and after the book came out, I started to take some time to do the things I wanted to do again.

I also needed a job, because the Pern book had kept me from doing any of the freelancing that I had been doing for so long. And I was on my own by then; the Army guy and I were divorced on Pearl Harbor Day in 1987.

So I called Terry at Llewellyn, and she immediately assigned the drawings for Donald Tyson's *Rune Magic Cards*.** That was a quick, fun job. Donald Tyson had explained in great detail what he wanted in the drawings, and instead of using my normal realistic style, Terry asked me to draw like a Viking. (Which is kind of like walking like an Egyptian, only different.) The Viking drawings were very stylized, and I had a great time doing them.

In fact, after I was finished, I asked Terry if she had any more cards she needed done. That was when she told me that Llewellyn was doing some Tarot decks, but she thought all the art was already assigned.

I told her that I had been working on a Tarot deck once, and had all the Majors and Court Cards done.

And she told me to send a few in, and they would have a look at them, and tell me what they thought.

By now it was 1989, The Year I Moved. (Four times. I lived in 3 different states that year. No Fun at Tax Time.)

I moved the first time, to Pittsburgh, and set up my studio. Then I settled down to work.

The first thing I wanted to do was convince Llewellyn to accept the cards as pen and ink drawings colored with colored pencils, so I wouldn't have to paint 78 little oil paintings.

So I did two renderings of the Fool, one using ink and colored pencil, and one as an oil painting, and sent them off to Llewellyn with a letter explaining that if they bought the the ink and pencil variation, not only would I certainly be able to meet the deadline (which I couldn't guarantee with paint, because of the drying time and other variables inherent in the medium) but they would have the black and white cards that they could use as line drawings to illustrate other books about

*People who are members of minority religions are often persecuted and hurt by those who are afraid or don't understand, as are people of any other minority. Just like members of the Gay community, many people in the Pagan community are "in the broom closet" for fear of the reactions of their family, co-workers, community and so on, or to spare their families etc. the pain such news might bring. As in all such groups, publicly exposing someone, called "outing" them, is considered not merely incredibly rude, but dangerous. It's not something I'm willing to do. Not all of these people are Pagans; but if I don't mention anyone's names, I feel it will help to protect those who are. So if I mention a name, you can be assured that person is already a very public Pagan, and you have probably heard of them in that context. Or they aren't Pagan at all, like Anne McCaffrey.

**Rune Magic Cards by Donald Tyson © 1988. Llewellyn Publications, St. Paul, MN. ISBN 0-87542-827-4

the Tarot. Besides, I explained to Terry, I really wanted to do them in the the more graphic style.

They replied that the ink and colored pencil would be fine.

Now, if you've been counting, you know that at this point, I had rendered the Fool 7 different times, and some of the other cards several times as well.

But after I got the assignment from Llewellyn, I took a good look at the cards and realized that they would all have to be redrawn. After all, it had been almost 10 years since I had started working on them, and I had learned many things about the Tarot and gotten much better at drawing in that decade.

So I sat down, and drew them all, all over again.

While I was doing this, I moved three more times, the last two with the man who became my new husband. (He and his two children wound up posing for many of the cards.) I ended up in Michigan. But I must admit that I don't recommend tearing down and setting up your studio four times while in the middle of a project as large as a Tarot Deck!

It didn't take me long to redo the Major Arcana and Court Cards, even though I changed many small details in all of them; and in some cases, such as the Court cards for Wands and Swords, I completely changed the design. (Originally, they had been seated. I decided that since they were active principals I would make them standing. I also put in all the "props" and redesigned the costumes. Animal X, a friend of mine in Pittsburgh who designs costumes professionally, posed for all the queens at this point, and I took some of the costume construction from her work.)

After that, I thought (for some reason that escapes me now) that most of the work was done, so when Llewellyn contacted me and asked to use some of the cards to illustrate Janina Renee's Tarot Spell book I said, "Sure. I haven't finished the deck yet, but any cards I don't have and you need I can get done by the deadline."

Then I got the assignment, and found out how many cards there were. And I pulled out my notes for the Minor Arcana cards which I hadn't drawn yet, and I found out that although most of the Majors have one person, doing one thing, many of the Minors have several people doing all kinds of things all over the card. So far from being almost finished with the drawings, I still had most of the work to do!

So I buckled down and started drawing like a mad thing. It was a good thing I had been designing the cards in my head for ten years, because I didn't have time to do much research at that point. It was also fortunate that Llewellyn only wanted the ink drawings, because that was all I had time for.

I made the deadline for the book; but I couldn't stop to rest, because Llewellyn had also given me a deadline for getting the entire deck colored and in.

I drew the remaining cards, and inked them all. And then I started at the beginning again, and colored them all in. In order to make the deadline, I had to work 14 hours a day, seven days a week, for ten weeks straight. But I got them finished!

Each card was designed in pencil on tracing paper, using a 3.7" x 6.9" format (which was the smallest Llewellyn would let me use!) After the drawing was finished, I placed another piece of tracing paper over it, and inked it using technical pens. Doing it this way not only preserved the original pencil (which is often important, since there was usually some shading and other information that I didn't want inked in on the drawing) but eliminated any problem with completely erasing the pencil lines after the inking was done. And if I really messed up the inking at some point, I could also throw it away and start fresh!

Once the inking was finished, I xeroxed it onto another piece of tracing paper and then colored it with Berol® Prismacolor® pencils on both the front and back. This preserved the fine line work, which the pencil would otherwise obscure. It also made it possible to achieve some effects, such as the silk gown on the Queen of Cups, which would have been extremely difficult to get otherwise.

While I'm on the topic, the secret to getting the bright, saturated colors with Prismacolor® pencils (the brand I use) is to bear down. Don't be alarmed when the point breaks off and shoots across the room. They're supposed to do that.

Ordinarily, the darker colors are blended by using one of the lighter colored pencils. But when I needed to keep the deep tones, and didn't want to lighten them, I used a paper stump (commonly used for charcoal drawing) dipped in Grumtine® (commonly used to thin oil paints) to blend. It works like a charm, in case you want to borrow the technique!

Once the coloring was finished, I very lightly and carefully coated it with a fixative spray. Lightly and carefully, because toner, such as that used in the xerographic process, melts and runs when sprayed with most fixatives! (In fact, it works best if you hold the picture vertically, and spray parallel to it. Then all that lands on the picture is the fine mist of the overspray. Do this several times, and it's coated without ever actually being in the line of spray. No big blobs, no running.)

When they were done, I shipped all the originals at once off to Llewellyn, where they made color separations, and did the other things necessary to make them into cards.

At some point in this process, we had to decide what to put on the back. At first, Llewellyn wanted a full color picture. I was more than willing. But when they found out how much extra cost that would be, they decided that a two color graphic would work out just fine.

The problem was, what kind of graphic?

I wanted something that would tie in with the Pagan/Wiccan/Nature theme, or else something that was Celtic. So I sent in three designs. The first was a pattern of leaves, taken from a piece of Zipatone™ shading film. The second was a spiral design, which I was very fond of since it represented the looking-inward idea that was behind the whole Tarot. Literally having it behind each card really appealed to me. The third was the knotwork that was eventually chosen.

I originally wanted the two ink colors on the back to be black and bright leaf green. But I was overruled, since the folks at Llewellyn thought the color too vivid for the rest of the cards, and a shade of jade green was picked instead.

I didn't argue about the back, truth to tell, because they had given me my own head completely on the fronts of the cards, where it really counted. They are all entirely my own design; no one told me to re-do any of it, or tried to influence me in any way.

Since I was used to doing covers and things, where almost all the art has to be approved by a committee (many of whom have strong ideas of their own,) this was a rare and wonderful experience for me, and one I am most grateful for.

After I turned all the cards in, it took Llewellyn about a year to publish, since they were trying to time the publication to coincide with the American Booksellers Association Convention. The ABA is where many of the buying decisions for the next year are made, and it's probably the most important show in the American publishing industry.

It was out on time, at least in prototype form, and my husband and I attended the convention, where I did readings.

And the rest, as they say, is history.*

If you want to see what some of this early work looked like, I have a pictoral history of my deck in Appendix E.

---

*Well, of course, so is all of this. But the rest is history that is still being written!

Chapter 5
Common Symbols

As I began to study and work with the Tarot, all those years ago, I slowly realized that the same symbols seemed to mean the same things on card after card.

I realized that all of the symbols were really just a kind of shorthand; a way of cutting through the thinking, rational, analytical part of the mind, and connecting directly with the other part, where emotions, feelings, and reactions live.

When you see a symbol, say an American flag, you don't think. "Flag, one, American. Designed in the eighteenth century. One star for each state, one stripe for each of the thirteen original colonies." You see it, and register it without thinking. Then your heart swells with pride, or you view it with scorn, or have whatever reaction you have (including no reaction) based on how you feel about the United States, and the government, and so on. Without consciously having to think about it at all!

Your reaction will be largely dependent on your own experiences and learning. For instance, if you are someone who immigrated to this country from another, and you are as pleased and happy as you can be to be here, and you were just naturalized last week, you will feel pride, and joy, and accomplishment when you see the flag.

If you have never thought much about the country at all; it's just where you happened to be born, then your reaction is likely to be along the lines of "Yeah, so?"

But then, if your beloved father, who was a veteran, dies, and they drape just such a flag on his casket, you are likely to burst into tears when you see the flag. Your feelings of grief and loss are triggered by the association which has now been made.

Do you see how it works?

Some symbols we are taught, and so they mean roughly the same thing to all of us. An octagonal red sign, for instance, makes most of us stop and look, even if it's not in the context of a road sign.

But even those symbols are colored by the experiences we associate them with. And we don't consciously think about them at all. We just react to them.

That immediate, visceral reaction is what makes symbols so very powerful.

The fact that they aren't the same reactions for everyone is why something that is largely symbolic, like the Tarot, needs to fit your own personal symbol set. It's why a particular deck may "speak" to one person, and not to another.

As I realized that, I realized that I could learn the symbols that the designers of the decks tended to use; if I understood the language, then I would have an immediate reaction to the card that included the things the designer was trying to convey.

I thought of it as the same sort of thing as learning a foreign language. Eventually, one hopes, if you are learning German, and someone says a word, like "*schlafen,*" a picture of a bed and the feeling of rest appear in the mind, instead of the word "sleep," and then the picture. The personal, emotional connotations will still be personal; but the language is understood. (And remember, words are symbols, too. They are really just a collection of sounds. What gives them meaning is the concept they stand for.)

In just such a way, I could learn that white roses stood for freedom and change. How I felt about freedom and change was still personal, and figured largely in how I would read the cards because of the visceral reaction I got when I saw them. But the basic meaning was there.

As I discovered those meanings, I was able to get deeper into the cards, and relied on the book less and less, in just the same way the student of a foreign language would rely on a dictionary less and less.

I'm presenting those discoveries here, in glossary form, because I think that's as useful as I can make it!

As with all the other symbols, these are my own interpretations, based on my own internal "symbol set." These are what I used while I was designing the cards.

But they aren't the only interpretations. Unlike a foreign language, you probably already have associations for some of these things. Don't try to force your symbol set to change; that's likely to make your unconscious unhappy, and you don't want an unhappy unconscious!

If your reactions to the cards aren't what I intended, that's OK too. (I'll be talking more about that all through this book.)

This list is to give you a jumping off point, to let you know what I meant in those instances where you don't really have any reaction to the symbols.

I suggest that you develop a list like this for yourself, as you study and learn more about the Tarot. Get a notebook, and write down the symbols that strike you as being common to several of the cards, and what sort of feelings or ideas they evoke inside of you when you see them. Doing this is one of the steps to winning free of the books, even if you don't want to design your own cards!

Apple (Fruit or Tree) - Fruitfulness, love, nourishment, nurturing. Also, the mystery hidden within the mundane (because if you cut one open crosswise, you see the Pentagram.)

Armor - protection, indication of status, authority. The Breastplate alone also stands for Truth.

Ash Tree - Wisdom, especially the wisdom that comes from pain or sacrifice, linking of the inner and outer worlds.

Athame - Sacred. Also symbol of God. See *Sword*.

Beech Tree - Gracefulness, beauty, stillness, peace, old knowledge, ancient wisdom, queenly attributes.

Birch Tree - Beginnings, purity, cleansing.

Black - Hidden things, the unknown, the unguessed at. Alternatively, mourning.

Blue - Spirituality, spiritual gifts, clear skies, sunny disposition.

Bluebells - Fairy bells, awareness of inner voice, silent singing, starlight wisdom.

Book - Knowledge, especially knowledge about the material world, or "seen" things.

Breastplate - Truth.

Burgundy - Joy, bounty, intoxicating feelings; perhaps even intoxication!

Butterfly - Rebirth, rejuvenation, transformation, metamorphosis.

Caduceus - Healing.

Candle - Enlightenment, spirituality, uncovering secrets.

Chains - Servitude, sorrow, subjugation, natural consequences of greed.

Circles - Unity, endlessness, perfection, intuition, feminine principles, looking inward. Also, the Circle of Life.

Cliff - Feeling of "being on the edge."

Clouds, Grey - Oppression, dreariness, foreboding, looming sorrow.

Clouds, White - Dreaming, summer days, imagination, flights of fancy.

Crystal - Purity, harmony, clarity. The seen world, things that are "crystal clear."

Crystal Ball - Unseen forces or knowledge, spiritual matters, hidden wisdom, esoteric knowledge, magic.

Cultivated Fields - Industry (as in hard work, not factories,) civilization, caring or planning for the future, delaying gratification, working with the Earth.

Cup - Femininity; a symbol of the Goddess (The Lady.) Also emotions, intuition, spiritual things.

Daisy - Freshness, purity, innocence, child-like qualities.

Dog - Faithfulness, loyalty, unconditional love.

Eight - wheel of the year, recurring patterns, cycles.

Feather, Red - Courage.

Feather, White - Accomplishment, purity, esteem.

Fir Tree - Vision, especially spiritual vision, reincarnation, persistence of beauty. Also Maid, Mother, and Crone.

Five - Senses, sensuality, material world.

Flowers - Joy, frivolity, celebration.

Flute - Harmony, beauty, balance, purity.

Four - Four elements. (Earth, Air, Fire and Water.) Also stability.

Gold: The visible, material world; the consensual universe, that which is seen, the sun, masculine energy. Also wealth, power, richness, warmth, success, fullness, luxury, rareness. Sometimes incorruptibility.

Grapes - Abundance, joy, wealth, plenty; party time!

Grass - Growth, lushness, health.

Green - Growth, vitality, earthy wisdom. Association with Goddess.

Grey - Balance, as between light and dark. Can also mean sterility, coldness, apathy, chill intellect depending on context, especially if it's grey stone.

Hand, Left - Intuition, the twilight, unconscious mind.

Hand, Right - Intellect, strength, the rational, conscious mind.

Harp - Harmony, grace, beauty, purity.

Hawk - Bravery, freedom, exhilaration, far vision, enlightenment, courage, power.

Hills - Gentle enlightenment, without as high a cost, but also without as much depth. Things gradually revealed. Also, ancient wisdom.

Horse - Forces of nature, or of self, harnessed and under control.

House - Home, family, security, nurturing.

Indigo - Psychic abilities, the unseen world, mystery.

Iris - Beauty, fragility, freshness, some of the connotations of the Rainbow, since Iris was the Goddess of the Rainbow.

Ivy - Introspection, turning within.

Laurel Wreath - Victory.

Lavender - Healing

Lemniscate (infinity symbol) - Symbol of the Adept. Mastery, magic, wisdom.

Light - Brilliance, purity, enlightenment, insight, recognition, perception, discernment, wisdom.

Lilies - Purity, chasteness, innocence, beauty.

Lion - Strength, pride, virility, majesty, nobility.

Mist - The unknown, uncertain, and unseen.

Moon - Mystery, magic, wildness, the hidden world, unseen forces, the passing of time or seasons, the fullness of time; also feminine strength, energy or power.

Mountains - Enlightenment, often purchased at a cost, but worth it.

Oak Tree - Strength, age, wisdom, protection, kingly attributes. Gate into otherworld.

Ocean - The unconscious mind, emotions, the whole concept of a universe that is beyond our ken or control.

Orange - Vitality, energy, passion.

Path or **Road** - Spiritual path, choices Seeker is making, life–decisions, life–direction.

Pentacle - Stillness, growth, depth of soul, wisdom, rest, plenty, rightness with the universe.

Pomegranate - Secret knowledge, rebirth, identification with the Goddess.

Poppies - Fertility, joy, virility, gaiety; often found growing with wheat, so represent nourishment of the spirit.

Purple - Royalty, majesty, power, richness, plenty, wealth.

Rain, Grey skies - Sadness, foreboding, sorrow, pain, melancholy.

Rainbow - Promise of end to hardship. Also, whole spectrum of possibilities, joy, mirth, beauty, effervescence, ephemeral qualities.

Red - Life, virility, passion, courage, boldness, resolution, pluck. Association with God.

Roses - The balance of sweetness and pain that represents life. Beauty and sorrow combined.

Roses, Pink - Love, affection, friendship.

Roses, Red - Courage and passion.

Roses, White - Change, freedom.

Roses, Yellow - Joy, laughter.

Scales - Balance, fairness, impartiality.

Ships - Far ventures.

Silver - Mysteries, the unseen, the moon, feminine energy, non-material wealth.

Spiral - Introspection, self-awareness, growth, contemplation.

Square - Perception, strength, linear thinking, masculine principles, honesty, sometimes rigidity.

Stars - Enlightenment, guidance, beauty, mystery, magic, hope, longing, dreams; the feeling of reach exceeding grasp.

Stone Walls, Rough - Security, boundaries, separation.

Stone Walls, Smooth - Being cut off from nature, separation from the Earth, setting self apart from others; coldness, aloofness, uncaring attitudes.

Stones in Road - Difficulties or hardship.

Sun - Joy, vitality, boundless energy, youth. The visible world or hidden things revealed. Victory. Also masculine strength, energy or power.

Sunflowers - Joy, vitality, mirth, radiance.

Sword - Intellect, austerity, power especially martial power, authority, responsibility, sorrow. Also symbol of the God (The Lord.)

Three - Past, Present, and Future. Also, Maid, Mother, and Crone. Or Body, Mind and Soul. Or Unconscious, Conscious, and Superconscious.

Triangle - Balance, religious principles, the spirit.

Two - Balance

Vegetables - Things in life that are good for you! Also abundance, fullness, feelings of good harvest; reaping what you have sown.

Violet - Youth, sweetness, vulnerability, shyness.

Wand - Will, vitality, growth, fiery attributes, cunning, sudden action.

Water - Emotions. The feminine, unseen, mysterious side of anything. That which carries us away, or exerts pressure upon us, without our intellectual agreement.

Wheat - Prosperity, food, goodness, wholesomeness, life, nourishment of the body. Also death and rebirth.

White - Purity, brilliance, lightness, clarity, newness (like an empty canvas,) freshness, spotlessness, renewal, the moon, feminine energy.

Wings - Freedom, enlightenment, joy, uplifting spirituality, soaring intellect or emotions, skillfulness, mastery.

Yellow - Vitality, vigorousness, energy, youth, joy, glory, triumph, the sun, masculine energy.

To some extent, the numbers on the cards also have common meanings. I'll warn you, though, that even though I've thought about these a good deal, and these are the best answers that I can come up with, they don't always seem to fit. In many instances, three of the cards would seem to be telling the same part of a story, and the fourth would not.

So I had to dig deep to find common ground. For instance, in the case of the Threes, I decided that the deep meaning of the number was Spirit or Mastery, because of the lessons about the attributes of the suit that are revealed here. For Pentacles, we learn that study leads to mastery. For Swords, we learn that knowledge or the thirst for power can bring pain. For Wands, we learn that part of willing is waiting. For cups, we learn that love brings joy.

If these don't make sense to you, feel free to draw your own conclusions. (Feel free to draw your own conclusions anyway!) I'm frankly not sure that they were ever set up to fit into categories like these!

King - Ruling principal. This is the element and affiliation of the suit, in its strongest and most dominating role. This one tells you.

Queen - Reflective principal. This is the element and affiliation of the suit, in its purest and most nurturing role. This one guides you.

Knight - Active principal. This is the element and affiliation of the suit, in its most active and explorative role. This one engages you in adventures.

Page - Learning principal. This is the element and affiliation of the suit, in its most absorbing and discovering role. This one opens new horizons.

Ace - This card is the beginning. It has all the attributes of the suit, concentrated and distilled into a single lesson. Although it's only one, it holds the entire suit within itself, as a bean holds a tiny plant inside.

Two - This is the card of balance. In this card, the attributes of the suit are held in tension against each other, and an equilibrium that reveals the first lesson of the suit is found.

Three - This is the card of the spirit and mastery. In these cards, the deepest attribute of the suit is first revealed.

Four - This is the card of change. In these cards, the flip side of each lesson is first explored. (activity becomes rest, joy becomes discontent.)

Five - This is the card of Reversal. Here, the negative side of the attributes of the suit are fully revealed.

Six - This is the card of Lessons Learned. In this card, the lessons learned from the Fives are translated into actions.

Seven - This is the card of Decision. In this card, the lessons of the suit are pinpointed, and the Seeker faces a choice.

Eight - This is the card of Challenge. In this card, the lessons of the suit are stripped to their most difficult.

Nine - This is the card of Revelation. In this card, the lessons of the suit are made most obvious.

Ten - This is the card of Logical Conclusion. In this card, the lessons of the suit are brought to their logical conclusion.

Chapter 6
The Major Arcana

I studied the Tarot for nearly a decade before I made this deck. I thought long and hard about the meaning of each card, and what symbols best represented that meaning for me. And I sketched, and drew, and thought some more. And I grew and matured, and the symbols that I needed changed, and still I drew.

At last I had drawn all the cards, and the symbols that I used became "frozen" at that moment in time. If I were making the deck now, it would be slightly different, because I have had another eight or nine years of experience and growth.

As I write these chapters I am working from the notes I made while I was studying and deciding what symbols to use for each card, supplemented by the things that I have learned since.

And yet, these are still just my personal interpretations and feelings.

As you are reading the cards, you are likely to have your own. These are not "wrong," even if they are not at all what I saw while I was making them! As I have said before, if I have done my job right, you are bound to see things that I didn't even know I was putting in there!

I recommend that you go over each card, much as I will do here, and write down what you see, and why you think it's meaningful. This doesn't mean that you won't see completely different things in some other reading. But it will help you to get into the habit of really looking at the cards.

I'm providing this material because a lot of people have asked for it, and because you might find it interesting to see what was going through my mind while I was designing the cards.

The Major Arcana are the Greater Secrets, the cards of power and mystery that touch on all the great powers in the Universe. They deal with what Jung would have called the Archetypes; the root images in the collective unconscious from which all other images spring. They represent the forces behind and within the life of the Seeker, over which the Seeker has no control. They are the Trumps, the portion of the deck that sets Tarot apart from regular cards.

When more than a few show up in a reading, then it becomes apparent that the reading is concerned with major forces, and all that the Seeker can do is hang on for the ride, and learn as much as possible!

I don't use reversed cards, so no meanings for reversed cards are given.

0 - The Fool

This card shows a young blond man dressed as a harlequin. He is playing the flute, and dancing near the edge of a precipice. Near his feet is a little dog.

Key – **Pay Attention**

The meaning of this card is thought-less innocence, and lighthearted folly. A lack of discipline. A lack of experience that can be dangerous. Great freedom, although with a connotation of foolish-ness. Idealistic youth, creativity. Seeing only the goal, and not possible difficulties along the way.

I dressed the fool as a harlequin to show that he is a lover, with sharp wits, although he may also be somewhat of a buffoon, and liable to be hurt in the end. I gave him a white shirt to show his purity. His vest is yellow and blue to show sun and shadow, light and dark. His moods may be mercurial, and vary between these extremes at the drop of a hat.

He wears red and white on his left leg for the Lord and purity. Red is often a color associated with the Lord, the God of the Hunt, and squares are also often symbolic of masculinity or rigidity. On his right leg are the green and white stripes of the Lady. Green and white are her colors for a good part of the year. But usually the right, active side is seen as masculine, and the left, intuitive side as feminine. He has them reversed to show that although he is aware of the forms, he doesn't really understand. Or perhaps he flaunts the convention in an act of youthful rebellion, to assert his freedom and independence!

He dances, carefree, to the sounds of a pipe. In many decks, he is carrying a staff which symbolizes the wand of will and life (we'll get more into that in the chapter about the suit of Wands.) In my deck, I decided to transform the wand into a pipe, because I see him as playing with his will and life; having fun, and making pretty tunes with them, but in a larger sense doing just as he wants with them, with little regard for the consequences. Far from a staff to steady his steps, he has made them into a flute to dance to! And dancing on the edge is very dangerous.

He wears the white roses of freedom in a wreath around his head. There are five of them, to symbolize the five elements; earth, air, fire, water and spirit. He knows of all of them, which gives him freedom in each. But the knowledge is still only at his head level. It has not penetrated to his heart, and he isn't paying attention to any of it!

Stuck into the wreath is a long red feather, symbolizing his courage. He is brave, even if it's mostly the bravery of ignorance. (He isn't afraid, because he has no idea how badly he can be hurt.)

He wears a pack on his back, strapped on with the white ribbons of guilelessness. In it he carries all the things he needs to get along in the world. But they are strapped down behind him, and not really accessible. I gave him five ribbons for the five senses. They are what he has bound his life up with. When he reaches for something he needs, he hits them first, and is usually distracted by their beauty.

He dances on bright spring grass, to show this is a youthful thing. The grass is strewn with pairs of red and white flowers for fearlessness and innocence. His eyes are on the distant vista of the mountains, which stand for knowledge and enlightenment. That may be a good thing, but in this case it means that he is completely unaware that he is about to dance right off the edge of a cliff!

A little white dog, which symbolizes his friends, or his own unconscious mind, is trying desperately to warn him of the danger. But so far he is not paying any attention. Sometimes, when this card comes up in a reading, the little dog looks like it's just dancing along with him, aware of the brink, but unwilling to disturb its master. In that case, I read it as people who are so enamored of his charisma that they are sure that he does really know what he is doing, all appearances to the contrary notwithstanding. If he is going to go over, then that must be the right thing to do, and they'll go right over with him!

Below him is the valley which symbolizes the deeper parts of his own soul, with the stream of his unconscious running through and watering it. In a very real way, it's the depths within himself that he is about to tumble into.

Three trees grow up from the valley to the level where he walks. These symbolize his body, mind, and soul. They are the parts of which he is made, which rise from his inner self until they are seen by all, although their roots remain hidden.

As he dances, three butterflies flit around him. Butterflies in the Tarot stand for transformation. If he doesn't watch out, he is going to have a transformative event! (Oh please, Gods, not another learning experience!) I gave him three to show the future, which is rosy; the present, which is a blank sheet; and the past, which is golden. He is facing the future, but the past and present are both behind him, and he isn't looking at them at all. In other words, he is paying very little attention to where he is now.

The sun shines brightly on him, and there are no clouds in his sky.

1 - The Magician

This card shows a smiling man with a dark beard and grey eyes, standing in front of a table with a pentagram, wand, sword, and cup on it. He is wearing a hood made from a deer's head, complete with antlers. His right hand is raised, and a lemniscate (infinity symbol) floats above it. His left hand is pointing down. Behind him burn two candles, one black and one white. The light from them fills the rest of the card.

Key – **Creativity**

This card means originality, great creative powers, imagination, skill, diplomacy, self-reliance. The opportunity to use any of these talents. The merging of the four elements. Mastery in the magical aspects of life.

I tried to give the Magician a look of quiet confidence, because that is one of the strengths of this card. This card shows up when you are well qualified to operate in an area, and are about to be given the chance to "show your stuff."

I gave him dark hair and light eyes, because he is an avatar of the God here, and I wanted to show that he embodies both the light and dark aspects*, and the balance between them.

He wears a hood made from the head of a deer, antlers and all, because that is the symbol of the Horned God, whom he serves, and whose Priest he is. And so, of course, who he is. I'm afraid that this makes him a Wiccan Magician; but then, I am Wiccan!

His robe is red because that is the color of courage and life. He embodies both of them. The lining is white to show his purity of purpose, and the absolute clarity of his thoughts and inspirations.

There is a double border down the front to show balance again, and to show the duality of the God, i.e., death and rebirth, the Green God and the God of the Hunt, etc. The background of the border is gold because of the mastery shown here, and the incorruptibility. Gold never tarnishes, or oxidizes in any way. The white roses of freedom and the white lilies of purity are intertwined on the border,

---

*Light and dark as day and night, or life and death, or visible and invisible. Not light and dark as good and evil. I never see them that way. Think about how much evil has been done in the name of the light, or how good and healing it is to rest in a dark room. Good and evil, in my worldview, aren't things that need to be balanced. In fact, good *is* being in balance, and evil is being out of balance! But that is really a topic for the Philosophy Book.

to show how he operates freely in both. They have bright green leaves, and look realistic, to show that they are alive and growing in his life. Also on the border are little drops of dew, to show the freshness of his perspective.

His robe is open to show that he is open to new things. He is naked underneath it to show that he is free, and unashamed.

His right hand is raised and visible, while his left is lowered and hidden to show that he operates in both the seen and unseen worlds. It also shows the principle of "as above, so below" as things are reflected between these two worlds.

His right hand is held in the position used to symbolize the horned God, but slightly more open. I did this to show that he is the representative of the God, again, and yet at the same time, he is himself, too. Above it he holds a shining lemniscate, an infinity symbol. This proclaims that he wields power in the realms of infinity and eternity. Nothing can stop this man; he can easily handle anything you give him, and have fun doing it!

On the table in front of him are the symbols of the four elements; the sword for air, the wand for fire, the cup for water, and the pentacle for earth. These show that he has control in all of these areas, and in the states of being that they represent. (To know, to will, to feel and to be still, in that order.)

If you look at them singly, the sword has a man holding the Tyr rune on it. This rune stands for the god Tiw, who dealt with oaths, legal contracts, and honor, and was known for his courage. So the handle of this sword symbolizes fairness, courage, and honor. The blade is steel, and mirror bright, because evil cannot stand mirrors, and iron is good for cutting through the sticky strands that evil creatures tend to bind things with. So the sword, as well as showing air and knowledge, shows knowledge extending into justice and honor, and the ability to overcome evil ie. things that would harm or hinder.

The wand, the symbol of fire, is made of crystal, bound with silver wire, and topped with a piece of amber. The crystal, once again, is for clarity. And crystal can be charged to hold energy. So the Magician has all the energy that he needs at any point. The silver is for magic and the moon, and all things mysterious and hidden. So the seen is wrapped in the unseen. The amber is for fire, and also because it is made from the sap of living trees, petrified through time. So, for me anyway, it also stands for life and for the permanence that time can give things. It's also sacred to the Lady in some traditions, and so gives more balance to this card.

The cup is very plain, to show that things may be very straightforward, and fancy trappings aren't necessary. It's gold on the outside and silver on the inside to show the balance between male and female energies, as well as that between the seen and unseen, day and night, etc. If you look carefully, it has water in it. I used water here because that shows clarity again, and because the cups stand for water. Also, if you are really thirsty, water is better than wine.

The pentacle has a silver star on a gold ground for the same reasons. The silver star is magical night, and the gold disk is the sun. Also, the silver pentagram is the symbol of a person (two arms, two legs, and a head) while the gold disk is a symbol of the earth, so it becomes a person on the earth, and shows that the Magician is at home here. The silver pentagram may also symbolize the five elements (earth, air, fire, water, spirit) with the golden disk allowing them to work as one, so it's another symbol of mastery in all the elements and of balance. Remember, the true meaning of any card is whatever seems true to you in any particular reading.

The corners of the table (which you can barely see) are piled with the red roses of passion and the white roses of freedom.

Behind the Magician are two candles; a black one on the left and a white one on the right. They stand for the conscious and unconscious minds. They are both burning, because he is illuminated in both aspects. Together, they fill the whole card with light.

2 - The High Priestess

This card shows a young woman, with black hair and deep blue eyes, standing in the open beneath a full moon. In her right hand she holds a crystal ball. In her left is an open book. Behind her are two trees, just beginning to bud. One is black, and one is white.

Key – **Wisdom and Compassion**

This card stands for aspects of practicality, good judgement, wisdom, knowledge, and mystery. Also spiritual leadership and maturity. An avatar of the Lady. All the things that one would ideally find in the HPS (High Priestess) of any group!

This is one of the cards that I found I wanted to change a lot. The position of High Priestess, carrying as it does the responsibility and privilege of being the representative of the Goddess, is very important to me personally. I tried to convey as much of that as possible in this card.

So I started with a woman who is young, but not too young, and who has a look of quiet joy and wisdom. (I hope!) I gave her black hair like the night sky, to show her affinity with the hidden, mysterious, sensual, healing and feminine dark. I left it blowing free all around her to show the freedom of her spirit, and her unbound femininity and sensuality. Her deep blue eyes show her spirituality, because that is the color of the intuition, and the third eye.

I gave her a crescent moon crown to show that she is the daughter of the moon. The horns are up, as they are in a waning moon, to show that even though she is young, she is full of wisdom. The silver circlet shows that she is capable of using circular logic and intuition. It also shows continuity; she has been a Priestess before, and will be one again.

She wears a silver pentagram to show that she is a Priestess, and also because a Pentagram (among many other things) is a symbol of secret knowledge and harmony with the universe.

Her silver bracelets are a symbol of her rank. In many traditions (including ours) silver bracelets signify third degree. So they show that she has already mastered the basics of the religion (first degree initiation) and has learned to see the patterns in the way the world works (second degree.) At this point, she can ply those patterns to further the work of the Gods. That is the level where she lives. That's the level of activity shown by this card.

In the first incarnation of the High Priestess, I made her robe white to show her virginity. But then I decided that virginity, and the naivete and inexperience that implies, wasn't right for this card. So I gave her a robe that encompasses all the colors that are normally associated with the Goddess; from the white of the maiden at her shoulders, to the green of the Mother of the Earth, to the blue that shows the spirituality and purity of the Goddess, to the deep indigo of the Queen of the Heavens and the Crone. There are no sharp dividing lines between the colors, because she is still the same Goddess, however we are looking at her.

Beneath her robe she is naked to show that she is unashamed of herself, and free. It also shows that she doesn't think of herself as vulnerable. She is unafraid.

In her right hand she holds a crystal ball, the symbol of mystery and magic, the unseen, mystic knowledge that can only come from within. Spheres are also a symbol of the feminine, so this symbolizes the intuitive, indirect side of a person, as well. It's in her right hand, although that is the active, not the intuitive, side, because that is the way she most often works. That is her strong suit, if you will.

In her left hand she holds an open book. This is also knowledge, but it's readily available, easily accessible, open to everyone. This is the carefully reasoned, practical side. The seen. The book has a black binding to show that it is filled with wisdom, as black is the color of the Crone. It has gold leaf on the pages, to show how valuable it is. Just because she is holding it open for all doesn't mean it's cheap or worthless. It just shows how much love she has, to freely give knowledge of such value.

I put her outside because this is a nature religion, and should, I think, be practiced out of doors as much as possible. It also shows once again how unfettered she is. There are no walls to hem her in, or hide her from the world.

It's night, because that is traditionally the time of mystery. The moon is full because it's during the full moon that the expansive energy is highest, and also to show the fullness of her knowledge. It's partially hidden by a veil of clouds, to show that her knowledge may be hidden by mystery. This gives me a visceral reaction of immanent disclosure and splendor. Because visceral reactions are what the cards are all about for me, that's important.

Behind her are two trees, just coming into bud to show that it's springtime, and the potential for growth is great. Although she is already a High Priestess, and has lots of knowledge, in a very real way she is just beginning to learn.

The tree on the left is black, because it symbolizes the feminine, the dark, and negative* life aspects. The one on the right is white for the masculine, light, and positive aspects. These are all brought together and balanced in her.

---

* Negative doesn't mean evil, or positive good, by the way. Negative is the side of things that are decreasing, drawing together, receiving, and winding down. Positive is that which is increasing, expanding, sending, and revving up. Too much of either one is unbalanced, and that is where evil comes in, I think. If you could never rest, you would quickly kill yourself. If you could never do anything *but* rest, it would be just as bad (although it might be slower!) It's time to take back the words, so people can understand the balance.

3 - The Empress

This card shows a pregnant woman, dressed in royal robes, sitting spinning beneath a beech tree. At her feet are baskets piled high with food, and a beehive. Hanging from the tree is a heart-shaped shield with the symbol of Venus, or femininity, on it. Behind her is a field of poppies and ripe wheat. Beyond that is a lake, and beyond that are hills that lead back to mountains.

Key – **Mother**

This card means fertility, safety, security, good advice. Great abundance, nurturing, and material wealth. Perhaps pregnancy. A woman who is competent and secure, and building a future for herself and her family. Plenty, joy, growth and success.

This card went through more permutations before it reached the present form than any other. At first, I just had her sitting on a throne, with her hands folded in her lap to show how patient she was. Then I decided that she should really be preggers, to show her extreme fruitfulness, and how full she is of generative life. Then I decided to make her spinning, instead of just sitting there, because ...well, we'll go into that later.

I should tell you, though, that I had a pregnant friend named Donna that I decided would be perfect to pose for this card. But when I called her, and told her I had decided to make the Empress pregnant and spinning, and would she mind coming over to pose, she informed me that was totally unnecessary. "Why?" I asked her.

"Because," she replied, "when you are pregnant you are quite dizzy enough without spinning!"

The Empress is smiling to show that she is comfortable, and friendly. She is pregnant to show the fruitfulness of this archetype, and also to show that she is full to bursting with procreative life. This doesn't necessarily mean a child, by the way. You can be pregnant with an idea, or a project, or something like that just as well. I also did this because one of the meanings of this card is pregnancy.

She is dressed in velvet robes the rich color of ripening wheat, because that shows again the richness and fruition that are such integral parts of this card, and also the softness and warmth that are part of her character. Her robe is trimmed in deep green for the color of the Goddess and growth. When a plant is no longer green, growth has stopped, and death isn't far behind.

Around her hem is a band of gold with a wheat motif. The gold is for richness and wealth. The wheat is a symbol of plenty, and of life and death. (The wheat grows, dies, is replanted, and grows again.) There is also a band of green for growth and vitality. It has a design of hearts for love, and the female symbol to show her motherhood. The band is continuous to show these things never end.

Around her sleeves are more bands, gold again for the same reason, and a motif known as "The Tree of Life" with luxuriant leaves, vines, flowers and fruits growing and twinning around, to show the richness and abundance of life.

Around her collar is another band, which repeats the same ideas, this time with green gems on gold. These gems form circles for the circle of life. From it hang ruby hearts, to show how freely she loves.

A band of gold goes from her collar to the clasp that fastens her dress across her breasts. On it is shown an Athame, the sacred knife of the Wiccae. On the clasp is a cup. The juxtaposition of these two is called "the Great Rite," and symbolizes the fertilizing of the female by the male, the act which brings forth life. It's very holy; and putting it right above her pregnant belly underlines the concept!

Her hair is a rich gold, like the wheat, and is bound to show that she has submitted to the responsibility of caring for a family. It's bound in gold, though, because these commitments themselves are a rich source of joy and happiness. On her forehead is a white jewel, to show her purity.

She is also wearing a crown, because she is an Empress, after all! It has a silver band with engravings that show all the phases of the moon, because she contains all of the aspects of the moon; Maiden, Mother, and Crone.

Above them are six shining stars, to show the six senses through which she speaks to us.

In the middle is a setting with four silver disks, for the four elements, with a golden one in the middle, for spirit.

In her ears are earrings shaped like a gold disk with three crystals hanging from it. (You'll just have to take my word for this.) The gold is for her love, and the crystals are to show that it springs three-fold to water the earth.

Over all she wears a transparent veil of deepest blue, with silver stars on it. This is to show that she is the Queen of Heaven, and crowned with the glory of the universe. It also shows that she is mistress of the night, intuition and hidden things. And that she reveals the hidden (the veil is transparent.) Her shoes are the same color, and also have stars on them, for all of these same reasons, and also to show that whatever is above is also echoed below.

Over her shoulders she wears a purple cape, lined with ermine. These colors show her majesty, and also her purity. According to legend, the ermine would rather die than be soiled. Her cape has gold disks with all the signs of the planets on them, to show her rulership in all of these areas. There is also one with a heart and one with a star to show her majesty there as well. It has gold trim with a vine pattern for abundant life and joy.

She is spinning the thread of life out of stars and air. This is what she does. Legends are full of women, often Queens, who spin in this fashion, and that is what I was trying to convey. My favorite is the Princess' Grandmother in George MacDonald's book "The Princess and Curdie." If you can, read it. She was wise, and gentle, and strong, and old, and wonderful in every way. And that is the reaction that I wanted to have when I saw this card.

Her wheel has eight spokes because it is the wheel of the year.* Around the outside of the wheel are the signs of the Zodiac, to show the year, again. As it turns, the thread of life is spun out, until it is perfect. On the frontmost leg of the wheel is a scepter, to show her majesty and mastery here.

She is sitting beneath a beech, because beech trees are the Queens of the forest to me. And in the Celtic tree system, the beech stands for old knowledge. So her knowledge is older than time. From the tree hangs a red, heart shaped shield, with the symbol of the feminine on it. This is to symbolize that her intuitive heart is the only protection that she has, and she has set even that aside to accept the Seeker with openness. It has a green ribbon for growth, again, and a gold border with a spiral pattern for introspection.

At her feet are baskets of fruit and vegetables, to show wealth and abundance. There is also a bee skep to show richness and sweetness.

The grass glows green to show the bright abundance of growth, sprinkled with small yellow flowers to show her joy.

Behind her is a field of ripening wheat. As mentioned before, wheat shows richness, and also the cycle of life. There are poppies mixed with the wheat for joy, sensuality, and fertility. Also, as the wheat nurtures the body, the beauty of the poppies nurtures the spirit.

Behind them is a deep and placid lake. This is the water of life, the unconscious, and emotions. It flows deep and pure in her.

Farther in the background are trees, which show strength and growth again, and then hills. These hills are old and rounded, and have fences on them. This shows that her wisdom is ancient, and also that it is tamed, and civilized. It is part of the home and society, not the wild, untrammeled knowledge that is shown in other cards.

Farther back are the mountains of enlightenment. These show her majesty and the depth of her knowledge once again.

---

*The Wiccan wheel of the year is divided into eight parts by the holidays that we celebrate. If you would like more information on this, it's in Appendix C.

4 - The Emperor

This card shows a man with a golden beard that is turning to grey, dressed in half armor and sitting on a throne made of stone. He is holding a scepter, and beneath his feet is a globe. There is a horn hanging from the corner of his throne. Behind him rust colored mountains rise to the sky. An eagle flies overhead.

Key – **Father**

This card means a father-figure, someone who is secure, successful, and stable, if a bit authoritarian. A powerful leader. Someone who is sure of himself, and who looks at the world with quiet reason. A virile leader. The embodiment of the active male principle.

I made this man mature, to the point of beginning to grey, to show that although he is still very virile, he is no longer ruled by his hormones. He tends to look at the world with calm reason, instead. His hair was once gold, though, to show his richness and also his association with the sun.

He wears a crown of laurel, because he has been victorious in many battles, and also to show growth and virility. It's the mark of a successful leader. Sometimes it also speaks a bit of the Green Man.

Beneath it is a golden crown, because he is the Emperor. The crown has a purple stone to show his majesty and royalty, topped by a golden trefoil to show the three parts of life, (youth, maturity, and old age) and his understanding of all of them. There is a white stone in the center for his purity.

He is wearing armor because of his martial nature, and his constant readiness to defend and protect. It is decorated with gold for wealth and richness, with a motif of leaves and vines to show life and fertility. On the breastplate is a two-edged sword. This shows his authority and fairness, and also his knowledge, which he carries over his heart, and which tempers his emotions.

The armor only covers half of his body, because he doesn't let his war-like nature cut him off from gentler things. It's decorated with golden ram's heads to show his virility, and his association with Mars.

He has a white belt to show his knighthood (I was in the Society for Creative Anachronism for too long) and so his nobility and chivalry.

His trousers are blood red, to show his courage, and also because red is the color of the God. It also shows that he rules death, bloodshed, and resurrection. And sometimes it just shows that he goes forth boldly.

He wears boots, because of his martial character. The Earth is beneath his feet as a reminder that the masculine principle rules the world just now.

He has two rings, one dark and one light, to show balance.

In his right hand he holds the scepter of his authority. The globe shows his dominion, again, and the ankh shows that he rules primarily through the life forces. The globe, if you look carefully, is held in an open flower, to show that he is in the flower of his prime. It's supported by another ram's head for potency and virility. The globe itself is quartered and cross quartered. This shows the wheel of the year, but mostly I did it to show that he tends to be a bit authoritarian. He's not really interested in freedom for everyone, control seems safer to him.

The ankh on the top has a circle and a square on it. The circle shows that this is part of the cycle, and complete. The square is for his stability, which can border on rigidity, as is shown by all the other squares, as well.

He wears a purple cape, with an ermine lining, for his royalty and majesty. The basic shape of this cloak is a square, to show his steadiness once more.

On top is a border of alternating red rectangles and green circles. These are masculine and feminine symbols, and show that he has some balance. As completely male as he is, he does acknowledge his softer side at some level. The bottom border is gold coins on a red ground to show his wealth and success.

It is fastened with a gold brooch that has a blood-red stone to show his passion and potency again, ringed with gold coins to show wealth and accomplishment.

He is sitting on a square throne made of stone, to show his stability and firmness. He is what my mother would call a "four-square" kind of guy. There are ravens carved on the throne to show his warlike attitude, and to call to mind the ravens of Odin. So they speak of his wisdom, intelligence, and self-sacrifice. The arms of the throne have rams again because of his virility and tenacity.

On the corner of the throne hangs a hunter's horn, because he is also the Lord of the Hunt. He has the lusty vigor and endurance necessary to bring down the wiliest prey, and the power of life and death once he has caught it.

Behind him are the rust-red mountains of Mars. They are dry, because the male principle is dry and cold, as opposed to the female, which is wet and warm. And they reach high, because his achievements are great, and because he likes a challenge!

The eagle shows the flight of his intellect, and his mastery over the element of air.

The sky shows yellow at the horizon, because there is joy here, and an abundant sense of humor, even if it is a dry one.

5 - The Hierophant

This card shows a bishop, shorn and shaven, standing in his stone church. He is wearing a gold miter with a crown at the top, and keys in the design, and carrying a gold scepter. At his feet kneel two acolytes with tonsured heads. One is smiling, the other frowning.

Key – **Conformity**

This card means repressive conformity, captivity, servitude, empty ritual. A concern for form over function. A desire to hold on to old things, even if they are outdated. A desire to control others, or a position in which you have allowed yourself to be controlled by others.

I realized, when I began writing this description, that not everyone has the same attitude about conformity I do. My thesaurus, for instance, uses words like "harmony, agreement, felicity, fitness, concord" as synonyms for "conformity." I have always thought of it more in the vein of "suppression, repression, smothering, squashing, extinguishing personality, limitation," Guess that's telling, isn't it?

So this card may not mean exactly the same thing in my deck that it means in others. I have never found conformity to be life-affirming. I tend to think it's something that was devised to more easily control others.

Rules, for me, are something for people who are too young and inexperienced to stay out of harm's way, to keep them alive until they gain the experience to make wise choices themselves. In other words, to keep children out of trouble long enough for them to grow up! After that, they don't need rules, just brains.

I made the fellow to symbolize stifling conformity a bishop in the Christian Catholic church, because that is where I, personally, have run into this unquestioning conformity the most often. Not to say that Christians automatically repress and try to control others. Some Christians are truly good people. And the Christian church is glad to squelch them, too. It's not Christians I object to. It's their Church! For someone who wants to control others, the Church is a ready tool. First tell people that they cannot question God. Then tell them you speak for God. And Hey Presto! They cannot question you, either!

In my opinion, any institution that has a guy at the top who, by definition, can never make a mistake has something seriously wrong with it.

And this card, to me, shows something seriously wrong in the life of the Seeker. He is throwing over all that he believes in for the sake of conformity.

Also, most of us former Christians go through a period when we are quite bitter about Christianity, just as one goes through a bitter period when anything that you have invested heavily in fails you. I designed this card while I was there. And I left it like this because I still find it scary that any religious group can control and manipulate people like that.

Anyway, that said, we'll go on with the description of the card.

I began by giving this man a sallow complexion, because I think this sort of activity is against nature. I don't think he gets out very much. I also did my best to make him look like he is disapproving of everything, and constipated, because that is what people who are forcing conformity on others usually look like to me.

His robes are very beautiful, because these forms can often be beautiful. But the designs on them are rigid, stylized, repetitive, and artificial. This shows that although he starts with a good idea, he has taken all the life from it by the way he treats it. They were supposed to be the lilies of purity and the red roses of passion; but now they are both dead and dried. Conformity may seem attractive, and may seem to contain the things you are looking for, but it's only a seeming. The act of rigid conformity takes all the life out.

They are rich, because this kind of control and manipulation often generates a healthy income from the people it preys on. But it all stays at the top.

They are the color of dried blood, as a reminder of the suffering caused by this sort of attitude, and how suppressing one's own individuality dries up vitality.

He wears gloves, so his hands won't become soiled with the cares of others.

On his head is a mitre, showing his position and authority. On top of it is a crown, to show that although he claims not to be part of the world, he is more than happy to tell you what to do in it!

Pictured on the miter are two keys, covering the spirals of introspection. One faces left, for the unconscious, and one right for the conscious mind. He has locked them both fast, and although you can see the keys, they, too, are not real. He has no intention of letting you get to true introspection, to the place where you actually use your mind. He would far rather you just do as you are told.

His miter has seven red stones along the bottom of it. This shows that he has used the traditional seven seals of the Church to help lock away any thought.

He holds a scepter with three rings and a sphere on it. The three rings stand for the past, the present and the future; or for the unconscious, the conscious, and the super conscious; or for any other three that pops into your mind. He will claim authority in all of them if you let him. The sphere is to show how complete and all encompassing his plans for you will be, if you allow it.

At his feet kneel two acolytes, dressed in white to show that they are still blank sheets that he intends to write on. They are children, because he is happy to keep everyone in that dependent state. They have tonsured heads, to show that they are already submitting completely to him. One is frowning and one is smiling for the masks of tragedy and comedy. This is really just a show, an act. There is no reality or substance here.

Behind him are stone walls, because he has cut himself off completely from nature. Real, growing things cannot touch him, because they are constantly changing, and he is against all forms of change.

There are two pillars there. The one on the left has a woman's head on it, to show that he oppresses women. It also has a frieze showing a bunch of sheep listening to someone preaching at them from a boat. This is to show that, like obedient sheep, the Hierophant's followers all listen to whatever he is saying, and go where they are told, and do what they are told, in spite of the fact that his platform is obviously unstable. Basically, he doesn't know what he is talking about half the time. When you think about it, what can a celibate man really know about living with a wife or raising children? And yet, they talk about it all the time, and tell people who are living it what to do. Makes you wonder, doesn't it?

On the right hand pillar is a man's head, showing that he oppresses men, too. At least he's fair, right? Also on it is a frieze showing people stumbling along under heavy burdens. This is the direct result of the scene on the first pillar. Not only does he not raise a hand to help them, he tells them that their burdens are good for them, and they should not complain. You may notice he doesn't get one.

Behind the pillars is a solid wall. This shows that such an institution is built with tradition and dogma until no breath of fresh air can possibly reach inside.

6 - The Lovers

This card shows a man and a woman walking with their arms about each other. She is holding a moon above her right hand, he a sun above his left. A rainbow connects the two of them. Behind them, two trees grow as one, with the sun just breaking between them; an apple tree on her side, an oak on his. Behind that are hills, rising to mountains. There is a home on her side, and plowed fields on his. Two eagles fly behind her, and two butterflies behind him.

Key – **Love and Companionship**

This card means love, respect, partnership, trust, communication, romance, beauty, honor, unity, perfect balance. It may mean a couple which has worked together to overcome trouble, or one that simply works very well together. Or it may mean a perfect mating of two other principles to bring forth something which is larger than either of them alone.

In the first incarnation of this card, back at the very beginning, the two figures were standing on opposite sides, reaching toward each other. As I came to understand the balance and harmony possible in a truly loving relationship, they came closer and closer together, until you cannot see daylight between them!

This particular design was first made for a magazine article about balance. I liked the woman holding the moon and the man with the sun so well that I decided to use it here. It really seems to me to illustrate the principle.

The two people on this card are the male and female principles, embracing and becoming one.

Because of that, I gave the woman long black hair, to show her sensuality, and affinity with the dark, feminine side of nature. Most of it flows loose and unconfined to show her freedom of spirit. But she has braided a single lock, to show that she has entered into a partnership, and is willing to make the compromises necessary. In it, she wears a green feather for the Goddess.

His hair is gold, to show his association with day and the light. He has a beard to show his maturity. Around his arm he wears two red feathers, for the God of Death and Resurrection.

She is looking straight ahead, while his eyes are closed, and he is following her lead. This is to show that in a perfect balance there is an exchange of attributes.

Now she is walking in the world of the seen and he is walking in that of the unseen. And she is taking the active role, while he becomes passive.

In her right hand she holds the full moon embraced by the old. This is to show that she is full of old, intuitive knowledge, and also to show her affinity with the secret, mysterious powers of the night. Using her right, active, hand shows the balance within herself.

In his left hand he holds the blazing sun. This is to show his grasp of the bright, new knowledge, and his affinity with the open, lucid powers of the day. Once again, using his left, intuitive hand shows the balance within himself.

Between them arches a rainbow, because when you have this sort of love, involvement, union and balance, everything becomes open and possible. There is also a very special kind of shining beauty here, and the rare, fragile, yet indomitable power of the rainbow.

They are walking together, with their arms around each other, to show that they are now going forward into their lives as one. From now on, they will follow their path together.

They are naked to show that they are unashamed in front of each other, and free to be whatever they are, without fear.

Behind them are two trees, growing as one. This shows that they, too, will grow together through their love. The tree on his side is an oak, which shows his strength. In the Celtic tree system, oaks stand for protection and strength. They also form the portal into the mysteries. The tree on her side is an apple, which shows her fruitfulness and beauty. In the Celtic tree system, the apple tree meant choice, and also youthfulness and beauty. And if you cut an apple in half cross-wise, you get a five pointed star. So her tree, too, is a door into greater mysteries. Together, they are very powerful indeed!

Through a gap in the tree shine seven sunbeams. Seven is a number of perfection, so this shows the perfection of their love. It also shows how bright and warm it is, and how it illuminates all around them.

They walk on soft, green grass, among little pink flowers. This shows that their love is growing and nurturing. The pink flowers, of course, show the happiness they find in their love and regard for each other.

Behind her are flying two eagles. There are a pair of them, because when you are this happy together, you want everyone to find someone as wonderful as you have, and to share this kind of joy. They are eagles to show her strength and freedom, which she can express without fear in this sort of communion.

Behind him are flying two butterflies. There are a pair of them for the very same reasons there are a pair of eagles. And they are butterflies to show his frailty and tenderness, which he can express without fear. They also show how this kind of love can transform a man (or a woman.)

Farther behind her is a home, with the hearth fire lit (you can see smoke coming from the chimney.) This shows the home that she is willing and able to make for them. On his side are plowed fields, which shows the work he is willing and able to do to provide for them.*

A stream comes down from the mountains to water the field, which shows that when a man is willing to open his intuitive side, he becomes nurturing, too.

Together, they till the soil and make a home in the fertile land of their love, which reaches ever toward new heights, as shown by the mountains. The mountains also stand for enlightenment, as always, so this kind of love can be enlightening for everyone.

There are no clouds, because nothing dims the brightness of their devotion to each other.

---

*Of course, in real life and when you are doing a reading, either of these roles may belong to either party, or they both may share both. I'm not trying to be sexist here; but the house and fields had to go on one side or the other!

7 - The Chariot

This card shows a young blond man playing a harp and singing, while riding in a moving chariot. Above him is a canopy hung with stars. The chariot is being pulled by two unicorns. One is black, and harnessed in silver. The other is white, and harnessed in gold.

Key – **Balance and Harmony**

This card means harmony, balance, triumph, leaving your problems behind. It may show that the Seeker can control conflicting forces, bringing them together into a harmonious balance, so they can work as one. It's the ultimate balance card, so in my worldview, it's a very good card indeed!

This card, too, deviates from the traditional in several ways.

The first thing I did was give the Charioteer unicorns. I did that because traditionally, unicorns are wise, but also fierce. I wanted to show that if he lost control, it would be bad. Also, they will only obey the pure in heart. If he can get two unicorns to pull his chariot, this guy must be a paragon of purity. And so he is.

One of the unicorns is black, and has a silver horn and silver harness, to symbolize the feminine, night forces.* I put a moon, and a female biological symbol (which also happens to be the symbol for Venus) on her collar to emphasize this. The other is white, with a gold horn and harness, to show the masculine, day forces. Once again, he has the male biological symbol (Mars) and the sun to reinforce the idea. They are mirror images of each other, to show that they complement and also oppose each other in every way. And yet, he has them working together to draw the chariot.

I made the fellow blond, with blue eyes, because of the general theme of yellow and blue that his entire dress conveys. (I thought blue hair and yellow eyes would be too weird.) Once again, that shows the balancing of the forces of night and day, dark and light, positive and negative.

---

* By this, I don't mean good and evil. I have encountered people who seem to think that good and evil should also be balanced. In my opinion, that is a tragic misconception. Don't think of it like two pans of a scale, think of it like a tightrope. Being balanced is itself good, because when you are balanced, you can continue. If you lose your balance, you fall and get hurt. And that is bad. So balance is good, and unbalance is evil. It's when people are unbalanced that they want to harm and hinder others. It's when you start to fall that you grab for other folks to try to save yourself. If you are balanced, you want to help and heal. If you are perfectly balanced, you can reach out to others who ask for help, and aide them in finding their balance, too!

He wears the blue of the night and intuition on his left, and the yellow of joy and perception on his right. In the same way, his armor is half the silver of the night, and half the gold of the day. There is a gold sun on the left side, and a silver moon (although you can't see it) on the right, for balance. He is wearing a breast-plate because it stands for truth. When you have perfect balance like this, the truth becomes the only protection that you need.

Around his brow he is wearing a golden circlet set with a green gem. The circle is perfection, of course. And the green in the gem is for growth and vitality. Balance like this isn't static. In fact, it allows you to change more gracefully than ever! There are rays shining out from it to show the perception, understanding, and brilliance of his spirit.

He is playing a harp because that is how he controls the unicorns that power his chariot. Through song, love, and harmony; not through brute force. You don't see any reins here, do you? It has eight strings because that is a full octave. And that makes music, and completeness. (ever try going up the scale from C to B, and not hitting that final C? Annoying, isn't it? Incomplete, somehow.) He is singing, too, because with the harp and the voice he can make beautiful harmony.

There are stars in the deep blue canopy over his head to show the celestial influences that guide him. After all, he's not just balanced, he is actually going somewhere, too! And the night forces on his canopy balance the bright day and golden dust all around him.

There are wings on the chariot itself, to show the freedom of spirit that such balance brings, with a blue jewel to show the purity and depth of his soul. And there is a yin/yang symbol, which shows balance, harmony, and unity (just in case you missed it in the rest of the card!)

Finally, the chariot is in motion, to show that even when balance is perfected, all things still change. And when balance is perfect, you can get where you are going more gracefully, and without as much trouble!

8 - Strength

This card shows a young maid, her blonde hair wreathed with flowers, closing a lions mouth. She is dressed in white, and her lap is full of flowers, too. Behind her is an alpine meadow. An oak tree is barely visible to the right.

Key – **Strength of Spirit**

This card means great moral strength and courage. Spiritual power, energy, and conviction. It may mean the gift of soothing other's grief or showing them a way to solve their problems. It shows fearlessness and love that can transform the world, or at least the way we think about it.

There is a controversy surrounding this card, believe it or not. It centers around whether this card should be Card 8, and Justice Card 11, or the other way around. When I realized this, I thought about it for quite a while, and listened to the arguments on either side. Then I decided that this deck was really the one I wanted to have, for me to use. And all the numerological and astrological arguments in the world mean very little to me; because I don't do numerology or astrology. (They both have quite a lot to do with numbers, and I have as little to do with numbers as possible, due to a bad experience with New Math when I was in first grade back in the late fifties.) So I decided to decide based on what I *do* use, which is Visuals. And I really liked the idea of the number 8, which is also the sign for infinity, as Strength. This kind of strength is infinite, and I liked the number to reflect that. I also liked the idea of the twin, balanced ones in 11 for Justice, which is a card of balancing. So that's how I left them.

I didn't change this card much from the traditional picture found in many decks, because it seemed just about perfect to me the way it was. It's a very simple card, and yet profound in its implications.

A beautiful woman, strong in her love and fearlessness, effortlessly closes the lion's mouth with her bare hands. I gave her short blonde hair, reminiscent of the lion's mane, to show that she has some kinship with the lion. She can understand it and empathize with it, although she isn't a lion herself. This is where some of her strength and love comes from. She is successful not because she is physically stronger than the lion; she probably isn't. It's because she has courage, understanding, and confidence.

She wears a wreath of flowers in her hair. I gave her daisies to symbolize the freshness of her spirit and outlook. Violets to show her sweetness. Forget-me-nots to show her caring. Spring beauties to show her joy, and babies breath to show her child-like-ness. Many of these are spring flowers, to show that she is young in her outlook. She wears them in a wreath to show that these qualities go on forever.

She wears a white dress to represent her purity. It's trimmed with the lemniscate that proclaims her an adept, with the forces of infinity in balance within her, and at her command. The trim is also yellow, to show her joy.

In her lap she holds even more flowers, to show that she has a wealth of spiritual gifts, which she is willing to give freely to others. They include all the ones in her hair, as well as white lilies for purity, pink roses for love, and a little yellow sunflower for joy.

The lion, of course, is the symbol of brute strength and pride. He is also the symbol of all the masculine qualities; vigor, virility, action, strong passions, etc. Yet he submits willingly, even gladly, to her. He allows his mouth to be closed, because she loves him. And such love evokes love and trust in return. That is the secret of this sort of strength.

She has put flowers in his mane, too, the same sort that she wears. Her good attributes are rubbing off on him, because of the association. And his qualities are even better when they are in control. (Out of control, they are often destructive and harmful.) So he learns self-control through her. She shows him what to do, and then he can do it himself.

There is an oak tree that barely comes into the picture, just in case you missed the other allusions to strength. The oak is the entrance to the mysteries, as well. So this strength can lead to even greater mysteries.

They are in an alpine meadow, because the mountains in the Tarot mean enlightenment. They are already there, although higher peaks still await them.

9 - The Hermit

The Hermit

This card shows an old man, with a long white beard, standing on a snowy mountain top. In his right hand he holds a lantern containing an eight-beamed star. In his left, he holds a staff with a red feather and two medicine bags on it. He is dressed in old, grey rags, and he smiles as he looks down the mountain.

Key – **Meditation and Contemplation**

This card means meditation, the search for truth, teaching, good counsel, wisdom, prudence, a withdrawal from life to find the center. Perhaps the Seeker has these qualities, or perhaps she is about to meet someone else who does.

I gave the man long, snow white hair and a beard to show that he is very old and wise. But he is strong with his age, which you can tell because he isn't stooped at all, but standing tall and straight.

He is dressed in clothes that look warm, but tattered. Appearance is no longer as important to him as function, and he isn't interested in material things anymore. This is something that happens with age and wisdom. His clothes are grey, because in him the positive, masculine, day forces and the negative, feminine, night forces* have finally become completely balanced and joined, and are one.

He has red shoes, though, because he steps out in courage. They are also new (you can tell, because they aren't faded) to show that the old knowledge is constantly expressing itself in new ways.

In his right hand, he holds out a lantern. This shows that having found enlightenment, he is willing to shed light on the path for others, too, if they are willing to look for it. In the lantern is a star (you might not recognize the shape, because it's too bright to look at. But that's the way I have always thought of it.) This is the star of knowledge, which shines with eight beams of light. This is to symbolize the eight parts of the year, and show that he is always standing there. It also shows the cycle, which never ends. Eight beams also show symmetry. He has followed this light, and now he bears it. Someone else is now following it, and will bear it after him.

---

* I don't mean good and evil here. I mean expansive and retractive, etc. See the footnotes for other cards.

He holds a staff, which is a symbol of will and life, to show that he is here by his own will, and that this is a vital, living thing itself. On the staff is the very same red feather that the fool had. In a way, the hermit is the fool, having come far and learned much on his journeying. Also attached to the staff are two medicine pouches, to show that his possessions are fewer now (compare this to the backpack the fool had) and yet, more powerful. As the fool's backpack symbolized his life, so the hermit's pouches symbolize his, distilled down to the most important bits, with all the fluff and drayage left behind.

He is standing high among the peaks of the mountains of enlightenment, because he has arrived there. And he is patiently waiting to help others arrive, too.

10 - Wheel of Fortune

This card shows a roulette wheel. It's divided into eight sections, and on each section is the face of a young woman. At the top of the wheel, she is ecstatic. At the bottom, despairing. Between, the colors change according to the spectrum, and her moods change, too. The wheel has a golden rim, with a silver ball in motion around it.

Key – **Roller Coaster Ride**

This card means change, and the inevitability of change. It's the card of destiny, fortune, luck, perhaps the end of troubles in sight. Moving on, for better or worse. Emotional upheaval.

When this card comes up in a reading I'm doing, it almost always means the emotional roller coaster. That's why I drew it the way that I did. I have a friend who refers to it as the bi-polar card. It's the card that comes up when you are just starting a new relationship, and are so on edge that you can be thrown into utter bliss if he sends roses, or utter despair if he breaks a date. It's the card that appears when things just matter too much! Change is inevitable; you can't let it throw you off balance like this.

When I was looking at the traditional cards, the images on them didn't convey that sense to me. So I redrew this card completely, to give it that feeling of emotional giddiness; that sense that life is going on, and there's nothing that can be done. You may wind up way on top, feeling like you have won the lottery, or you may wind up feeling that it's run over you like a semi truck. But you are likely to wind up reeling in any case. Time to find some stability here.

And you can find it, by realizing that the change is a pattern, and that it repeats endlessly. I put a lot of things into this card so that I can explain that to the Seeker, and show him what I mean.

I started with a roulette wheel, to show that the whole thing is a gamble. All that you can really depend on in this sort of situation is that the situation is going to change. But there is a pattern to the change. And the pattern is constantly revolving around a fixed center. This demonstrates the interplay between stillness and motion. Between the principles that don't change, and the things that do.

Change is a matter of position, more than of substance. The ball falls into the top slot, and you are happy. It falls into the bottom, and you are full of despair. It falls someplace in between, and you are calm and content. But it's the same ball, on the same wheel. By accepting the idea that it will land in a different section another time, you can gain balance. Whatever is going on now, this too shall pass.

Things swing from positive to negative, from joy to sorrow, from light to dark, from expanding to contracting, and back again, never stopping. If all you ever did was inhale, you would burst. If all you did is exhale, you would run out of air and die. Change is necessary; you can balance it by accepting what comes for what it is, learning whatever you can from it, and going on.

The eight spokes symbolize the wheel of the year, from summer to winter and back to summer again, over and over in endless turning.

The silver ball stands for the unconscious, from which our thoughts and feelings spring. It travels the golden rim which is the path of change. The speed of travel may vary, but the path repeats. This illustrates the underlying order in all things. It travels clockwise, deosil, in harmony with the motion of the universe.

The young woman in the card is going through the emotional roller coaster. In the picture at the top of the card, she is blissful, and everything is coming up in gold stars and yellow light. Here, she is wearing white, because she is completely full of the bright, expansive, daytime forces.

In the next section, she is still happy, and looking back towards the good times. But things are starting to cool a bit, as shown by the green background.

In the next section, she is pretty well balanced. She is calm, and serene, and her robes are grey to show the balance between the night and day forces.

Next, she begins to look ahead, and realizes that there is trouble coming up. This makes her unhappy, and she changes her robes to dark grey, and closes her eyes, to begin introspection. Her background is blue.

Then she is in the depths of despair. No longer looking outward at all, she covers her eyes so that she will not see the things that are troubling her. Her robes are black, as she becomes totally aligned with the dark, introspective, night time forces. And yet, even now, remember that night time is when you sleep and heal.

As the wheel continues, she makes the same transitions again, in the reverse order, until finally she is back where she started, in boundless delight once more.

The important question is, what has she learned from the journey?

The wheel spins, and round she goes, and where she stops, nobody knows. But if she can grasp the concept that wherever she stops it's just a temporary thing; that the wheel is going to go round again; then she can keep her balance, not get dizzy, and not invest too heavily in the ball stopping in any particular place.

And that's the secret of this card. That's what I tell the Seekers who come to me, and get this card in a reading.

11 - Justice

This card shows a woman sitting in front of two pillars. In her right hand, she holds an upraised sword. In her left, a pair of scales. She is crowned with a laurel wreath. Her eyes are open, not blindfolded. Behind her, trees and hills stretch to a clear blue sky.

Key – **Fairness**

This card means fairness, balance, justice, equality, rightness, equitable negotiations. Total justice untempered with mercy. It may show up if there is a legal matter pending. It's the card of balanced reasoning, and of completely unbiased thinking.

There is some controversy about whether this card should be number 11, as I have it, or number 8. When I learned this, I spent quite some time thinking about it. Now, I suppose that I should have been thinking about it from the viewpoint of numerology, or astrology, or something. But I don't do numerology or astrology, because I have never really made friends with numbers. (New Math in first grade in '59. It's a long story.) So I made the decision based on what the numbers look like, not on what they mean. And I liked the visual image of the two identical numerals, standing straight and balanced. It seemed to be more in keeping with the other images on this card. And I wanted the infinity symbol to stay on the Strength card. So that's the way I left it.

I gave this woman blonde hair and a light complexion to show that she is fair. (Alright, I know it's a pun. My mind often works that way!) On her head is the laurel wreath of victory, to show that in this instance clear, impartial, dispassionate thinking will prevail.

She is seated, to show that she is considering things over time, not rushing, not thinking on her feet. This may be a bit slower, but it's truer, too.

Her eyes are wide open, because she isn't blind a bit. She sees both sides, and what they need, clearly. And when she has seen all of it, and gone over it all impartially, then justice will be done.

She is very calm, because passion plays no part in her decisions. And she is looking directly out of the card, because her approach is direct.

She is wearing red robes because of the courage with which she does this. She isn't faint hearted, or weakened by fear. Fear has no part in the equation she is building here. It's also the color of the God, of animal life, and of death.

Her cape is green, to show growth and vitality. This isn't some static thing, judged by rules. She considers everything on a case-by-case basis, and makes her decisions based on what is best for everyone. It's also the color of the Goddess, and of vegetative life, and of growth.

I used both red and green to show balance, between the God and Goddess, between animal and vegetable, between life and death.

Both of her garments are lined with purple to show the depth of her wisdom, her authority, and the majesty of her justice.

Her cloak is fastened with a silver square set with a red jewel. The silver is for intuition and looking inward, and the square for perception and looking outward. So the silver square means that she has both the unseen and material worlds at her command. She can see through any argument, and discern the truth of the matter. The red jewel is the same, but in reverse. Its circular shape stands for the feminine, and its red color the masculine. So it, too, is perfectly balanced between feminine, circular logic and masculine, linear logic. As a whole, then, this clasp means that she has it covered. She understands the whole thing.

In her right hand, she holds the shining silver sword of truth and knowledge. This sword can cut both ways, and nothing can stand against it. In the hilt is set a blue stone for purity of heart. The blade catches the light, and reflects it back because truth is like that. It mirrors what is in each of us, and illuminates the world.

In her left hand, she holds the golden scales of knowledge and judgement. They are perfectly balanced, because her discernment is perfectly balanced. The handle is set with the amber stone of will, because what she wills will happen here.

If you look, the juxtaposition of the scales and her open sleeve mirror the sword. This shows balance once again. And because the bright sword is pointing up, and the dark sleeve sword is pointing down, it also indicates the concept of "as above, so below."

She is sitting between two pillars to show that she is perfectly aware of both sides of any argument.

Behind her is open air, trees, hills, and sky. This shows that her justice is calm, considered, peaceful, and ancient as the hills. But it's also fresh, vibrant and alive. The birds show that this kind of open-minded thinking can give you wings to fly!

12 - The Hanged Man

This card shows a young man hanging upside down. He is wearing red trews and a white shirt, and has one leg over the branch of an ash tree. His other leg is crossed on his ankle, and he is holding his hands behind his back. The background of the card is grey, and there is a nimbus of light around his head.

Key – **New Point of View**

This card means suspense, change, looking at things from another viewpoint. It may mean willing surrender to higher wisdom, or sacrifice to gain this wisdom, especially in occult or spiritual matters. An inner search for the truth.

In many decks, the hanged man is tied up. I thought about that, and decided that if he was doing this voluntarily, that should be shown by a lack of ropes. So the first thing I did was make all the ropes go away.

He is hanging upside down, by one knee, because he has chosen to look at things in a totally different way, from a whole new viewpoint.

The trees that he is hanging from are living, because this is a growing experience. I made them ash trees to bring to mind Yggdrasill, the world ash, from which Odin hung to obtain the knowledge of the runes. (That's also why he's blond, by the way.) In a similar fashion, the discomfort he may feel in this position is something that he is going through deliberately, in order to gain knowledge and wisdom.

He has his hands behind his back, and one ankle crossed over the other to show his total surrender to this attitude. Also, this makes his upper body (arms and head) into the triangle which is used as a symbol of the first degree of Wicca in our tradition. So it illustrates that he is on a new path of wisdom, and is changing his priorities. His shirt is white to show the purity of his resolve in this.

His legs, too, form a triangle; but with one point up, not one point down. (OK, it's a little cockeyed, but that's what I meant.) Together with his red trews, this makes the symbol of fire, or will. He is doing this through his own free will. The red trews also stand for his courage in taking this step. (If you don't see the second triangle, don't worry about it. I tried to draw him with his second leg not crossed at the ankle, but it looked like he was going to fall any second, so I did it this way instead.)

Around his head is a nimbus of light, or a halo. This is to show the spiritual radiance that this position has given him, which glows against the greyness that surrounds him.

That greyness, of course, is for balance. The night and day forces mingling equally. But sometimes, when I'm reading this card, it seems to be the drabness of the viewpoint he had before, which is being lightened and purified by his new outlook.

As always, it's how the card hits you in a reading that really counts.

13 - Death

Death
13   13

This card shows a figure completely hidden within a hooded robe, standing at a fork in a pathway that runs through a birch wood. He is holding a black flag with a white rose on it, and blocking one fork of the path. With outstretched arm, he points down the other one. A butterfly is going that way, too. And it's spring.

Key – **And Now, for Something Completely Different!**

This card means sudden and complete change. A discovery that brings about such a change in the Seeker's life direction. The end of an era, and the beginning of a new one. Change that is inevitable, and profound.

In most traditional decks, there is a skeleton on this card. Since the meaning of the card never has anything to do with skeletons, I decided that I didn't want one here. This card doesn't mean physical death. None of them do. In my experience, the Tarot doesn't care about that. It means change, complete and irreversible. It happens to everyone. And even though it can be frightening, change is often for the better in the long run.

I made the central figure completely cloaked and mysterious, because that is the scary part of change. By its nature, you can't really tell what its face is until its over. All you can tell is the general shape, and that's all you can tell about this guy.

His robes are the color of heart's blood, because that is where change generally strikes you. And yet, it's also a very vital, energizing thing, as you can tell from the bright red lining of his robes. This takes courage, but he will lend you all you need. That's one bright point about not having a lot of choice in the matter. It's easy to be brave when there is nothing else you can do!

He holds a flag showing a white rose on a black field. The white rose is a symbol of freedom and rebirth, the black field is mystery and the unknown. So the seeker will find freedom and rebirth by going through the unknown, and following the path he is now shown.

The flagpole is white, for purity. It's better if you take this way with purity in your heart. The flag is grey where it meets the pole, for balance, and there are 13 nails because this is card 13, and I'm compulsive.

He is standing in a birch wood, because birch trees are the trees of beginning, rebirth, and cleansing in the Celtic tree system. It's spring to reinforce that idea, with violets growing in the verge, and a little maple tree springing up for sweetness. This is the beginning of something that can be sweet, and new, and wonderful, as well as a passing away of the old stuff.

Behind the figure is the path the Seeker was on, stretching away into the distance. That route is closed now. From now on, she belongs on a different path. Both are equally stony. No one said this was going to be easy. But both are also equally clear. It's not going to be too difficult.

Accompanying the seeker on the new path is a yellow butterfly. Yellow is the color of joy in the Tarot, and butterflies are a sign of transformation and rebirth. So the new path will have unexpected joy, and will transform the seeker.

14 - Temperance

This card shows a blonde man with golden wings juggling three balls. One of his feet is on land, and the other is in the water. Near him grows a clump of yellow irises. Behind him is a path between fields of bright green grass, leading through a fog bank to mountains in the distance. The sun is just coming up through a gap in those mountains.

Key – **Moderation**

This card means economy, moderation, and patience. Perhaps the Seeker is going to achieve security by clever juggling of his resources. Perhaps she is going to go through a time when she *has* to juggle her resources! It may also mean meditation. Increasingly, to me, it means the ability to move gracefully and easily through life, not beset with uncontrolled appetites and avariciousness that can pull you off course. Everything in moderation (including moderation!)

Wings, for me, are a potent sign of freedom, skillfulness, and mastery. So I started by giving this fellow wings. This shows that his ability to juggle, his temperance if you will, has given him freedom. I made them golden to show that his temperance and freedom are incorruptible. (Gold alone, of all the metals, cannot tarnish.) That's the same reason that I gave him golden hair.

He is wearing a white robe to show his purity. But he has the sleeves rolled up, because he is not adverse to hard work. On his chest is the square of reality and the material world. Within it is the triangle of the spirit. This is to symbolize the spirit in the flesh, which is life.

He stands with one foot on the land, to show that he is firmly grounded in reality and in the seen, consensual universe. The other foot is in the water to show that he is also established in the unconscious, instinctive, intuitive universe.

Between the freedom of movement he has in the water and on the land, and his wings which give him movement in the air, and the symbol of the fiery sun on his forehead, he has freedom of movement in all the elements. I did this to show that when you are practicing moderation like this, you are balanced, and that gives you freedom at least, and perhaps mastery, in all the elements.

As further evidence of this, I made him juggling three balls. One is silver, one is gold, and one is crystal (you can tell by the inverted reflections, and the shadow against his robe.) The silver ball stands for spiritual wealth, the subconscious mind, and the present. The gold ball stands for material wealth, the conscious mind, and the past. The crystal ball stands for mental aptitude, mystery, and the future. He coordinates all of these, so that they will go around. (I know, but my mind works in puns!) He also handles all of them easily, and can control these forces within himself.

The idea of having him juggle was actually the brain child of my then roommate, Elisa Firth. She thought of it after a long night discussing this card, which I was having some difficulty with. (Well, I was having difficulty with Temperance at all at that point in my life!) As soon as she mentioned it, I realized that this would solve the problem, and was perfect for the card. Thanks Elisa! Love you!

Next to him is a clump of irises. Iris was the Goddess of the Rainbow in Greco-Roman mythology. So I put them there to symbolize that this was very beautiful, or that an end would come to the period of hardships that necessitate this frugality, depending on how the cards feel. I made them yellow for joy, and also to contribute to the whole feeling of brilliance and light that I intended this card to have.

Behind him a path leads to the mountains of enlightenment. It's got some rocks on it, so it may not be the easiest path in the world when you begin to travel it. But when you get up into the mountains, it'll be much easier to be on the path of balance and coordination.

It leads among fields of bright green grass to show growth and vitality. This temperance is not the dry, dusty, dead-end world of the miser. This is fresh, and vital, and growing. This is balance that feeds the spirit and revitalizes the soul.

The fog bank is to symbolize the uncertainty that is so often encountered on this path, where you can't really see clearly. But if you stay on the path of temperance and balance, you will be fine.

Past the hardship and enlightenment of the mountains is the sun. This shows the dawning of a new day, bright with promise. It also shows the mastery which can be reached if you follow the path of temperance.

The Devil

15 - The Devil

This card shows a man and a woman struggling over a chest. The lid is open, and all kinds of treasure spills from it, but it's chained to the wall; they aren't going to get anywhere. They are in a long, dark tunnel. At the end, you can see a glimpse of bright sunlight, grass, trees, mountains, and birds flying.

Key – **Greed**

This card means greed. Bondage to desire, lust, avarice, appetite, gluttony, excess, etc. The opposite of the Temperance card; the Seeker is unwilling to settle for less than everything, and it's really hurting him, and holding him back. This is a "clear warning" card. It says as plainly as possible that the Seeker needs to change his attitudes, and let go, or be seriously hurt.

This is one of the cards that I found it necessary to completely redesign. Traditionally, this card has shown a Devil character; a malicious being who causes people to be greedy and intemperate. As a Wiccan, I don't believe in any such being. Besides which, I don't think that people need any help to be greedy. I know I certainly don't! So I decided to show this card the way I saw it - naked greed.

I kept the name, The Devil, for two reasons. One was because after some discussion with a number of Tarot practitioners that I know I decided that most folk would simply be more comfortable with the names they were familiar with, and the other was because I am making a statement here. From my point of view, the Devil is our own greed and appetites, gone completely out of control. And I wanted to show that.

The central idea of this card is the Monkey Trap. This is a trap actually used in South America, where monkeys are eaten as food. A jar with a narrow neck, or a box with a hole in it, or some such container is set out with a piece of fruit inside. A monkey comes along, and puts his hand in the container to get the fruit. The problem (for the monkey) arises when he tries to pull his hand out. His little fist full of food won't go back through the hole that his empty hand went through. So the monkey begins to scream; but he won't let go. And he continues to scream, and not let go, while the people come calmly up and club him to death. If he could let go, he could escape; but his monkey brain won't make that leap, so he's dinner.

That has always seemed to me the most elegant description of your own greed killing you that I have ever heard of. And since that is what this card means, I put it on the lid of the chest.

On the end of the chest I put a drawing after Hieronymus Bosch, who painted more pictures of people being punished for their greed than any other artist I'm aware of!

Inside the chest are all kinds of treasures. Among them is a cup with hearts around the border, showing love; and a golden crown for leadership. There are also ropes of pearls and jewels for wealth; and the corner of a book for knowledge. All of these are good things, just like appetites are good. The problem doesn't arise until you let your appetite get control of you. We should be people with appetites, I think, not appetites with people! So the pearls, which usually mean purity, are beginning to look like tentacles. Letting your desires rule you like this eventually spoils the very things that you desire, turning them to dust and ashes.

The lid is open, in fact it's *chained* open, to show that these people are free to take as much of the treasure as they can carry, and leave. But they won't, because they want the whole thing. It's their greed that has trapped them here, and as soon as they can overcome it, they will be free.

I made them naked, because I wanted to show that this is naked greed. (I know, but I've warned you.) I gave them light hair so that you would be able to see it against the dark background. It's also the color of fire, and the will. It's a perversion of their will that has them trapped here. They aren't balancing their emotions (what they want) with their intellect (what they know is good for them) and so they cannot see clearly. Thinking with only one is like closing one eye; it eliminates depth perception and perspective. The woman's hair is covering one of her eyes to emphasize this point.

The chains of the chest would make an inverted pentagram if you followed them out. This is to show that this sort of attitude is anti-life, and works against the harmony of the universe, just as they are working against each other.

Overwhelming, avid greed like this is actually very lonely, because the universe contracts to a single point with just the Seeker and the object of his desire in it. There isn't any room there for anyone or anything else. I tried to show this by having the two people put their backs to each other, and pull in opposite directions. They probably aren't even aware that someone else is there. That's why I put a desperate expression on the woman's face, and the other reason I covered her eye.

They stand in a long, dark tunnel to show the narrowness of their outlook. It is open to the sky, and the mountains of attainment. You can even see the birds that show freedom of spirit if you look carefully. All open, ready for them to just walk out. But they won't, because they can't take the whole chest with them. Just like the monkey, they are determined to have their prize even if it kills them.

16 - The Tower

This card shows a ziggurat standing on an eroded piece of rock. It is being destroyed by earthquake, storm, flood and fire. Two figures are falling from it into the raging sea. They are losing their crowns as they fall.

Key – **Now to Lose the False Premises**

This card means sudden, catastrophic transformation. Broken friendships, lost security, disgrace, the overthrow of ambition or status. But this loss, though sudden and painful, is a good thing because what is being lost was built on false premises, and doomed from the start. Now it will be over, and something new can be built.

If this card shows up among the cards showing the future, I would recommend that the Seeker determine what false assumptions they are making. Perhaps the change can be made less traumatic. If it's in the past, then point out that clearing away mistakes is good, even if sometimes painful, and the worst is over now. If it's one of the cards that explains the current situation, I have found that it helps people to know that what they are going through will be of benefit in the long run.

This is one of the cards that I wrestled with in the beginning. Because the tower is supposed to be built on false premises, I wanted to make it a Tower of Babel, just like the ones shown in all those Bible stories that were read to me so often while I was growing up. But I'm no longer a Christian, and don't believe the stories literally any more; and many of the things that they represent are principles (like the value of unquestioning obedience) that I now disagree with. And then I realized that the very fact that I had found those stories to be untrustworthy, not the firm foundation for building one's life on that I had been taught they were, made the use of an illustration from one of them an even better symbol of a tower built on faulty ground.

So, here you have a ziggurat, representing something that the Seeker has put a great investment of time and effort into, crumbling into ruin before his eyes. The spiral goes widdershins (counter clockwise, the decreasing direction) as it's built from the ground up, to show that it was constructed backwards, that is, without thinking through the really important things first.

I gave it five sections for the five senses. There is a better than even chance that this faulty construction was based on a sensual appeal, and not to the higher senses!

It has eight windows, because it was meant to be balanced; but they are placed almost randomly, because that plan failed in the beginning.

It's being attacked by the four elements; all of nature, as shown in the earthquake (cracks in the foundation,) air (hurricane, shown by the lightning and the circling clouds,) fire (bursting from the top, and shooting from the windows,) and water (raging waves and flood.) Nature won't stand things set up against its rules for long, and this was. So down it goes, taking its builders with it.

The man and woman falling from it are wearing blue and gold clothing. These colors stand for spiritual things, and wealth, and show that they had the highest intentions when they were doing the construction. But they didn't choose the site wisely, so their efforts were doomed. They are also wearing purple and red cloaks, to show that they were acting as royalty. (Whether they really were trying to rule their lives wisely, and just made unwise choices; or were acting as despots and simply wanted every whim granted depends on how it feels when this card shows up in a reading.) They also had golden crowns, but they are losing them. This shows the Seeker losing his lofty position, or maybe just his big ego.

Sometimes, in a reading, it will be obvious to me that the entire structure is actually a monument to someone's ego. In that case, no wonder it's being destroyed. That sort of thing can really slow your progress along nearly any path, and needs to be removed.

17 - The Star

This card shows a woman kneeling by a pool. She pours water from a crystal bowl onto the grass, and from one of silver into the pool. Behind her are distant mountains, icy and clear under the light of a huge eight pointed star that shines overhead, surrounded by seven smaller stars.

Key – **Starlight Vision**

This card means hope, inspiration, starlight vision. Bright prospects, an awareness of two worlds, mastering the occult arts. Moving freely in both the conscious and unconscious universes. Meditation and contemplation, or gaining the ability to reach a state of meditation.

In our tradition of Wicca the Maiden is that which is complete within herself, needing no other. So I kept the Maiden on this card. She is nude, because she is free, and practicing her rites.* Her hair is blonde, in contrast to that of most of the other figures that directly represent the Goddess, to show that she also has the sun/light aspects, since stars are really suns, after all.

She is kneeling with one foot in the water of the unconscious, hidden, unseen, spiritual world, and one knee on the land of the conscious, overt, seen, physical world. This is to show that she is perfectly balanced between them. The actual position of kneeling with one foot up is used in our tradition when you dedicate yourself to the Goddess; so she is in the act of dedication.

She gazes down into the pool, showing that she is currently contemplating the unconscious, the mysteries. She is engaged in meditation.

The bowl in her right arm is silver, to show the hidden, spiritual world, and yet it also is reflective, as contemplation often is. A star is reflected in its depths, to show that meditation on the unseen can yield insight into the highest parts of the seen world, as well. The bowl in her left arm is crystal as clear as glass, to show the tangible, physical world. And yet, she sees it with crystal clear vision. The arms are reversed (left normally being the unseen, and right the seen) to show that she has balance here.

The bowls are hemispherical; if they were put together they would make a perfect sphere. This shows that the seen and unseen are both halves of a whole, and

---

*From a line from the Charge of the Goddess, written by Doreen Valiente. "And as a sign that you are free, you shall be naked in your rites."

together they make the sphere of all that is. It also shows the concept of "as above, so below," because they are identical except in materials.

The maiden is pouring the water of the unconscious equally from both, because the unconscious operates not only in its own hemisphere, but also in the worlds of the conscious, in ways we can only imagine.

The water she is pouring back into the pool shows how meditation, contemplation, and dreams recirculate, and how they refresh the unconscious.

The water she pours on the ground separates into five streams, for the five senses. This shows how the senses are enlivened and nourished by the very same meditation, contemplation, and dreams. They are necessary for physical health, as well as spiritual growth. One of the streams runs right back into the pool, to show that the senses also contribute to the unconscious. It's all part of an interactive system, and cannot really be separated, although we often do look at just one part or another. Still, isolating part of anything is really illusion. The reality is that the universe all works together.

She is kneeling on a broad lawn to show the openness of vista that such knowledge can bring. The grass is bright green because it's spring. And it's spring to show that such knowledge, although very ancient, is always new and fresh.

In the foreground grow bluebells. When I was a child, I used to call these Fairy Bells, and I *knew* that if you listened quietly enough, you could hear the fairies ringing them. So I put them here to symbolize those quiet tones that you can only hear with starlight ears. They are mixed with tiny white flowers to represent purity.

She is kneeling below a tree, which represents thought. I made it a beech, because beech trees are my favorite. They are the Queens of the forest, as oaks are the Kings, and represent old knowledge and ancient wisdom. I gave it the first tiny leaves of spring to show that through this kind of contemplation and awareness of the starlight the old knowledge is constantly renewed, and grows.

The white bird symbolizes pure thought, and freedom of the spirit. It's just landing in the tree, to show that a wonderful thought is just entering the mind. A thought that comes from the mind of the Goddess into that of one of her children is inspiration. So being in the starlight state is being open to inspiration.

Far behind the maiden is a line of trees. This shows all the other minds that also border on this state, and how all can benefit and grow together. Behind them are the mountains of higher knowledge, shining pure and white in the starlight.

The stars themselves each have eight points, to show the circle of the year, and the recurring pattern of that cycle. That is also the reason that there are eight of them. One is very large and far outshines the others, because there is one point that the Seeker is focused on right now. Which part of the cycle that is will be explained by the other cards that surround this one in the spread.

18 - The Moon

This card shows a dog and a wolf, on either side of a path, howling at the moon. In front of them a tiny crawfish crawls from a pool, making ripples among rocks where mushrooms grow. Behind them, two ancient monoliths stand in long, wild grass. The path continues through misty hills into the distance. Overhead the new moon holds the full moon in her arms.

Key – **Wildness**

This card means restlessness, wildness and change. "Going Fey," when all the trappings of the civilized world look unfamiliar and confining. The struggle between wildness and domestication in all of us.

One of the traditional meanings for this card is deception, although it never seems so to me. Some people also think of it as showing psychic powers, although I admit that I don't. For me, it's way beyond that. At this point, all mental things, and the value that those things hold, are gone; the Seeker is running wild and free as an animal, and no longer cares about powers, psychic or otherwise!

The very foreground of this card holds the pool of the unconscious; hidden stuff that we all partake of to some extent. Deep within, you can barely make out obscure shapes moving around. (Well, OK, they aren't really moving, because it's just a card. But if I could animate it, they would be.) This represents the deep unconscious, and the hidden things within it, many of which are not "nice" at all.

It's bordered by large rocks, which represent our society trying to keep the unconscious stuff safely walled away. Since this card represents the struggle to observe those walls, or to drop them and respond to deeper instincts, the pool is lapping at the edges of the rocks.

Around them grow mushrooms. I put them there because this card also means going Fey, and mushrooms have long been associated with the Faeries, and other Fey folk. If you step, or especially sleep, in a fairy ring of mushrooms, you leave the concerns of the consensual universe, the "normal" world, behind, and you can easily lose yourself. Time, also, doesn't exist the same way within the rings.

Mushrooms are also things that can spring up in a single night, as this attitude can seize you when you thought you were resigned to your life. And they don't need any sunlight to thrive, showing that this wildness has usually been relegated to the hidden, shadow sides of our personalities. It isn't trotted out in polite society.

A tiny crayfish crawls from the pool, symbolizing primitive thoughts and tendencies. It is also a creature that can survive both in the water of the unconscious, and the land of the conscious. So it symbolizes those thoughts and feelings that cross from the unconscious to the conscious mind.

Crayfish are a very potent symbol of the wild for me personally. When I was 5 or 6, we were visiting my grandparents, and my dad took me to the stream where he had played as a boy. It was beautiful; crystal clear and cold, shaded by ancient trees. We played there for a wonderful afternoon, catching crayfish (which my dad called crawdads) by putting one hand behind them, and the other in front. They would see the hand in front, and shoot backwards to get out of danger, right into the other hand. I must have picked up dozens of them, holding them in the air to watch them waving and snapping their little pincers before putting them back into their watery home.

When my dad said it was time to go, I was heartbroken, and resolved to extract a promise that we would come back the next time we made a visit to his folks. But my dad said that was impossible. It wouldn't be here next time; that was why he had taken us this time. They were putting up a shopping center, and this whole area would be destroyed, the trees cut down, the land paved over, and the stream would be turned into a drainage ditch that ran through a culvert. "That," he told me, "is Progress."

I was stunned. The stream was far better than any number of shopping centers. And I realized then that I hate Progress.

So, for me, crayfish mean the all the sun splashed afternoons in the wild, paved over and tamed.

But the crayfish on this card is winning! So it's the triumph of the wild over the unseeing forces of civilization that would destroy everything without even noticing, in the name of Progress. And the ripples that he creates, waving his pincers in freedom, stir the whole of the unconscious, and grow and spread, washing at the confining rocks.

They create the beginning of a rocky and difficult path, that leads between the wild on one side, represented by the wolf, and the tame represented by the collared dog. The dog's collar is red, for courage, but he is still the product of generations of domestication. He was a wolf once, but he has been bred to please and serve man, just as we have been to please and serve society. And yet, he is out baying at the moon, exactly like his cousin. This shows how thin the veneer of civilization actually is. Given the moon, we'll all be out there howling. I've done it. Haven't you?

The trick to this card is staying on the path, as difficult as it is. Acknowledging the wild, and reveling in it, but not losing oneself to it entirely. If you do that, then you can no longer reach those who have lost it, and help them.

The grass is long, uncut, and wild, to show that these are not tamed lands. But it's grass, so they once were. They are feral, and have reverted to a wild state.

Two ancient monoliths stand on either side of the path. At one point in the design process, I had made these trees. But I decided that I wanted to show "the hand of man," and yet still get across the ancient nature of this struggle. So I made them monoliths, one on either side of the path. They have moss growing on them, and are weathered now, but still they were once put there as a sign of civilization in ancient times. This shows that we have been treading this path between our wild and conventional sides for millennia.

Beyond them, the path continues into the misty mountains. That way is full of uncertainty and probably hardship; but still the path beckons. Eventually, it does reach the mountains of enlightenment.

Above all hangs the moon, in a purely symbolic phase that is called "the full moon in the arms of the new." This shows its changeable, restless nature. It doesn't rise at the same time of day, or set at the same time in the evening, and it changes its phase constantly. So this card has a feeling of change, and restlessness about it. But there is also a sense of continuity. The phase of the moon changes, but it always shows us the same face.

Sometimes, in a reading, when I see this card I will feel not the freedom that wildness brings, or the restlessness that comes from being too long confined in a strict regime, but instead a kind of canny hunter feeling, with no care for the prey, such as feral dogs engage in.

This may be someone who has forgotten all about ethics (or who never understood) and is about to make the Seeker prey. Or it may be the Seeker herself, on the pendulum swing from being too "nice" who is about to become completely unbalanced in the opposite direction.

In either case, the seeker needs to be warned. If you have questions about this, please see the chapter on Ethics.

This card, like the moon itself, can be either bright or dark, and needs to be examined carefully when it comes up in a reading.

19 - The Sun

This card shows a little child on a white pony. He is naked, except for a wreath of white roses and a red feather, exactly like the fool has. His right hand is outstretched, and his left holds the a huge red flag, with golden songbird wings on the pole. Behind him is a stone wall, with sunflowers growing over it. Over all shines a glorious bright sun.

Key – **Joy**

This card means success, happiness, freedom, contentment, the end of troubles. Joy, pleasure, etc. It can also mean a good marriage, or the birth of a child with a bright, sunny personality.

The child on this card is naked, to show unconfined joy and freedom. If you have ever taken care of one this age, you know that they love to run about untrammeled like this. A healthy child this age isn't troubled by modesty, or other conventions of society, and that's what I wanted to show in this card. A spirit that is totally innocent and pure, childlike in his joy and delight and wonder, and unashamed of that joy.

He is wearing the white roses of freedom, and the red feather of courage, like the fool. But he is an entire lunar-solar cycle further along in his development. (My notes from when I designed the deck say that after 19 years, the full moons fall on the same day of the year. I don't know if that information is accurate, because I didn't write down where I got it from. But I do know that the Jewish calendar has a solar-lunar cycle of 19 years, according to Grolier.)

During this time, he has passed through the Hermit, and has been reborn as a young child. No longer worried about enlightenment or knowledge, he is full of boundless joy, and content simply to play in the sun.

In his left hand he holds the red banner of life and courage. This is the hand of the unconscious, and he is holding the banner with it to show that life is no longer something that he needs to concentrate on. He simply lives it, effortlessly. For the same reason, the standard has the wings of freedom of spirit on it. And the wings aren't the huge wings of a raptor, they are little happy songbird wings, to show that there is a song in his heart, and that is what lifts his spirit.

With his right hand, he reaches out, showing his loving, happy nature.

He is riding bareback on a white pony, to show his complete comfort and mastery of the bright daytime forces. There is no hint of the unseen here, this is pure seen energy, that glories in its very physical tangibility. The pony has blue eyes to show its purity, as well. And it wears a golden bridle, with the symbol of the sun on it, in case you missed the allusion.

Underfoot grows bright green grass, with happy little yellow flowers of joy in it.

Behind him is the wall of security. It's that security that enables him to run around like this, totally unafraid.

On the other side of the wall bloom sunflowers. Besides the obvious reference, notice that they are not pointing up towards the sun, they are pointing at the child. This implies that he is shining brighter than the sun. There are also four of them blooming, for the four elements, and one in bud, to show that the best is yet to come.

Above him shines a brilliant sun. It's gonna be a great day!

20 - Judgement

This card shows a woman standing in a fiery cauldron. Behind her rises the Phoenix, reborn in glory. She is holding out her arms, in the position of the Goddess, with her hands showing the phrase "I love you" in American Sign Language shorthand. She is wearing the silver bracelets of a High Priestess, and all around her are clouds of glory.

Key – **Rebirth**

This card symbolizes rebirth, rejuvenation, reward, transformation. A spiritual awakening. A changed state of consciousness. A revitalization, or reclamation. A renaissance.

This is one of the cards where I kept the name, in spite of the fact that the concept named has no place in my worldview. I don't believe in Judgement, any more than I believe in the Devil. In my philosophy, people aren't judged and either damned or sent to heaven forever. My gods are interested in growth, not obedience. So we aren't judged, we are reborn. I decided to keep the traditional name for the card, though, because the people that I spoke with thought it would be more comfortable and cause less confusion, and because I wanted, once again, to make a statement. In our "Judgement," everyone wins, because ours is rebirth, not punishment; and there is no failing, just lessons learned.

A naked woman stands in the Goddess position in the Cauldron of Ceridwen, to show that she is one with the Goddess, and is part of the circle of rebirth. She is naked, to show that she is free and unashamed, and has cast off the trappings of the world. She has silver bracelets to show that she is a High Priestess, and has attained a high level of spiritual awareness. Her hair is white, to show that she is old. And yet her body is lithe, and her face unlined, to show that she is strong and young even in her age. This symbolizes the sort of agelessness and wisdom that are attained with great spiritual growth. Besides, she is between the worlds just now, and infirmity has no place there.

Her hands are held in the position that is shorthand for "I love you" in American Sign Language, to show her great love for everyone.

She stands in the midst of the fires of purification, which she has gone through. This experience has transformed her, and tempered her spirit; now she is wiser and stronger than ever.

The Cauldron of Ceridwen is another symbol of rebirth and renewal. It is the womb of the great Goddess, from which all things are reborn.

Behind her, overshadowing her, is the light shadow of a Phoenix, which symbolizes her new self, reborn from the ashes of her old self. In ancient stories, the phoenix was known for its wisdom as well as its beauty. So here, too, she is both beautiful and wise. It has six feathers on its crest, for the six senses. She is crowned with all of them. It also has a red eye, which stands for its courage.

From the heart of the woman shoot 13 beams of light. (Follow them back, and they really do all center in her heart.) This shows her enlightenment, and also completion. It will soon be time to venture into the world again, and continue her journey along her path.

21 - The World

This card shows a young woman effortlessly leaping through a wreath of fruit and flowers. In each hand she holds a wand. She is dressed in a flowing white cloth. Behind her are the stars. Around the borders of the card are the four elements.

Key – **Wholeness and Mastery**

This card means completion, success, the attainment of desire. Since every ending is also a beginning it also means a fresh start, a change for the better, hope for the future. It is the card from which all things are possible. If this one comes up in a reading, the only limits the Seeker has are those she sets herself.

Once again, most of the traditional designs on this card felt right to me. The only things I removed were the animals that were usually found in the corners of most decks. Those didn't seem to mean the various elements nearly as much as plain drawings of the elements concerned, so I used them instead.

The figure on this card is female, to show the potential of giving birth that is inherent to this state. Even if the seeker is male, he can give birth to many things. Not all births are babies! She is dressed only in a pure white wrap, to show that she is free, and unashamed of the possibilities that are here. The wrap is white to show her purity, and also the endless opportunities available. White is the combination of all colors of light, and it's also the color of a blank sheet of paper or canvas. To reinforce this, I made the wrap flow around her in a figure eight, the shape of the lemniscate, or infinity.

She is leaping easily and gracefully through the wreath, full of joy and freedom. This also shows balance and coordination. Her posture as she leaps is reminiscent of the hanged man, with one leg bent back behind her, and one in front. Her posture is more open, though. This shows that she has incorporated the new, more spiritual outlook of the hanged man into her life, and is now at ease with it.

In her left hand she holds a silver wand, in her right one of crystal. These show the unseen and seen worlds, respectively. Also, one has a pink stone, and one a green, to show both animal and vegetable life. In all these ways, she is well balanced, and has mastery.*

* Whenever I use the term mastery, I mean that she has mastered the lessons to be learned here, and can work in this area without stumbling or making too many mistakes. I never mean that she has power over the things that inhabit the area. I feel that "power over" is unethical, and shows neither balance nor spiritual development.

The wreath that she is jumping through represents the world, and her victory over it. The elliptical shape shows the action of the higher self, which is often shown as an ellipse, or egg shape. (It also shows an acceptance that the world isn't perfect, and it fits on the card better!)

It's composed of all kinds of fruits, vegetables, and leaves to show that there is plenty of everything. The world is a very rich place. You can look through it all carefully, and draw parallels and illustrations from each bit, if you want to. Briefly, I included roses; pink, white and yellow for affection, freedom and purity and welcome and joy respectively. White lilies for purity, pink lilies for tenderness and yellow lilies for joy and sunshine. Pomegranate for secret knowledge and identification with the Goddess. Apples for youthfulness and beauty, and also for mysteries. Oranges for the sun. Poppies for fertility. Oak leaves because oak is the king of trees, and represents strength, protection, and the door into mysteries. Beech leaves because beech is the queen of trees, and represents beauty and ancient wisdom. Wheat for plenty, fertility, and rebirth. Grapes for richness, bounty, and joy. And the list can go on and on.

The ribbons on the wreath are red, to show the vitality, passion, and courage of the world. They are shaped like infinity symbols, to show that she has mastery in all of this. And there are two of them, one at the top of the wreath mirrored in the one at the bottom to show the concept of "as above, so below." All things in the seen world are mirrored in the unseen, and when you move in balance with one, you move in balance with the other as well.

Behind her is the starry sky. This shows the limitlessness of her position, and also that she is very much at home in the starlight world of mystery and the spirit. The five stars stand for the five senses. (Sometimes, though, they look more like the five elements, or the five points of a pentacle. Whatever you see is what you are supposed to see. Go with it.) Each has four points, for the four elements of the material world. This is where the material world meets the starlight, and true vision, ability, and competence are born. That's why there are no limits here.

Around the outside of the card are representations of those four elements. Air is in the upper right hand corner, fire in the lower right, water in the lower left, and earth in the upper left. Together they make the corporeal world, and support the physical aspects of it. In the center is the fifth element, spirit, represented by the stars, and the woman. When these are combined, you have all the world, both physical and non-physical aspects, and anything is possible!

Chapter 7
Pentacles

This chapter is all about the reasoning behind my choice of symbols for the suit of Pentacles. I chose all of them, ultimately, because they meant something special to me. And I'm going to share those meanings with you. But as you read this, remember that the very same symbols might mean something very different to you. And that's fine.

It's my opinion that many of the problems all over the world can be traced to the fallacious reasoning that if one person is right, then everyone who doesn't agree must be wrong. In actual fact, lots of people can be right, even when their opinions on any given matter are wildly different. It's not so much a question of right and wrong as of different points of view.

When I'm trying to explain this to people, I usually tell them the story of the blind men and the elephant. (If you don't know the story, it's in Appendix A.) In this story, all the men were right, though none of them agreed. If they had compared their viewpoints, instead of arguing, they might have come up with a much clearer picture of what an elephant actually looked like!

So, if your interpretation of the symbols on these cards isn't the same as mine, that's great! Go with yours! After all, something that has real meaning to you is bound to be more in touch with your inner, unconscious mind than something that is foreign to you, but means a great deal to me. Keep a notebook, write down what the symbols and colors on the cards say to you. This will get you into the habit of really looking at them, and that is the first step, from my point of view, to becoming a top-notch reader.

The suit of Pentacles is aligned with the element of Earth. This means, of course, that it's also aligned with all the correspondences of that element. In Wicca, which is my background and tradition and the point of view from which I drew all these cards (and everything else, for that matter,) this means that this suit stands for quietness, rest, and peace. It also stands for richness, wisdom (as opposed to knowledge, which is the purview of the Swords,) and sensuality. The season is winter, and the time is midnight. This entire suit deals again and again with rewards after the job is finished, with waiting, with material things, and with gaining wisdom.

Compared to the frantic activity in some of the other suits, the people in this one are all engaged in quiet, restful, creative pursuits. This is a reflection of the feeling of the suit as a whole. There is also not as much interaction among people on these cards. To a large extent, solitude is necessary to build wisdom. After you have knowledge, you need time alone to digest it; to incorporate it into your worldview, and to draw correlations among the various things you have learned. And that is where wisdom comes from.

King of Pentacles

King of Pentacles

This card shows a king with black hair, seated on a throne. In one hand is his scepter, in the other a golden pentacle. He is dressed richly; but wearing bedroom slippers. Ancient grapevines surround him, and the grass grows thickly underfoot. In the background, cultivated fields lead toward his castle. Behind that are misty hills, and a sky the deep blue of twilight.

Key – **Riches and Comfort**

This card means a rich man, spiritually, materially, or both. A father figure, who is dependable and generous. Someone who is steady, reliable, earthy, helpful, sensual; A place or situation in which these qualities become apparent around the seeker.

When I started to design this card, I wanted to convey both a feeling of great wealth, and a feeling of ease and sensuality. I wanted the king to somehow look like he was completely comfortable; both in the sense of surrounding himself with comfort and being comfortable with himself. So I decided to dress him richly, and then put slippers on his feet. No tight, pinching shoes for this one!

His cloak is a rich grass green to show his alignment with green, richly growing things. The border is brown for the earth, with a design of golden grape vines for richness, abundance, and joy. It's lined with brown fur for richness, sensuality, and the earth.

I gave him a coat of the richest purple I could make to show his majesty and wealth. It's lined with brown fur, and quilted, to show earth again, and opulence, and comfort. The quilting pattern is squares, to show that even though he may be acutely aware of how things feel to him, he isn't totally hedonistic. There is something about him that remains "four-square." His head is still on straight.

There is a pattern of a bull's head wreathed in flowers worked on his breast in golden thread, to show his connections to the earth again, and his strength and virility. The flowers show his love of pleasurable things, as well. And there is also an overtone of stubbornness, which often comes out in someone who is represented by this card.

His belt is gold, and has a square buckle, to show his strength and reliability. There is an oval inside the square, to show unity and completeness.

I made his undertunic cloth of gold, to show that deep inside, this man is pure gold. It shows again his steadiness and reliability, and also his generosity and mental, emotional, and physical wealth. The design on it is known as the "Celtic Tree of Life," and is there to underline the whole theme of flourishing growth, prosperity, and living. It also has grape vines again, to show the joy, abundance, and pleasure that these vines symbolize all through the Tarot.

His stockings are burgundy, as an echo to the wine that can be made from those grapes. And he is wearing slippers, to show that comfort is very important to him. He may be a king, and he may be in a position of importance; but that's no reason to suffer! They are grey to show the balance this gives him. He enjoys luxury, but he isn't ostentatious. He's not doing this to impress others, but because it feels good.

On his head he wears a crown of gold that is shaped like a bull's horns, with a spike in the center. The horns, of course, are there to underscore the whole connection with the bull, and earth, strength, and virility. The spike is what crowns used to be about; it's there to show the divine light that shines upon a king, and his connection to deity.

He is wearing a wreath of grape vines and wheat that almost obscures the crown. This is because living things are more important to him than symbols. The vines, once more, show the love of life, prosperity, and pleasure. The wheat symbolizes prosperity as well, and goodness, wholesomeness, and the whole life/death mystery* (which is one of the aspects of the earth, and north in my tradition of Wicca.)

His hair and beard are black and curly, because that is the traditional coloring for the suit, and some people use that when they read the cards.

In his right hand he holds a scepter, to show his authority. Never mistake this man for anything other than a king, in spite of his geniality and good nature. He may be warm, generous, and kindly; but he's also used to having everyone obey him!

In his left hand, he holds a Pentacle. Besides being the symbol of this suit, it shows his connection with the Earth once more. His is made of silver and gold, to show his richness extends into both the spiritual and material planes. It is decorated with a pattern of leaves to show growth and vitality. This connection isn't a concept; it's a live thing!

He is sitting on a throne that is really a comfortable chair. Its broad back is decorated with purple, gold, and burgundy to show his wealth and sensuality.

He sits in a bower of ancient grapevines, which are covered with leaves and fruit. Grapevines, according to legend, never die unless they are killed. There are vines in parts of Italy that are hundreds of years old, and are considered immortal. They have been producing year after year for centuries. So these vines are a potent

---

*Wheat is symbolic of both life and death, because as the staple food for most of Europe it was necessary to live. And yet, in order for there to be more wheat, it had to "die," and be buried in the ground. Legends concerning this property of grain are prevalent all over the world, from John Barleycorn in England to the Penobscot stories of the Corn Mother in North America, and virtually everywhere else on the planet where the people planted grain.

symbol of reliability and stability. This is someone you can really depend on. He will always be there for you. And the vines themselves, of course, also show all the things that grapevines always show, symbolizing love of life, joy, abundance, and so on.

Grass is growing richly beneath his feet, to show great abundance again. Near his right foot bloom two yellow primroses. They are there to show the joy that underlies all the rest of the things on this card, and also because sometimes this man is shy. If those flowers are very obvious when you see this card in a reading, you can probably bet on it.

Behind him are cultivated fields, to show that this kind of wealth has to be cultivated. This guy isn't a Wild Child (who needs his Teeth Filed!) Adventures and wildness are often uncomfortable, and he simply doesn't enjoy that sort of thing. He likes a steady, predictable sort of life. And in order to have that you have to plan, and set things aside for the future. Which, really, is what farming is all about. Saving the grain, instead of consuming all of it, so that there is something to plant the following year. Weeding and hoeing now, so that there will be a good harvest in several months. Rotating your crops, so that the soil won't be exhausted. Basically, delaying your gratification.

Since delayed gratification is one of the marks of wisdom, and is so often necessary for stability and comfort, it is one of the primary lessons of this whole suit. And so it's shown here.

At the end of the fields stands his castle. For this man, home really is his castle, with all that implies.

Beyond it, gentle hills rise through the mist. The hills show enlightenment, as they do all through the deck. But these are gentle, so the enlightenment is also gentle, and not the result of traumatic experiences. They are wreathed in mist, because this man is wise enough to know what he does not know!

The sky is the deep blue-violet of twilight, because that is the time of rest, and midnight is the time of the north, which is aligned with the earth and pentacles in the first place.

Queen of Pentacles

This card shows a queen in a golden crown, sitting on a vine chair in a garden. Flowers bloom around her, trees and vines bear fruit, and a basket of harvest is at her feet. She contemplates a pentacle she is holding. Behind her misty hills rise into a deep blue twilight sky.

Key – **Abundance and Practicality**

This card means a warm, generous woman, who has the seeker's best interest at heart. Monetary gifts, intelligence, thoughtfulness, caring. A careful, insightful, practical person. Someone who is not afraid of hard work. A situation or place that embodies these characteristics, or brings them out in the seeker.

This queen is sitting, because the suit of Pentacles is aligned with the element of Earth, and therefore is restful. I gave her a satin dress that ranges in color from the palest spring green at the shoulders to the deepest forest green at the hem. This is to show that she is concerned with all stages of growing things, since, at some level, she is the Earth Mother. The lining of her gown is deep purple, to show majesty and richness. But her sleeves are turned up, because she is practical, and not afraid of hard work.

She also wears a brown velvet apron or tabard. If it looks like an apron to you, it shows her practicality and ability to get things done. If it looks more like a tabard, it shows her nobility. I chose brown, because it's the same color as rich soil, or the earth itself. It's velvet because of the softness of her character, and also for richness. All along the hem is a border of fruits, flowers, and vegetables. They show abundance, richness, and the gathering of nourishing qualities. This is to symbolize her wealth, generosity, and her ability to nourish and care for those around her. It also has two green stripes, to show tenderness and care for all things, no matter their stage of growth.

Her belt is a sash of purple, with more of the harvest theme, and golden fringe. Purple stands for richness, royalty, and wealth; and that's what it means here too. The fruits, flowers, and leaves are for all good and wholesome things. The golden fringe is to show her wealth, and her love of luxury; for she shares that quality with the King of Pentacles.

If you look closely, you will notice that she is pregnant. I did that to show her fertility, and also her role as mother.

She has black hair, and dark eyes (although you can't actually see them) because those are the traditional colors for this suit, and there are people who use that. Also, I liked giving her hair the color of midnight, because that is the time of the north, the earth, and pentacles in my tradition of Wicca.

Her crown is golden, to show her majesty and richness, and decorated with a pattern of wheat to show goodness and plenty, and also to show the whole death/rebirth mystery of the grain.

Her hair is braided into a bun at the back of her head. This shows her identification with the Great Mother, the Goddess, because of the three strands of the braid (Mother, Maiden, and Crone) and also her practicality. She wears two bright red poppies in her hair, to show her courage, fertility, and joy. Poppies have long been associated with pleasure and fertility, and red is the color of courage. She also wears a white fruit tree blossom, to show her purity and sweetness, and the promise of nurturing.

In her hands she holds a Pentacle, the symbol of her suit. It is made of silver and gold, to show that her wealth is both material and spiritual. And it has the pattern of twinning leaves to show that she is concerned with growth and life.

I drew her contemplating this symbol, because I wanted to show that although she is quite willing to work very hard, she also has a quiet, insightful side to her nature. She thinks about things a great deal, and has grown wise as a result.

The throne she sits on is of simple woven vines, to show that she is not really concerned with the outward show of wealth at all. The interlocking framework of all growing things is much more important to her. If you look closely, you will notice that these vines are still rooted in the ground, and growing. This is to show that everything she does, she does with an eye to how it helps growth and development. That sort of thing is fundamental to her.

The weaving is actually done with several different kinds of vines, as you can tell from the leaves that are growing out of her chair, to show the interdependence between varied things. One of the vines used in her throne is honeysuckle, to show her sweetness. (It's the white flower, blooming next to her sash.) Another is ivy, to show introspection. (The green leaves next to the honeysuckle.) Another is clematis, to show beauty. (The pink flower right next to where the seat begins.) All of these things together also show the beauty, strength, and flexibility that comes from diversity.

The grass grows rich and luxuriantly green beneath her feet, to show the richness and vitality apparent all through this card. There is also a clump of flowers, to show beauty and sweetness again.

On the ground are a pair of snakes, and a pair of rabbits. The snakes are to show feminine qualities and wisdom, both of which were associated with the snake from deepest antiquity. The rabbits show softness and fertility. I show a pair of each for balance, and also because, in my experience, this card often comes up for someone who is a matchmaker, and who likes to pair people up with each other. When the thing that strikes me first is a reading is that she has paired the animals up, I know that this is true in that reading.

She sits where grape vines meet the branches of an apple tree. The grapes, of course, stand for wealth, plenty, joy, and the love of life. Apples stand for choice in the old Celtic tree alphabet. They also stand for beauty, youthfulness, and the revelation of secrets. (If you cut one in half cross-wise, the pentagram is revealed.) All of these things are present in abundance on this card, as the vine is covered with grapes, and the tree with ripe apples.

Behind her throne is a garden filled with various flowers, and with a basket of fruits and vegetables laid on the ground. These once more show beauty, grace, diversity and so on. And the fact that there are vegetables mixed with the fruit in the basket shows that besides providing what you would like, this queen is also going to give you those things that are good for you, even if you don't care for them much at all!

Beyond the garden lie cultivated fields, as in the King of Pentacles, to show that she is a person who plans, and cultivates the things she would like to have manifest in her life.

Beyond them again are the misty hills and deep sky found in all the court cards of this suit, symbolizing enlightenment and yet the wisdom to recognize that enlightenment is not total. The sky is that of twilight; the time of day that is given to rest and contemplation, and a space to grow wisdom.

Once again, though, remember that although these were my intentions while I was making the cards, if any of these symbols mean something different to you when you are reading then you are right!

The Knight of Pentacles

Knight of Pentacles

This card shows a fully armored knight on a heavy horse. He's holding a Pentacle in his right hand. The horse is standing on the bare ground of a newly plowed field. Behind him are more fields, leading back to woods which give way to misty hills in the distance. Over all is a clear sky the deep blue of twilight, with two birds flying in it.

Key – **Dependable Help**

This card means a person who is responsible, reliable, practical, utilitarian, dependable, trustworthy. A person who will help the Seeker. Someone who is solid and honorable. It may also mean travel.

After a lot of thought, I decided to put this knight in full plate armor. He is the only knight who is dressed like this; but I wanted to give an impression of absolute dependability and strength. Putting him in full plate showed, to me, that he has no weakness or susceptibility. No matter where an attack might come from, he has it covered! It also added to the general feeling of "Knight in Shining Armor." This guy might not be flashy or exotic; but he's as dependable as they come, and he'll always be there when you need him to be.

At times, too, all of that armor makes him seem very closed in. Since he might be amazingly stubborn, and not at all open to new ideas, that also fits. Which of these is actually going on, of course, is something that you will have to decide based on how you feel about this card when it shows up in a reading.

His armor is patterned with a motif of leaves and vines to show his alignment with the earth, and with growing things.

His mount is a heavy horse (in fact, it's a breed known as Italian Heavy Draft) to show the great dependability and solidity which are attributes of this card. This particular breed is not only very docile and amenable, but is also extremely quick and active for its size. I chose it for these characteristics, to show that his steed (representing his instincts and nature) may be quiet now, but it can be very active indeed if that is necessary! I made him a dark brown (actually dark liver-chestnut) to echo the color of the earth. His mane and fetlocks are the color of ripe wheat, for richness, plenty, goodness, and all the self-sacrificing life/death stuff that wheat represents. His eyes are green (not a color found on the real horse, I'm afraid,) to show once again his correspondence with the earth and green growing things.

There are oak leaves in his mane, to show the strength, stability, and protection that have long been associated with oak trees.

His chamfron (the armor a horse wears on its face) is decorated with vines and leaves, once more for the whole growing earth motif. On the boss is the symbol of the earth, done in green enamel, so there can be no doubt.

His reins are also decorated, with gold on green, in the pattern that shows a vine bursting from a pomegranate. The gold is for wealth, of course, and the green for the earth. The design itself symbolizes the seasons, and femininity. The pomegranate is the fruit of the Goddess, and of course it was the pomegranate seeds which Persephone ate that mean that we have winter. (If you don't know that story, it's in the Appendix B.) The vines growing out of the pomegranate also mean life, and plenty.

The back of the reins are hung with purple cloth, to show richness and plenty.

The horse is also caparisoned all over with various bits of cloth decorated in these same patterns and colors. His saddlecloth and the decorative cloth on his chest are both made of green fabric, decorated with gold vines and flowers. They are cut in a pattern like crenelations on a castle wall, to show that this knight is so strong and reliable that he is just about a mobile fortress. They are trimmed with gold to show his richness, and purple tassels to show his love of luxury. Once again, they are lined with purple, to show royalty and wealth.

Over his saddle he has a plain green cloth with a purple border. This is to show that he's not particularly interested in opulence just for the show of it. A great deal of it may simply be hidden, because it's more practical that way. Since saddles were ordinarily quite ornate, and the stirrup that can be seen is decorated, it's a pretty safe bet that the plain cloth conceals ornate decorations. And that is in keeping with his character, too.

In his right hand, he holds a Pentacle. This is the symbol of his suit, and, like all the other court cards, it's made of gold and silver, to show that his wealth is both material and spiritual, and has a design of leaves on it to show his concern with growing things.

He is standing in a newly plowed field, to show that he is very concerned with the cultivation of things. He doesn't expect them to just appear; he's willing to put in the effort necessary to get them. This covers everything, from friendships to business relationships, to new cars! You will know what is meant in any particular reading by looking at the other cards that show up in relationship to this one, and by following your own instincts.

But the field has just been plowed. The cultivation process for this particular thing is just at the beginning. Nothing has grown yet, and it will take a good deal of care for any growth to occur, let alone flourish.

Just beyond the field is a meadow that is growing thickly with lush green grass and yellow flowers. These show that the conditions for growth are there, as well as showing that vitality and joy are already present.

Beyond that are more fields, already beginning to produce, interspersed with woods. If the woods are the most apparent thing when you look at this card, then it's possible that this character has a darker, wilder, mysterious side to him. Otherwise, they are just there to show contrast with the fields, and to underline the whole aspect of vigorous, healthy growth.

The fields and woods give way to misty hills in the background, as they do for all the court cards of this suit, to show gentle enlightenment, wrapped with the wisdom to know that all is not known!

High above, the sky is turning the deep blue-violet of twilight, to show that the time for rest and contemplation is approaching. Two birds fly in the sky, to show that although this knight is heavy, and solid, and rooted to the earth, his spirit may still soar, (especially if it's joined by another.)

Page of Pentacles

This card shows a young girl, with her black hair in three braids, standing in a field holding up a shining Pentacle. She is dressed in green and brown, and barefoot. A book dangles from her belt. A fir tree is behind her, and beyond her stretch cultivated fields that eventually give way to misty hills under a sky that is the endless deep blue of twilight.

Key – **Studious Scholarship**

This card means deep concentration, scholarship, news, a bringer of messages. A young person who makes the Seeker very proud. A careful, studious child. Someone who is methodical, or deliberate; who considers every move carefully.

Page of Pentacles

Like all the other pages, I made this one a young woman, so that there would be more balance in the deck. Two males and two females just felt better to me than three males and one female!

I gave this one a brown tunic, with the same sort of pattern on it as the Queen of Pentacles has on her apron, for the same reasons. The brown stands for the earth, and the richness and promise of the soil. The yellow border is for joy, and the pattern of fruits, flowers, and leaves on it are to show the beauty, growth, richness, goodness, and nourishment that the earth provides. Even though this person is still very young, she has a mothering, nurturing nature.

She wears a green shirt under her tunic, to show the vigorous growth that underlies all of this.

Her belt is very wide, to show that she is a sturdy thing; not easily swayed or confused. From it hangs a book, bound in green and purple, with a design of gold and gold leaf on the page edges. When I first began to read the cards, I had problems with all of the pages; I couldn't remember what they were supposed to mean. So when I made my deck, I gave them symbols to help me remember. This one has a book, because this one is involved with study, and learning. It's bound in green and purple for the growth and richness that are present in all these court cards. On the front of it is a pattern that shows an old fashioned rose in gold, with scrolls above and below it. (Honest. Look carefully.) I did that to show her sweetness, and also because this child is often seen as being a little "old fashioned." The scrolls are to show that she has an announcement, one of the alternate meanings of this card. The pages of the book have gold leaf to show that the contents are precious.

This page is barefoot, to show that she is in touch with the earth; she studies it, too, and is very aware of where she is going and what's underfoot all the time. She can sense the moods of the land, and knows when it's happy and when it isn't.

Her hair is black, as is that of everyone else on the court cards for this suit, to help the people who expect that tradition and also to echo the midnight which is the time of the North and Earth in my tradition of Wicca. She has it braided into three braids to show that she is growing into the tradition of the Mother, Maiden and Crone. She is very Earth-oriented, and honors the earth in all that she does. Although braided, her hair is unbound. That's to show the freedom that she enjoys, in spite of her studious temperament. She is like this because it's her nature, and she wants to be this way.

She holds her Pentacle proudly in both hands, to show that she is using both her intellect and intuition as she studies it. She gazes at it intensely, with a slight smile on her face, to show that she is enjoying her study. It responds by glowing, and sending out eight beams of radiance. The study of the Pentacle, and, for me, of magic and the universe in general (since, for me, that is part of what the Pentagram symbolizes, and the Pentacle is the material form of the Pentagram) illuminates her life in all its seasons, since the eight rays symbolize the eight spokes on the wheel of the year. (If you need to know more about that, it's in Appendix C.) The eight beams of light may mean something different for you, of course. And if they do, as always, go with your own meaning! Not only will it be easier for you to remember, but it will be more meaningful.

She stands in the shadow of a fir tree (as you can tell not only from the bits of the tree that you see behind her, but also from the shadows on her.) In Celtic tree symbols, this tree stands for the Maiden, Mother, and Crone. Because of its height, it's also considered a tree of vision, especially spiritual vision. And because it's green all year round, it also connects life to life. All of these things are present in this card, or represented in the life of this person, or the position or situation this card is talking about.

All around her feet grows an abundance of long grass, sprinkled with yellow flowers. The grass is to show energetic vitality and growth. The flowers show beauty and joy. Although she is standing quietly now, this child is not always sedentary.

Beyond her are cultivated fields, meadows filled with sheep, and woods. The fields show that, as young as she is, she has learned to delay her gratification; to work to get the things she wants or knows she needs. This is the primary lesson of this suit, and she is already grasping it. The sheep show that she is working with both plants and animals; with both sides of any question. There are three of them to reprise the other groups of three found in this card. The woods show that she is not completely tamed, in spite of her studious, and often serious, nature. There is wildness in her yet!

Beyond the woods are hills, wrapped in mist, that rise into the deep blue of the evening sky. These mean once again that this card shows gentle enlightenment, and the wisdom to know that learning isn't over yet! Several birds fly in the sky, to show the freedom of her spirit. That sky itself is crystal clear, and yet it's growing dark with the ending of the day. This whole suit reflects a time for quiet labor, or for rest; for things winding down, as they do at the end of the day, in preparation for sleep and a new day to come.

Ace of Pentacles

This card shows a golden disk with a silver pentacle entwined with vines that bear green leaves and red fruit. It floats above a rich garden full of roses, lilies and wisteria. A path leads through the garden to an empty pedestal. Beyond that lie misty hills, fading away to the horizon.

Key – **Reward and Riches**

This card means pure contentment, attainment, prosperity, bright prospects both material and spiritual. Plenty, luxury, peace, magic.

This card is an Ace, of course, and so it holds all the meaning of the suit, distilled down to its essence. At the same time, it symbolizes the beginning of the things represented by this suit; a certain newness, as they first start to enter (or reenter) the Seeker's life.

So the Ace of Pentacles shows all the richness, plenty, luxury, earthy pleasures, and downright hedonism of this suit. And yet, at the same time, it shows clearly that there is work involved in getting these things. Gardens like this don't just happen!

That's why I designed the Pentacle on this Ace the way I did. It's made of gold, for the richness, wealth, and luxury denoted by this suit. The pentagram itself is made of silver, though, because it's more in the lines of spiritual richness, since it shows so many things. It's a symbol of the five elements; air, fire, water, earth, and spirit, with spirit at the top. So it symbolizes the idea that all things should be in balance, with spirit above the other elements. I believe that if you don't arrange your life in this fashion, if you are ruled by your appetites instead of that part of you that constantly strives to be better, you are heading for serious trouble.

It also is the figure of a person, with a head, two arms, and two legs. Once again, the person is standing upright, proud and vigorous.

And it shows a star, which is where we all came from. Every atom in our bodies is really star-stuff, and we would do well not to forget that.

It means other things, besides; but I don't have the space here to go into an exhaustive discussion of the Pentagram. Meditate on it yourself, if you are interested, and see what truths you can learn. It's always possible that you might be the first to discover them!

I put a vine threading all through it, to show its vitality and beauty as a living symbol. The vine also symbolizes looking within, which I find is an incredibly valuable exercise. This one is bearing fruit to remind me that when you contemplate this symbol, and look within, your pondering will often bear fruit that will nourish you spiritually. Each vine has three leaves, for the Maiden, the Mother, and the Crone, and two fruits for the Green Man and the Horned God. Together, these make five, which is once again the number of points on the Pentagram.

This is what I was thinking when I designed this symbol. I'm sure that you can find more there, if you want to.

The path, of course, is the path that the Seeker is on right now. It's well maintained, which shows that he has been caring for and about it, and leads through a beautiful garden. There are lilies for purity, bluebells for awareness of the hidden side of nature, and purple flowers for health. Over it all hangs yellow wisteria, for joy and beauty. Altogether a beautiful place.

It leads to a pedestal, which is empty and waiting for whatever the Seeker wishes to put on it. Monetary, spiritual, or emotional rewards; anything is possible from here. You will know what is going up there by looking at the other cards that surround this one in the spread, and by listening to your own intuition.

You may also want to ask the Seeker what they would like to see on this pedestal! Remember, this is supposed to be a co-operative effort; the Reader and Seeker should be working together to unravel the Seeker's Question. So don't be afraid to ask the Seeker for input and feedback. We aren't trying to prove anything here!

Beyond the pedestal are hills, shrouded in mist. These stand for gentle enlightenment, still shrouded in mystery, and wisdom to know that all is not known. It's a wise man indeed who has the measure of his own ignorance.

These go on as far as the eye can see, because there is no end to enlightenment.

Two of Pentacles

This card shows a young woman dressed as a juggler, walking a tightrope and whistling while she balances two Pentacles in her hands. A flute hangs around her neck. Below her are white, puffy clouds. Behind her two bird ships sail through the sky in front of a full moon.

Key – **The Juggler; Balance**

This card means the ability to easily handle two (or more) things at once. Harmony in the midst of conflict and change. Fun and games. Knowing the ropes. Balance in self and life; being in control, and making it look easy.

Like all the twos, this card deals with balance. That's why I decided to put a tight-rope walker on it.

This young woman is dressed like a performer, like a more advanced representation of the Fool. Like the fool, she wears the red feather of courage in her cap. But unlike him, she is aware of exactly what she is doing. In her case, this is a role she has chosen to perform; she has put on a costume and makeup, and gone for it.

Her cap is green, to show growth. Her dress is blue for spiritual enlightenment. Her underdress is white for purity. Her trews are red for courage, and her stockings are yellow for joy. All of these qualities are hers.

She whistles as she balances the two Pentacles, because she understands harmony. Harmony and balance often go together, and she has them both down pat. She wears a wooden flute around her neck to emphasize that point, and also to echo the wooden flute of the fool. It has seven finger holes, to show perfection.

Her feet are bare, because she is in touch with her balance point. Her arms and shoulders are also bare, which gives her freedom of movement. She is ready for anything.

Her Pentacles are gold, to show that they are precious things that she is holding in balance here. The act of balancing is creating a glowing lemniscate, showing that she is a magical being, and has mastery here.

The element of the pentacles is earth. She is out of her element, out of contact with the earth. And yet, she is still in complete control. Her profound understanding of balance has allowed her to do this. And to show how wonderful and valuable this sort of understanding is, her rope is also made of gold.

This is the balance that I think is the secret to the universe. Not balance like a scale, with an equal number of things on each side, but balance like a tightrope. Good doesn't need an equal amount of Evil in order to maintain the balance. It's far simpler than that. Balance is good, and loosing your balance, falling off the rope, is what is evil. It's when you feel yourself falling, and start to grab at anything around to save yourself that you harm yourself and others. And doing harm is what evil is!

This person understands all of that, and that is where she gets her strength and power.

Behind her fly the ships of her imagination, free to soar to the moon, which seems almost close enough to touch. It's her balance that gives them this ability.

They are shaped like birds with their wings outstretched, to show their kinship with spirit and air. Their bird bodies, wings, and sails are all spotless white, to show their purity. The beaks and crests of the birds, and the boat part are all golden to show how rare and marvelous they are. Each also flies a red banner to show bravery and fearlessness. It takes courage to let your creativity take off like this, to leave all expected and normal limits behind.

But if you have that courage, and that balance, then there are no limits anymore.

Below the ships are the puffy white clouds. These also symbolize imagination to me, since I spent so many, many summer afternoons as a kid seeing shapes and pictures in the clouds.

The moon behind it all is full. This means that this is a time of magic, that anything is possible. It also means that one cycle is hitting its peak. What this means in a specific reading, of course, will be determined by the other cards that surround this one, and by what your instincts are telling you. As always, trust your own inner voice.

And don't force any meaning onto the card. It's possible that time, for instance, may have nothing to do with this card when it shows up in a reading. In that case, the moon won't look like any kind of time at all. It'll just be the moon. It may seem more important that the juggler has black hair. If so, go with it! I made her hair that color so it would contrast nicely with the white moon. (Sometimes esthetics are just esthetics!) But if it looks to you like it echoes the High Priestess card, for instance, and it seems to you that this card is the High Priestess playing the Fool, then that is what it means in that reading.

Three of Pentacles

This card shows a grey bearded master craftsman, with a hammer and chisel, putting the finishing touches on a sculpture. All that is visible of the statue is part of one wing. Behind it are golden rays, and a red arc with three pentacles on it. He leans for balance on an intricately carved stone arch.

Key – **Master Craftsman**

This card means the Seeker's skills and abilities will be appreciated and rewarded. Care and effort will lead to success. Artistic ability, achievement, recognition. Also increase in rank or power as a result of doing outstanding work.

When I started to design this card, I knew that I wanted to have wings in it because, I feel, learning your craft really well, and becoming a master of it, gives you wings to fly with. And I wanted the wings to be Big, because that is what the joy of rendering the pictures without loosing anything in translation feels like. But I also wanted to be able to clearly see the face of the Master, so that it was obvious he was enjoying himself.

In order to do this, I had to crop the image, so that only a tiny part of the sculpture was visible; little more than a few wing feathers. But I like this better anyway. Now it's left to the Reader's instinct to decide what it's a sculpture of!

So, sometimes, it'll look like the wing of a bird, and sometimes like the wing of an angel, and sometimes like a pair of wings that the sculptor can put on and fly away with! If it does that for you, go with it. Remember, follow your instincts.

I made the sculptor a mature man, with grey in his hair and white in his beard, to show that you don't reach this level until you have had years of practice. These years have given him such prodigious skills that he doesn't have to worry about the mechanics of how to do things anymore. He just does them.

He's smiling as he works, because he really enjoys what he is doing. He would do this anyway, just for the love of it. And when you have that kind of attitude about your work, the rewards just seem to follow. He clearly is paid well, because he can afford to wear nice clothing to work in! (Unless he was dressed like this to show the client, and decided to just touch up that wing a bit. This might imply Perfectionism. (Which I prefer to think of as Care, and Good Craftsmanship, and Pride in Your Work.))

His jerkin is of indigo velvet, the color of the brow chakra or the third eye, to show that he sees beyond the surface of things, and his work is inspired. The cuffs are the red of courage, decorated with the gold of wealth and power. The decorations are in the form of trefoils, for the Triple Goddess, and flames for inspiration.

His shirt is white, to symbolize the purity of his vision.

He wears a green kerchief on his head, decorated with bright pink and yellow flowers. This shows that he is careful, because it protects his head and hair. The green shows growth, and the pink and yellow show love and joy. For me, in particular, this kerchief means something more. It's actually one that a former employer brought back for me from Russia. So it's also a symbol of caring that reaches beyond cultural boundaries; of art and craftsmanship as the universal language.

The white feather that is tucked into the band made by a fold of the kerchief stands for purity and vision, and also shows that this project is another "feather in his cap." According to my notes, a feather in the cap means achievement and truth. In this case, being true to his craft.

He leans on an arch. When I was designing this card, I assumed that was part of a doorway, and put it there to show that he was fixed on this path right now. Other doors were below him.

The interior of the arch is filled with gorgeous stonework to show his consummate skill. But the arch itself shows the steps used to make Celtic knotwork, in a pattern as if he had been showing someone. I put that there for two reasons. The first is because when you become a master of your craft, a logical next step is to begin to teach it to others. The second is to show that even when you have achieved mastery, things still need to be accomplished one step at a time.

The wings he is carving, as I mentioned above, symbolize the freedom and uplifting of the spirit that come with mastery. They may also show the heights he aspires to, or the lofty position that he is building for himself.

The painted ground just behind the wings is deep blue, for insight and illumination. It has five tiny white stars on it to show the five elements, and the five points of a pentagram.

The red arch that holds the three Pentacles stands for courage and bravery, as well as for virility and vibrant life. You need courage to become a master of whatever craft you aspire to, because part of mastery is breaking new ground, and that means taking risks; risking failure, risking ridicule, risking your reputation. In this case, the risks have all paid off.

Behind this arch are carved and gilded rays. These represent rays of golden light, and show the brilliance of his achievements.

Behind them again is more stone, this time gray to show the balance that he has achieved with his work.

The whole effect I was trying to achieve was a man who was really happy to be making truly beautiful, glorious things.

Four of Pentacles

This card shows a richly dressed old man, who looks unhealthy and ill-tempered, clinging tightly to a Pentacle. He wears a golden crown that is topped by another, and has two more under his feet. He sits in a tiny stone niche at the top of a tower. Behind him is a town decked for a festival, but he doesn't see it.

Key – **Miser**

This card means miserliness, greed, selfishness, avarice, suspicion, distrust. An inability to let go of anything. Someone who is an emotional black hole, who absorbs affection, attention, wealth, etc, but never returns any. Shortsightedness, imbalance, desperation.

This is a desperately unhappy man. He wears a golden crown, which should imply that he has power and wealth, but the stone in it is black. He absorbs everything that comes his way, and returns none of it. He is misusing both his power and his wealth, and it's likely to slip through his fingers, hold it as he will.

He grasps his Pentacles in an iron grip. One is balanced on his head, to show that money (or whatever the Pentacles seem to represent in this reading) is the only thing on his mind. Two are beneath his feet, because money compromises his entire under-standing. (Get it? Sorry.) One he clutches to his heart, because all he loves is money.

He is all alone, and cold. Note the fur that lines his clothing, and the way he sits huddled in spite of it. His clothing is black, to greedily absorb any light or sunshine that comes its way, while reflecting as little as possible.

The tops of his sleeves are dark purple and burgundy, the colors of richness and royalty. But he has them almost hidden. They are bordered with gold, to show his riches; but the design on them is nothing but currency symbols in different languages. That is all that is really important to him. There is no growth shown here.

His boots are also black, but they have red soles. Actually, they have crimson soles and crimson linings, for the slippers of Little Black Sambo (who was East Indian, of course, and not black at all, and who was also the hero of his story.) In case you aren't familiar with the story, it's about a little boy who lives in India, and his adventures when he encounters a group of Tigers. He persuades them to take his clothing instead of eating him. (The tiger who gets the slippers with crimson soles and crimson linings wears them on his ears.) And then they become so jealous of the finery that the other tigers got that they throw it all off, and rush around and around a tree, chasing each other, until they are all turned into butter. Which, of course, Little Black Sambo scoops up and takes home to his mother.

This story seemed to me to have all the elements of greed that is so complete that it destroys even the one who is greedy. And that seemed entirely appropriate for this fellow, so I gave him the slippers.

He has used his wealth to build a great castle around himself, and made walls to separate himself from all other people. Now he is trapped within these walls, as I have shown by putting him in a bare, grey stone place. It's not only empty, it's narrow; as the life of all misers becomes narrow. It has crenelations, because he wishes to defend himself from any who might try to breach his walls.

And there he sits, with his back firmly turned to anything which might open his world, or take his mind off his obsession.

Behind him is a village; bright, clean and shining. Banners and flags are flying, as if the town is decked for a festival. The air is bright, with puffy white clouds, and birds flying. A perfect day.

But he sees none of it, because he refuses to.

And no one sees him, either. The windows that face him are all dark, and no one looks out of them. If you close yourself off like this, and keep snarling that you want to be left alone, eventually you will get your wish.

If this card comes up in a reading in a position that shows that it represents the Seeker, you should probably warn her that she is doing herself quite a bit of harm by behaving like this. Before you do that, though, you might want to read the chapter on Ethics. And remember, whenever you have to give someone a hard truth like this to be as gentle and understanding as you can possibly be.

Five of Pentacles

This card shows two beggars - ragged, cold, filthy and hungry - in the snow outside of a stone building; perhaps a church or college. Inside, light is shining, causing the five stained glass Pentacles in the window to glow brightly.

Key – **Misery**

This card means destitution, loss, loneliness, being "left out in the cold." Lovers who cannot find a meeting place. Poor health, spiritual impoverishment, etc.

These two people are miserable, indeed. I often see this card as the logical extension of the previous one. If you are unwilling to help others, then you frequently find yourself in need of help, with no one to give you a hand.

They still retain that same selfish attitude, in spite of their penury on this card. They are asking for help, but unwilling to help each other. Notice that they aren't even looking at each other. In fact, the figure in back has a hand out, but other than that has withdrawn completely. Their very indifference to each other shows that they are emotionally, as well as monetarily, destitute.

The standing figure has lost a leg, and perhaps an eye as well, but at least he is still struggling. He still has a bit of fight left in him, which is why I gave him a plaid blanket over his shoulders. It's a shabby, faded reflection of the Seven of Wands; but if you notice it, it is a reflection nonetheless. (If you don't notice it, of course, it probably doesn't mean anything in that reading. The cards are like that.)

He has made himself a crutch, to try to help himself along, and he has used rags to make up for the fact that his clothing is inadequate. And yet, if he would turn and help the other beggar, he might find more comfort and solace than he has with these.

The building behind him is also alight. This might mean several different things, depending on the other cards in the reading, and how the whole thing feels to you while you are reading the cards.

Perhaps it shows that the large institutions really don't care.

Perhaps they could enter the building, and find warmth and shelter, but they are too proud.

Perhaps the people in the building would ask them to give up the only thing they have left - their freedom - in order to get warmth and comfort.

Perhaps the building is locked, or open only to those who already have wealth, and they cannot gain entry.

Perhaps it's a college, and they are not ready to learn, so they cannot go inside.

Perhaps it's the home of the Seeker, who has no idea that there are beggars outside.

Perhaps it's an unknown, and they should be knocking at the door to find out.

Perhaps they aren't even really aware that it's there!

I purposely left few clues as to the identity of those in the building, or their motives, so that all of these things can be read into it. As a play I went to in college once said, I left it "purposely vague so as to exclude little."

The pentacles themselves are made from beautiful stained glass. The actual pentagram shape is made from yellow glass, to show warmth and joy. The center of each one is blue, to show spiritual harmony. The points are green, to show growth, and the background is red for warmth and courage. The green and red together like this also show balance and both animal and vegetable life, as well as representing both the God and the Goddess.

In the corners of the windows are golden petals. These are there to balance the design, and also to show how precious transient things, like flowers, can be.

The five pentacles are contained in three stone panes. This is to show the Maiden, Mother, and Crone, or any other "three" that seems appropriate at the time you are doing the actual reading.

Glass is also fragile, as life and beauty can be fragile. Sometimes, that is the most obvious thing about this card; how fragile life, prosperity, and warmth really are.

Taken as a whole, the window is meant to convey an impression of glowing warmth, beauty, and hope. It's right there, it's easily within reach, but for some reason these people are ignoring it.

So they shiver, out in the snow. I made some of the snowflakes beautiful, to remind myself that even in hardship, there are still beautiful things that can give our spirits a lift, if we take the time away from concentrating on our misfortunes to enjoy them.

The lesson of this card, I think, is to learn to see the good that is there, and to help our fellow sufferers, so that this exercise can be learned and put behind us.

You may find a completely different statement in this card, of course, and that's alright. Remember, the purpose of the cards is to unlock the knowledge that is inside of you.

(By the way, for those who are curious, I got the basic design for this window from one of the buildings at Princeton University; not from a church!)

Six of Pentacles

This card shows a richly dressed man, with a chain of office on his chest, holding a scale. Beggars cluster around his feet, kneeling as they wait with upraised hands out for alms. He drops a coin into one of the outstretched hands.

Key – **Gratification**

This card means help, especially with financial matters. A favor returned. Gifts, either given or received. Gratifying your own desire to help or repay someone else. Riches enough to give away.

This card went through several metamorphoses. Originally, it was just a hand with a fancy cuff dropping a coin into another hand, which had a large safety pin holding the sleeve together.

Then I decided that it was important to show that there were a number of people vying for the one coin, so I added more hands.

Finally I came to the conclusion that I also wanted to show the face of the man who was handing out the cash, and so I arrived at the current design.

I gave him dark hair, because that is the coloring normally associated with this suit. He is dressed richly, because he has plenty of wealth; more than enough to give away to those who deserve it. The designs on his coat are the white roses of change on a gold and blue ground to signify spirituality and wealth, and the purple grapes of joy, abundance and the love of life on a gold ground to show wealth again. The grapes are arranged in a pattern that is composed of four leaves (for growth) and four bunches of grapes (for plenty,) with a red border. The four is for the four elements, or for "foursquare," or for any other four that seems right to you. The red border, of course, stands for courage. Where red borders overlap, they are purple. This color, besides connoting wealth and riches, is also the color of healing. Either giving or receiving rewards like this can be very healing. There are gold dots all through the border, which stand for gold coins.

The coat also has a border of red-brown fur to show warmth and wealth.

He wears a gold belt which is an unbroken circle, to show his wealth doesn't end, and a red shirt for courage.

On his head is a red hat with a cream plume and a purple brim. The red is for courage, and the purple for wealth or healing (or both.) The "feather in his cap" is for the good work that he is doing, or the reward that he is handing out. It's cream colored for richness again, and because the cream rises to the top.

On his hat brim is a white jewel shaped like a heart with a red cross in the center. The white is for purity, and the heart for the love he has for the people. The red cross is to show that he's here to help and heal. There are two little white pearls at the bottom, to show the same kind of balance that is shown by the scale.

Around his neck, five pentacles are arranged in a necklace like a chain of office. This implies that he isn't just handing out the alms on his own; this is his job. If it doesn't look like that, that's fine! It may not be the case in the actual reading that you are doing. They are all gold because chains of office usually were.

In his left hand, the hand of intuition, he holds a bronze scale. This is to show that the gifts are not random or handed out on a whim; they are carefully chosen, and are just. When these people get a coin, it's because they deserve it according to some plan. The pans of the scale are perfectly balanced. There is fairness here, and equity.

With his right hand, he passes a coin to one of the petitioners. While he does this, he looks into the person's face. This act may be official, but it's also personal. This isn't an institution giving the Seeker a reward, it's individual recognition. And this fellow isn't giving it grudgingly, either. He enjoys giving these rewards.

The coin itself is glowing, sending out beams of radiance, to show that it is bringing light into the person's life. It's not just money, it represents more than that. In any reading, it may become obvious exactly what this coin is, just as it will be apparent whether the Seeker is the one who is giving or the one who is receiving the gift. Remember not to get tied to what you think a card *should* mean. Just look at it carefully, and report what it seems to mean to you at the time.

From the angle of the hands in this picture, combined with the tousled head of a child in the front, it is evident that the petitioners are kneeling. (In fact everyone who was helping me that day, including my two stepsons, knelt with their hands out for this one.) There are many more hands than there are coins. When you are reading, and this card comes up, you may feel that there are enough, he is just handing them out one at a time. Or you may feel that this is all there is, and most of these people are going to have to do without. If you get either feeling, you will probably also get a feeling of why this is so. If you do, go with it!

They are all dressed in rags, which has always given me the feeling that this is a continuation of the card before, the Five of Pentacles. But now the sense of desolation and isolation is gone. Now people are helping each other. And that means that a valuable lesson has been learned.

The background of this card is formed by trees, for growth and the earth. Behind them is a clear blue sky. The Seeker's problems are over, at least for now. Now they will receive (or give) the well-deserved help that is so sorely needed.

Seven of Pentacles

This card shows a farmer in smock, hat, and gloves, leaning on a tool and watching his garden grow. His vines are bearing seven Pentacles.

Key – **Material Progress**

This card means cleverness, skillfulness, a handy person. Growth achieved through hard work. Surprisingly good news. Help which proves useful. Waiting for a plan to come to fruition. Patience.

This card shows a gardener at work. He is wearing a smock, the traditional clothing of English farmers. It's brown, as is his hat, to show that he is not wealthy, but he is closely connected to the Earth. His green scarf shows that he understands growing things.

He wears gloves to protect his hands from the hoe, which shows that he is used to this work, careful, and not afraid to take advantage of help. I used to know someone who was too proud to wear gloves; he thought they weren't "macho." He often declared that he would rather have blisters than look weak. (Well, he was very young.) This man isn't like that. In fact, I gave him these gloves to remind myself that he wasn't. He will use any tool that helps to get the job done.

The only part of the tool that I actually show in this picture is the handle. I did that because sometimes it feels as though he's using a hoe, and weeding. Sometimes it feels as though he's using a shovel, and transplanting stuff. Sometimes it seems as though he's using a rake, and clearing out the dead growth. Since only the handle shows, I can fill in the business end of the tool with my instinct and imagination. Please feel free to do the same! As always, let your instincts guide you, so that you can see as accurately as possible.

I gave him dark hair, because that is the color associated with this suit. He has a thoughtful, waiting expression on his face, to show that he is contemplating the harvest, and waiting patiently for it.

I put the pentacles on vines because the vine, with its spirals and twisting, represents turning within and soul-searching; discovering hidden depths within yourself. That is part of what he may be waiting for here, as the harvest ripens.

If you know a lot about gardening, you may recognize these vines as cantaloupes. I chose to use them, because they have leaves that have five major lobes, and so they echo the pentagram theme. If you know about cantaloupes, then you know that the vines usually run along the ground. This gardener had to train them to grow vertically. Which means that he was willing to put in quite a bit of work in the beginning, to make his work easier as the job went on. This is an important facet of this card to remember, I think.

This whole suit deals with the rewards of delayed gratification, and working hard to harvest a rich bounty later, as well as the times when it is necessary to wait.

This card shows all of that; without the planting and the work put into caring for the fruit, there would be no crop. The part that is actually shown on this card was the hardest for me, personally, to master. For now the farmer must just wait patiently, and do nothing. If he picks the fruit at this stage, before it's ripe, then once again he has no crop. I can't tell you how many things I've ruined because I couldn't leave them alone to ripen, or set, or dry.

So this card is also about patience.

Finally, the sky behind him is a summer sky, promising fair weather. There are clouds, so no drought is likely to burn the crops. But there is also sun, so they can grow.

When I first drew this card, I had a sunset behind him, to show that the time of waiting was almost over. But it didn't feel right, and I had to change it. That was just my own impatience coming out! From the look of the sky now, there is still a long wait to go. But this fellow has the fortitude, wisdom, and equanimity to take it. He can enjoy the moment, and rest while he watches the ripening fruit. And there is a lesson to be learned there, too.

Eight of Pentacles

This card shows a young lad, learning to carve a pentacle. In front of him on the table sit the tools of his trade, and another pentacle all laid out ready for him. Behind him on the wall hang six finished pentacles. In the wall is an open window, through which may be glimpsed a castle, and hills, and clouds. There is another castle in the clouds.

Key – **Learning**

This card means learning, apprenticeship, gaining new knowledge or skills, creation, productivity. Or working very hard at low-paying levels, or keeping the nose to the grindstone.

The child on this card is eagerly learning, and taking joy in the experience. He is learning more than how to carve; he is learning how to work. He is carefully and studiously carving along the lines that his master or teacher has laid down for him. Or perhaps he has developed this design on his own. Once again, trust your own feelings when this card comes up in a reading. I purposely didn't put a master in this card, so it could go either way.

In front of him on the worktable is another pentacle, exactly like this one. It's there to show that it's through practice that you gain mastery in any skill. And practice usually implies a good deal of repetition. But, as in most of the cards of this suit, the hard work necessary is a price this lad is willing to pay.

Also on the table are several of the tools of his trade, as well as the shavings that are evidence of the work he has been doing. The vise, just visible in the extreme lower left corner is to show that he works at holding things together. The plane, in the middle of the table, but almost off the card to the right, shows that he works hard to smooth things out. The two additional carving tools next to the pentacle show that he isn't afraid to change tools if the job requires a different one. The whetstone, which is the white thing near his right elbow, is to keep his tools sharp. In a reading, you may feel that his tools are his mind, or his skills, or his technology, or anything else that can be used as a tool. If you do, then go with it. That's why I put in all the subtle stuff that can be easily overlooked in one reading, and then be the most important thing on the card in the next. It's all there to help your unconscious mind get your attention!

He wears a red shirt, for his courage and passion. He really cares about his work. He also wears brown coveralls, and a brown undershirt, to show his kinship with the earth.

His entire concentration is bent on his work, to show that being totally absorbed like this really facilitates learning.

Behind him on the wall hang six finished examples of the same sort of pentacle that he is carving now, in six different kinds of wood. They may look like examples that his master has laid out for him, or they may look as if he has been experimenting to see how different kinds of wood behave when they are carved. Or it may look like he has been doing this forever, with no break in sight. Whatever they look like, pay attention to that feeling, as always.

Also in the wall is a window. It has glass at the top, so the light can never be cut completely off. I did this because no matter how tedious the drudgery in repetitive work may be, as long as the act of creation is happening, the light can never be completely stifled. There is always something there to take delight in, if you look for it. (And yes, I have worked in a factory, and I do know what I'm saying. Honest.) The panes at the top of this window are diamond shaped, to show that this kind of pressure can produce the rarest and most beautiful of jewels.

The bottom of the window has a wooden shutter, with iron hinges, and many nails. I put that there to show that it is possible to cut yourself off from the air too much, if you are engaged in this kind of intensive or repetitive work. It's necessary to know this, and to make sure that the window is opened, at least a little bit.

The window opens onto the wider world, to show what is out there away from the work table. If you look through the window, you can see the water, which stands for hidden knowledge. If you fathom the hidden knowledge, you may reach the castle, which stands for achievement, wealth, power, etc. All those things that the lad is working so hard to reach. Beyond the castle are the hills of knowledge and enlightenment, as shown in so many of the other cards of this suit, with the mist of wisdom that acknowledges its own ignorance.

Above them is the sky, with the bright puffy clouds of the imagination. If you look carefully in those clouds, you will see another castle. This cloud castle stands for dreams, which are a vital part of the creative process, and of the learning process as well.

Birds soar through the sky, because learning can set your spirit free to fly to places beyond imagination.

By the way, if you are interested, the lad who posed for this card was my stepson Tony, when he was eight years old.

Nine of Pentacles

This card shows a richly dressed young woman, with a hooded hawk on her arm, picking a grape in a garden full of roses. Behind her, an ornate and beautiful gate stands between her and the rest of the world.

Key – **Solitary Wealth and Luxury**

This card means accomplishment, discretion, safety, material comfort, love of nature, solitary achievements, working alone, security, femininity. Or perhaps security and luxury purchased at too high a price.

This is the card of affluence mated with self control, and security with solitude. There are also overtones of femininity. So I chose to follow tradition, and draw a picture of a young woman in a garden, enclosed by a gate.

I dressed her in white for purity, purple and gold for prosperity and power, and red for courage and passion. I gave her black hair, as is customary with this suit, and put it in a golden net, to show that she is in control. Order is very important to her.

Around her neck is a choker that has a golden strand that goes to her bosom. This shows that she can sometimes strangle her emotions, in order to coolly do what she considers the proper thing at the time.

On her left hand, the hand of the instinct and the unconscious mind, she holds a hawk. It symbolizes her passions, and her freedom of spirit. She has these things, and she accepts them, but she is keeping her hawk hooded; her passions and freedom under strict control. She may loose them if she so desires, but right now they are restrained. Whether she is about to free them or not is something you will have to discover by being sensitive to your own instincts and feelings when this card comes up in a reading.

The red feathers on the hawk's hood are there to underline the feeling of passion. The light color of the hood is to contrast with the bird itself; but as I was just writing this, it also seemed to me that it could mean that you can use an appearance of light to keep your passions in the dark, as well.

Her glove matches the hawk's hood. If you look at it carefully, you will notice on the cuff a female biological symbol, which is also the glyph that means Venus, with leaves instead of a cross bar. It's there to show both femininity and growth.

Control doesn't always mean stagnation: it's very possible this young woman is flourishing under the self control she has discovered here.

She is plucking a single grape from the vine that grows among her roses, to show once more that she is not greedy. She has plenty, and she enjoys it, but she doesn't give in to any form of gluttony. Perhaps that's why she is so prosperous.

She stands in front of a great bank of red roses. They, too, are tamed and ordered. You won't find any stray sprays, or suckers poking far above the hedge. But they are red roses, and so they show her passion, and courage, and sweetness, as well as her bravery and willingness to fight. Remember, roses have thorns. But all of that is banked now, as a fire is banked. And, just as banking a fire preserves it, controlling her passions doesn't mean that they are lessening at all. If anything, a strongly passionate nature, firmly controlled, simply builds the passion higher.

Behind the roses stands a beautiful gate, all gold and iron filigree. I designed it with arches because I wanted to give this card the feeling of a cloister; a place of beauty, peace, and harmony, shut away from the cares and bustle of the outside world. I put gold in the gate, because I wanted to convey a feeling of richness, plenty, and luxury as well. And the iron is there because her will is also implacable. It may look delicate and ethereal, but there's no use tying to break it. Astrologically, the suit of Pentacles corresponds to the earth signs; Virgo, Taurus, and Capricorn. And if you have ever tangled with one of them (particularly with a Taurus, and I can say this because my husband is one) you will know that once their minds are made up that's that. There is no budging them.

But this is a gate, not a fence. Sometimes, when this card comes up in a reading, it seems to me that there is a path beyond the roses that leads up to the gate, and the young woman could easily go there and open the gate if she wanted to. She is inside, here where it's safe, by her own free will. She is at home; as safe as houses.

Sometimes, it seems that the roses have grown right up to the gate, and she can't open it any more. Then I get the feeling that she may have chosen this garden to start with; but now she is trapped in it. She has bound herself, and hooded her hawk, and although her life may look pleasant and prosperous, she is actually screaming inside.

If that happens for you, then listen to your instincts, as always. I designed this card so that either of those things could be read into it. And anything else that you find in it is great, too. That's what the cards are for.

Behind the gate, the sky is a serene blue, just beginning to turn to dusk at the zenith. I did that to add to the feeling of serenity and calm. For this card is very calm, even if it does look like the calm of rigid control and repression.

Normally, however, it looks like a haven. An island of peace and security. A place most sought after.

Ten of Pentacles

This card shows a wealthy patriarch, with his grandchildren on his knees and his dogs around him. Behind him is a rich garden, and an archway that gives a glimpse of a lovely home and a loving couple. It's a picture of familial harmony.

Key – **Prosperity**

This card means home, family, riches; positive domestic changes. Comfort, abundance, ease, plenty, contentment.

I designed this card so that the Seeker could be represented by different people on the card; and that is how it works, at least in my experience.

Sometimes, it seems that the Seeker is the grandfather, with success and abundance all around him.

Sometimes, the Seeker will be one of the children, loved and cared for, and learning to be generous in their turn.

Sometimes, the figures that resonate are the ones in the background; those in the prime of their lives, with the wealth of experience, or wisdom, or material things that they have gotten from their parents, and are passing on to their children in a beautiful, unbroken chain.

Be aware that this can happen, and listen to your instincts (as always) when you are reading; for this card is one of those that can open different vistas at different times.

The grandfather has a white beard, but an unlined face, to show that although he has many years behind him, they have been pleasant ones. He is portly to show that he has lived a very good life, and not known want. (At least, not for some time!) In fact, he looks a bit like Santa. I did that to give the reader the impression that he is very loving and generous, (and also because my husband, who posed for this figure, looks like that.)

He is dressed in purple, gold and burgundy to show richness, abundance, and power. If you look closely at the design on his coat, you will see that the gold is a pattern of vines and songbirds. That shows growth, and also shows that his spirit is singing within him.

He has a white shirt, and white trim on his clothing, to show his purity.

His grandchildren and their dog are leaning on him, to show that he is well loved.

The grandson is dressed in blue and white to show the pureness of his spirit, and in red to show his passion and courage. His clothing is trimmed with gold, to show wealth, decorated with a pattern of trefoils inside of circles. These show the past, present, and future all tied together into one moment. And, to some extent, that is what children are.

He is giving his grandfather a little basket filled with blue and pink flowers. This shows his generosity, and underlines the fact that he is learning how to be giving from the gifts that he receives every day as a matter of course. The blue flowers are for spiritual gifts, and the pink ones are for love.

His grandfather is accepting it with as much joy and pleasure as if it were a far more expensive gift, because he recognizes how precious any gift is, when given with love.

The granddaughter is kneeling, and leaning on her grandfather's knee, to show that she also loves him, and recognizes that he has wisdom to share with her. She is dressed in white for purity, and green for growth and femininity. Her clothing is also trimmed with gold, to show the wealth and luxury these children enjoy. But in her case the gold has a spiral pattern, to show introspection. There is a pattern of three loops at the top of the sleeve, though, because she represents the past, present and future as well as her brother does. There is also a square there, to show balance and stability.

At their feet, a puppy looks up to see what they are doing, and farther away another dog stands partially hidden behind them. These dogs stand for faithfulness, loyalty, domesticity, etc. The one in front is for friendliness, and devotion. The one in back is a greyhound, and stands for speed. But he is mostly hidden, and is not moving right now anyway. I did that to show that things have slowed down here; this is one of the still moments, when peace and tranquility reign.

Beyond the dogs is an archway, which leads from this sheltered place into another walled garden, and which affords a glimpse of the house beyond. At the bottom of the arch is a pedestal, from which ten pentacles run up the arch. This is to show that the principles of the pentacle are firmly established in this home. You will know which principles (spirituality, religion, money, etc.) when you have this card actually show up in a reading.

At the top of the arch on the left is the sun. I put it there to show that the sun always shines on this household, and also because all the attributes of the sun (warmth, joy, light, and so on) are present. If you look at the extreme right corner of the card, you will see a couple of stars above the arch there. From them, you might extrapolate that there is a moon on this corner of the arch. And you would be right. So all of the moon attributes (mystery, wonder, magic, and so forth) are also present, although they are hidden. Which, when you think about it, makes sense.

The shape of the arch itself echoes the rainbow that is found on the Ten of Cups. In fact, these two cards have a lot in common. The main differences are that this family is more established (it has another generation forming part of it,) and it is also more likely to have material wealth (compare the two houses.) Nonetheless, that same feeling of endless possibilities and promise exists here.

There is a vine growing up the side of the wall next to the arch. That is for introspection, again; a sort of quiet soul searching that will enable the whole scenario to become even richer.

Beyond the doorway stand the parents of the children, or the son or daughter of the grandfather. She is dressed in bright colors, in yellow and pink and orange. These stand for joy, love, and warmth. She has a basket over her arm, to show that she has been gathering good things for the family. It also echoes the basket that the boy holds, and so can easily stand for another gift.

The man who is facing her is dressed in deep blue for intuition and inspiration. He has a red hat, which shows his passion and courage, and a burgundy cloak, which shows his wealth, abundance and liberality.

They are facing each other, and he has his hand on hers. I did that to show that there is deep affection here, and caring. It adds to the feeling of conviviality and love that is shown in this whole card.

Beyond them is a wall, with trees espaliered onto it. I drew trees that have been trained to lie flat against the wall to show that these people are capable of gently shaping their environment to serve their own purposes. It isn't often important in a reading; but in case it is, there it is!

Beyond that wall stands the house; a rich mansion, with large windows, to show that they let air into their lives and relationships, and they thrive in the light and sunshine. Tall chimneys show the warmth here. Steep roofs show that they shed problems that would cause them trouble. and crenelations show that they are quite capable of defending themselves if the need arises.

All around the house are trees, to show growth and longevity.

Above it all, the sky is a lovely blue, without a cloud visible, to show that there are no clouds in their sky, and the sun shines brightly for them. Three birds fly there, to show the lightness and freedom of their spirits.

In general, I meant for this card to give the reader a sense of love, plenty, beauty, and support. It's a fully functional family, and a safe and happy place to live, with no lack of anything spiritual, emotional, intellectual, or material. This is what Home should be.

Chapter 8
Swords

Once again, the symbols chosen here were chosen because they are the ones that best expressed my own feelings about the meanings of each card.

They may mean something different to you. If they do, don't hesitate to ignore why I chose them, and use the meanings that are important in your own personal symbol set.

Towards that end, you may want to keep a notebook while you read this. Write down your own interpretations as we go over each card; what you think the symbol means, and why it is important in expressing the meaning of the card for you. If you wind up with the entire card meaning something different, my advice is to go with it. This may upset the purists among us, but in my experience when one card shifts meaning, another generally expands or shifts to take its place. So the entire range remains unchanged. That's what growth and change is all about, after all!

The Swords are one of the suits in the tarot that is (believe it or not) fraught with controversy. Some people say the swords are ruled by the element of air while fire rules the wands. Some reverse that. In my deck, air rules the swords, and fire the wands. When all the other arguments were over, I decided to do it this way partly because that is what I was originally taught, and so it was most comfortable for me. But also because as air cards, they have all the magical attributes of air. In other words, they also correspond to knowledge, which often cuts two ways. When you think of them as knowledge, remember that knowledge doesn't necessarily contain wisdom (that is for the north, and earth; in my Tarot deck, the Pentacles.) Knowledge that isn't tempered with wisdom can be pretty dangerous stuff.

So, in my deck, Swords are the suit of air, which also means knowledge and beginnings. Their direction is the East, and their time of day is morning, and their time of life childhood. (The real stuff; not the idealized one. If you really think back on childhood, it was relatively violent, wasn't it?)

Swords usually stand for pretty serious stuff; trouble, strife, courage, authority, health, etc.

The lessons of this suit are about handling knowledge or authority. They also deal with sacrifice, redemption, and transformation.

King of Swords

This card shows a solidly built man with dark brown hair and beard standing with his legs apart, and his arms crossed over his chest. In his right hand he holds a sword. He's on a windy hilltop that is covered with half-dead grass. The sky is stormy, and filled with thunderheads.

Key - **The Boss**

This card means a mature person of military bearing. A commander, with the power of life and death (or work and unemployment!) Perceptive, strong-willed, intelligent and firm in either friendship or enmity. He may also be suspicious, over-cautious, cruel, and overbearing. Either way, he wants to control the situation.

Court cards are often read to represent people; which person it is representing may be shown by the physical attributes of the card (in this case, a mature man with dark hair and light eyes,) or sometimes by the personality shown.

I think they may also symbolize attributes that are appearing in the Seeker's life; things the Seeker is becoming, or the way in which many of those around her are behaving towards her.

Please remember this as you read the descriptions of the court cards.

This king has a firmness and intellect that overrides his emotions. So I made him standing, to show that he is the embodiment of an active principle. I gave him dark hair because that is traditional for this suit, and a beard to show his maturity. He is scowling, because that is the way he tends to look at the world - as a series of problems to be overcome. This may mean that he helps the Seeker to overcome them, or that he sees the Seeker as one of them! It will become apparent which of these is in effect when you do an actual reading.

His feet are wide apart, because he is firmly planted, and ready for combat at any time. This one is not nonconfrontational! I crossed his arms on his chest to show that he is not really likely to be open to new ideas. In my experience, not many people who really want control want to hear what others have to say.

Starting from the top, he is wearing a helmet because this is a martial sort of guy. The golden crown shows that he is a king. I gave it raven's wings because ravens are the bird of war, and also the bird that was sacred to Odin, who brought learning (knowledge) to the Norse. They also show the element of air, which is important in all the Sword cards, but most of all in the court cards.

His cape is square, to show that he can be very rigid, and also to show that he can be very dependable and steady. It has two sides; the outside is the bright sky of day, and a living atmosphere to show light and life. The inside is the night sky, or the vacuum of space, to show darkness and death. One is the flip side of the other, and this character deals in both. Or, if you are of a more Science Fiction bent, the outside can show the warmth and hominess of a planet, and the inside can show the adventure and excitement of space. Once again, it all depends on how you look at things!

The double penannular brooches are made of gold to show his royalty and nobility. I used penannular brooches here because they fit with the cloak (sometimes a cucumber is just a cucumber!) and also because they have the sharp pointed bits that are exposed, just as the thorn of a rose is. In fact, I use roses with the swords a lot, and the design on the brooch is also a wreath of roses, although you can't really see that. But now you know it anyway! The chain shows that he may be a prisoner of his own intellect, or he may be trying to make the Seeker one.

His arms and hands are covered with mail because, once again, he is warlike, and imparts that feeling to everything he touches.

He is holding a naked sword upright because that is the symbol of this suit, and also because it shows his authority, his virility, and his readiness to fight. He is not one who is going to try to compromise.

The grip of his sword is red because that is the color of courage, and also the color of blood. He has plenty of courage, and he doesn't mind blood at all. The pommel is a rose, again, because roses are symbols of air (the scent) and of sharpness (the thorns.)

His undertunic is red as well, to show his underlying courage, with gold brocade to show the richness that he is capable of.

His tunic is the air, going from the rich, cloud-filled air near the ground to the thinner, deeper blue of decreasing atmosphere. This shows his affiliation with the element of air again, and also that he is comfortable in the rarefied intellectual realms. This guy is sharp!

The gold trim and belt are to show his royalty.

He wears his sword on a baldric slung over his shoulder to show that it's high up in his estimation. The baldric and scabbard are grey to show the storminess that he is capable of. In fact, the scabbard has lightning bolts on it, to show that he can become very angry, and that he is likely to be violent or intellectually cutting when he is. The hardware on the scabbard is gold to show his royalty again.

He wears thigh high boots because the sword cards also show movement. He is capable of moving very quickly, and I wanted the boots to show that. He is also capable of walking all over someone, and the boots show that, too. (I guess I listened to too many popular songs in the sixties!)

They are tight, and show his muscles, because this is a fellow who is never afraid to show his muscles, if you know what I mean.

He is standing in a field of long half-dead grass because that kind of field has always felt closer to the wind to me. When I was designing these cards, I thought about making all of the court cards in this suit have spring backgrounds, because spring is the time of the east and air. But I decided not to, because pretty spring scenes didn't seem to fit in with the swords very well. And then I realized that in the very early spring, when the winds are the strongest, the long grass is still mostly dead. The bright green spring stuff isn't showing yet! So I made the hills the color of mostly dead winter/early spring grass, and it felt right to me.

The hills show the depths of this card, and the intellect. But they are eroded hills, because the wind has been scouring them for many years.

The stormy sky is to show that this guy can be pretty stormy. It also shows the element of air very clearly.

The birds show the flights of the intellect that he is capable of. Or perhaps they are the ravens of war, again. Did you know that a group of ravens is called an "unkindness?" So this fellow might be unkind.

Queen of Swords

This card shows a tall, strong woman standing in profile on a windy hilltop. Her right hand holds a sword, with the blade pointing up. Her left hand is held out and open. Behind her is a red rose bush.

Key – **Cool and Confident**

This card represents a quick-witted, intensely perceptive, confident, strong woman. She may have suffered loss, and become stronger because of it. She may also be controlling, cruel, or sharp-tongued.

I put mail on her head, to show that she may have a martial frame of mind, and also that she may use her intellect as a weapon. But I also put a veil there, to show that she may still retain some softness. Her hair is tightly bound, to show her control. But the net is gold, to show her royalty. The crown shows her royalty as well.

She is in profile because although she is very sharp of wit, she may choose not to approach all of her problems head on. This person may use a more unconventional, sideways approach to things; based partially on intuition. That's why she is a female on the card, although she may represent anyone with these attributes in a reading, regardless of sex.

Her left hand is stretched out and open to show her openness to intuitive knowledge, as well, since the left side often means intuition, as the right side means action.

And, in her right hand, she holds a sword. She isn't adverse to action at all! In fact, she is armed and ready for it. The sword has a red grip for her courage. The hilt is gold for her nobility, and is decorated with two seated sphinxes (even though they are hard to see) to show that she excels in all kinds of knowledge, and can solve all sorts of riddles, puzzles, etc.

The pommel of her sword is a rose, because roses are symbolic of swords to me, since their scent is like incense, and so is part of air, and their thorns are sharp, like a blade.

Her cloak, like that of her consort, shows the bright daytime sky on one side, and the dark night sky on the other. Skies, of course, are symbolic of air. And this also suggests that she can show both sides, light and air, which is life; and the darkness and quiet in the vacuum of space.

The white satin puff of her sleeve is like a summer cloud, and the open sleeve below it is white, because that is one of the colors of dawn. It's covered with butterflies of transformation, because knowledge can transform things. They are many colors to show that her knowledge is in many areas. (This can also be quite a colorful woman, since our society tends to disdain women like this. A woman with this much courage is likely to be unconventional in lots of different ways.) Below it opens into the deep blue of an endless sky, because even the sky is no limit.

There are two buttons to show the duality that may be present in this card (brilliant/cruel or scholarly/intuitive or controlling/tender; whatever it looks like while you are reading it.) and to warn you that this woman has buttons; be careful how you push them! They have yellow tassels because yellow is the color of the air, and to show that there is some part of her that remains free and wild, in spite of the constraints that she may have imposed on herself.

The golden butterfly at the top of the sleeve shows her royalty, and also shows that transformation is something she does openly.

Her undersleeve is blue, for the sky and purity. It is encased in a silver web to show the restraint that she uses.

She wears a ring because she understands the power of the circle, and to show her intuition once again.

Below her cloak you can see the tip of one blue-booted foot. This is to show that although she may look stationary now, this lady is going places!

The grass she stands on is dried because this is very early spring; and besides dry seemed more appropriate for wind and swords!

Behind her are the red roses of courage. Roses I've already explained, and red, too. As I wrote in my old notes, "This is a strong woman, but she has her prickly side, as well."

The hills go on into the distance to show the depth of this card.

The sky is bright, although filled with clouds, because she is bright, although she may have a hidden side. The sun is low, because it's morning. That is the time of the east and air. It's about to burst forth in full glory to show that this person may be on the edge of an intellectual breakthrough. Birds fly through this sky, and the one on her cloak, to show her freedom of spirit.

One interesting note on this card. When you are drawing things, they don't always come out exactly as planned. So with this picture. In the pencil sketch, her nose wasn't nearly that close to the sword. But when I did the inking, the ink lines were both so thick (which is done to show depth, and to isolate the main subject of the drawing from the background, or other details) that they appeared to touch!

I narrowed the line of the sword just there so they no longer met, but it still looks to me like she has her nose almost against her sword. This has always looked like "nose to the grindstone" to me ever since! And since this person is one who may be working too hard, I guess that's appropriate!

Knight of Swords

This card shows a young, beardless man on a flying horse, charging across a stormy sky. He carries his sword aloft, and lightning crackles around it.

Key - **To Boldly Go**

This card means a soldier, or someone who is heroic and brave. It can also mean righteous anger, triumph over opposition, or a practical solution to a problem. Or it might mean someone who tends to be a bit over-enthusiastic!

When I was doing all of the knight cards, I tried to put them on mounts that were somehow connected with the element that the card represents. So I put this

one on a flying horse. (Besides, I love to draw flying horses. Or anything else with wings. My secret soul name is "Wing-Nut." Shhhh. Don't tell anyone!)

I made the horse dappled grey to look like clouds and storm, because that is the basic theme of all these court cards, and also because this fellow isn't afraid to face any storm there is! He has pale green-blue eyes because he is a creature of the sky and storm. If you notice, although he is flying as fast as the wind, he is hardly extending himself. There is no foam on him, and his nostrils, although wide, aren't showing any red. He is at ease at this speed.

His tack is blue, the color of the sky and of purity. His chamfron (the armor on a horse's face) is silver with blue trim. I did this to show his oneness with the sky. But the eyeguards have a red lining, to show the courage that underlies his attitude. On the top corner of the chamfron is the alchemical symbol for air, picked out in blue.

The knight has brown hair and eyes because that is the coloring that goes with this suit, and some people use that.

His helmet is made of silver (over steel, we presume) to show his affinity with air, and his shining spirit. His noseguard is shaped like a bird in flight to show the flights of intellect that he is capable of, and his freedom of spirit. For the same reason, there is a motif of flying birds on the sides.

The front of his helmet is decorated with lightning bolts, because his wit is quick, and to show that he may have a temper, as well.

There are white bird wings on his helmet to show affinity with the air, and also to show his purity.

I drew him with his mouth open because he often seems to me like he is calling a joyful sort of war-cry as he flies. (Although sometimes he just looks like he is so excited that he has opened his mouth to get more air.)

His eyes are straight ahead, because he is looking forward to whatever challenge is coming up.

In his right hand, he is waving a sword. This is the symbol of the suit, of course. It's also a symbol of his bravery and his willingness to go full tilt into whatever battle offers itself. Knights are active cards, and air is an active principle; so between the two of them...well, you can imagine!

The grip of the sword is red to show his courage, and his willingness to deal with bloodshed if need be. The guard is decorated with wings, again, in case you missed them someplace else! The pommel is a kind that is known as a wheel pommel. I gave him one to show that this kind of activity has its place on the Wheel of Life, and is neither something to be feared nor something to be suppressed. Sometimes, things are simply worth fighting for! I set it with a blue stone to show purity and spirituality.

Lightning crackles around the blade, to show the sheer energy and power that this kind of righteous anger has. There is enough voltage there to do anything necessary. The only trick is directing it in an appropriate fashion.

He is wearing chain mail on his arms because this is a martial card. I used mail instead of plate to show his flexibility.

Page of Swords

This card shows a young girl running down a hill. In her hands she holds a naked sword upright. On her belt she wears a spyglass. Behind her, hills covered with grass go back to the horizon. The sky is filled with clouds, except the area around the sword.

Key – **Running with Scissors**

This card means grace, dexterity, diplomacy, intelligence (or intelligence work i.e., spying.) Service done in secret, or secrets uncovered. An unexpected happening; something that is too quick to react to. Vision and agility, but with an edge of danger.

Like all the pages, this one is a young girl. She is running, with her sword held in front of her, to show her swiftness and dexterity, and also to show that she is living on the edge. She is smiling as she runs, because she really enjoys this! Her grace and good balance may enable her to run easily, and safely, in spite of the inherent dangers. (In some readings, though, all I can see is the sword. In those cases, I remind the Seeker that he is doing dangerous things, and may get hurt.)

She has brown hair because that is the coloring that traditionally goes with the suit of Swords, and there are people who use that. I made her hair long and loose so it could be streaming behind her in the wind of her running. Yellow is one of the colors of the east, which is associated with the air and Swords, so I gave her yellow ribbons. She has four of them for the four winds, because this is the suit of air. She also has three white feathers in her hair, to show her purity and freedom of spirit, and that she will retain these throughout her life; now as a maid, later as a mother, and lastly as a crone.

Her tunic has long sleeves, because she likes to feel them billow in the wind, but is short, so it won't interfere with her running. This shows that she really likes the sensations, but is still practical enough to protect herself in some ways. It's blue, for the sky, because this is an air card, and has clouds on the hem and cuffs to show affinity with the sky as well. Pretty, puffy ones, though, to show her imagination and because in many ways she is still just playing. There are birds there, too, to show the freedom of her spirit. It's lined with yellow, to show the correspondence with the east, and the dawn, and also to show her essential joy.

Her boots are short, so they won't hamper her, and blue for the sky. The cuffs are made like wings, to show that her feet really fly! They are white again for her purity, of course.

She wears a long white belt with a motif of feathers on it, once again for the freedom, beauty, and swiftness of a bird in flight. It streams behind her to show how quickly she is moving, with a spiral motion to show that the vision which is also a part of this card may be turned inward.

Attached to it is a spyglass, to show that vision, and also to remind me that this card also stands for secrets revealed, or spying. I gave all the Pages little mnemonic devices like this, because I had a hard time remembering what they meant.

She holds her sword upright in both of her hands, to show that it is her primary focus; she isn't putting a hand to anything else. At the moment, knowledge (which is the primary lesson of the Swords) is more important to her than anything, and she is pursuing it wholeheartedly. Maybe even past the point of prudence. Her right hand is on top, to show that the knowledge she seeks is primarily that of the overt, tangible, physical world.

The sword itself has a mirror bright blade, to show that the knowledge is bright, untarnished, and new (at least to her.)

The cross-guard is of gold, because it's precious, and is shaped like wings to show the freedom that this knowledge will bring her, and her freedom of spirit in searching for it. It has a blue stone, to show her purity and also the correspondence to the sky, again. If you look at the guards of the other swords with winged guards in this suit, you will find that they are all upright when the sword is drawn. Hers is inverted. I did that to show that she is likely to look in all kinds of unexpected places, using unexpected ways, for the knowledge that she seeks. She is likely to be unpredictable in the search, and it will be in a fashion that is totally unprepared for. This is especially important if the card is in a position that represents someone who is not the Seeker, but who is trying to ferret out the Seeker's secrets.

The grip is red, for her courage. She isn't worried or fearful about the consequences of this search at all. Maybe not even as much as she should be.

The pommel is a wheel pommel, to show that while she is finding things out, she should remember that what goes round comes round; that is, if she wants to find out the secrets of others, she shouldn't be surprised when hers come under scrutiny as well. It has a yellow stone, for the east and joy.

As the sun hits the edge of the blade, it sends out seven rays. These symbolize perfection, and show that she seeks perfect knowledge. Or they may symbolize the days of the week, and show that she never stops seeking. Or they may simply look unbalanced, and show that she isn't seeking in a balanced fashion. Once again, what you see when you really look at the card during a reading is the meaning. (If you want to know why I originally decided to use seven, it was for perfection.)

The sky all around is full of clouds, except for the area around the sword. This shows that the knowledge gained is clearing up the clouds of confusion, misdirection, and uncertainty, and revealing the sky. In other words, all the secrets are being revealed.

Above her head, there is a flock of birds flying. If you look carefully, you will notice that the flock takes on the shape of the lemniscate, the infinity symbol. I did this to show that there is no end to the freedom that the search for knowledge can bring. In her headlong pursuit of the truth, she finds mastery. Because the symbol is made of birds, it also shows that fearlessness and freedom of the spirit yield infinite possibilities. But it's very subtle, and seldom stands out in a reading.

She is running over the same kind of grass that is found in the other court cards of this suit, for the same reasons. Behind her, the hills of knowledge go on to the horizon. There is no end to the knowledge that is waiting to be gained.

Ace of Swords

This card shows an upright sword against a background of clouds. Around the top is a laurel wreath from which hang a garland of olive and one of roses, making a double helix. Sun strikes the edge of the blade, and shoots beams of light throughout the card.

Key – **Knowledge Victorious**

This card means success, attainment, victory, or the beginning of all of these things. It may mean that the Seeker is or is about to become a champion, hero, or leader. It may show the birth of a valiant child. It may also show the beginning of an intellectual venture.

Like all the aces, this is the beginning of the suit of Swords. All the other lessons in this suit follow from this one. But it is also the culmination, or perfection of the principles of that suit. In effect, it is the most perfect statement of the fundamentals the entire suit is based on. Think of it as a sort of unified field theory. The simplest possible expression of a complex topic.

So this single sword has within it the idea of the pursuit of knowledge, and all that can be gained, both pain and healing. It encompasses the whole of war and of peace. It speaks of storm, fear, and depression and the bright, clean skies after the storm, the hope and joy that relieve the gloom.

Quite a lot for one card, and more opposites than I found with any other suit.

So; first I made a sword, double edged to show that knowledge can cut both ways. It is often painful to learn things, and innocence is often destroyed to gain wisdom.

The blade is very bright, because the quest for knowledge is so very attractive. It's something that all of us share. All you need to do is to watch a small child, who constantly asks "why?" to see that the need to understand is one of the major forces that drive us. We often lose a great deal of this in the Public Schools, at least in this country, where they make the acquisition of knowledge boring and senseless by presenting it in a vacuum, but still it's there. How many children are endlessly curious about everything that they aren't studying in school? So, the sword, or new knowledge, is shiny and pretty; and we forget that it cuts.

The hilt has golden wings, to show the freedom and joy that knowledge can bring. The more you know, the more you are free, and realize that the only limits are those that you impose on yourself. And, of course, the higher you fly, the more you can see. So the more you know, the more you realize there is yet to learn!

They are gold, to show that knowledge is precious. Sometimes, when I am reading, the gold makes the knowledge look like it has been dearly bought, or will cost a lot. If that happens, of course, go with it. Remember, you see what you need to see when you look at the cards.

The stone is the blue of a calm and untroubled spirit. This shows that there is peace between the two edges of the sword. Knowledge, coupled with wisdom, can bring great peace.

The grip is the red of courage, blood, and life. All of these things are illustrated here. This knowledge is vital, not boring.

There are two crowns on the grip, one at each end. These are for the mastery and riches that knowledge can bring. They reflect each other to show again the principle of "as above, so below" that runs through so much of the Tarot.

There is a rose on the pommel to symbolize the air, and swords. The scent of the rose is very sweet, as is the quest for knowledge; but the thorns can tear you and cause pain, once again just like the quest for knowledge. I think it's worth it, though, as a visit to my garden in summer would tell you!

The tip of the sword is crowned with a laurel wreath, to show that the fight was victorious! This is the champion's sword, or the sword of someone who will be a champion. If you take up this sword, then victory will follow because your cause is just. Remember that although the swords are sometimes knowledge, sometimes they really mean a fight! And since there are things worth fighting for, it's good to know that you will win.

From the wreath hangs an olive branch, meaning peace and fruitfulness, and a garland of white roses. White roses are a sign of freedom of the spirit and of thought. They are pure, and lovely, but not without the prospect of pain, shown by the thorns. So victory will bring peace, beauty, and freedom; although there may also be pain.

These hang in a double helix for two reasons. One is because this is the way in which the snakes twine around a caduceus. Knowledge, although it may bring pain, also brings healing. And the victory and ensuing peace bring healing as well. The second was to show the double helix of DNA, the beginning of new life. This is a card of beginnings, as well, and new life can rise from the old.

Behind the sword are the clouds. They show that this card is associated with the east, and with air. And they also show the clouds of confusion and ignorance that the sword is about to dispel.

The sun, which is caught reflected in the blade, also shows the hope that the victory or learning will bring, and the joy that is about to be discovered. I meant this card to have a clean, bright, sharp, bracing feeling. The idea of taking up the sword, and completing the quest victoriously!

Two of Swords

This card shows a woman with black hair in a long white gown, sitting on the ruins of a wall, holding two swords in her hands. Behind her, a restless ocean foams among black rocks and cliffs. Above, the new moon floats in a cloud wracked sky. She is blindfolded.

Key – **Balance**

This card means precarious balance, a dangerous spot, a choice of the lesser of two evils. It may also mean that the Seeker is in a position that seems impossible, but actually has the knowledge needed to balance the situation and make the best of it.

This is a card of balance, like all the two cards. In this case, the balance is a balance of knowledge, and implies danger and/or fear. So the balance is between two swords. If you look carefully at the hilts, one has a triangle pointing up, and the other has a triangle pointing down. This is to show that even though the two things may seem very similar, there are indeed differences between them, and that needs to be considered.

Both have silver hilts, because I wanted this card to be almost monochromatic; it's all done in shades of indigo, with the scale running from white on the one end to black on the other. This is to show the very starkness of the choice. At this point, there's probably not a lot of distraction in the Seeker's life. She is probably very aware of the problems that caused this card to come up in the reading, and its lack of color underlines the lack of possible choices. But the color used is indigo; the color of the brow chakra and the psychic sense. She knows intuitively how to get out of here without too much damage; she has the swords, which stand for knowledge, and she is balancing them.

She may have more than intuitive knowledge, too. She may know exactly what to do. In that case, it's more likely to be a question of courage. This is a scarry place to sit, after all.

She has black hair, to fit in with the monochromatic color scheme, and also to show that she has hidden, secret, intuitive knowledge that she can find here. She is dressed in white, once again for the barrenness of this position, but also to show that if her heart is pure, she will find her way out. Her dress is long, because it's possible that she can be tripped up easily if she isn't very careful.

She has a blindfold on, because part of her problem is that she can't see her way out of this mess. She isn't sure where she is, or what she can safely do. So it's important to point out to her that she is holding both of the swords herself; she has more control of the situation than she thinks. If the card represents someone in the Seeker's life, and not the Seeker herself, the blindfold may also show that that person isn't thinking clearly, or doesn't have all the facts about the Seeker's situation, and is about to act, possibly against the Seeker, out of fear or desperation. In such a case, it may be wise to counsel the Seeker to open up to this person, and explain her side of the case. As always, follow your own instincts when you are reading the cards.

Her feet are bare, because she is still in touch with the knowledge of the earth.

She is holding her hands crossed on her chest for several reasons; the first is that in this position, the swords take on the shape of a pair of calipers; a tool used to measure things. If she concentrates, she has the measure of the problem. She just needs to face the facts that she knows. This is also the "God" position, used in our tradition of Wicca when drawing down the God. This shows that she has plenty of active power and advice ready, if she listens carefully to her inner voice.

She is sitting on the ruins of a castle, because she probably feels like her life is in ruins around her, or about to be. This also shows that her position is becoming untenable. (OK, I know, but I have warned you that my brain often works in visual puns.) It has two arches to show the balance, and also to show that there are open doorways, if she looks for them. Her feet are firmly planted on a pillar. She may feel like there is firm ground underfoot, as long as she doesn't move. But she needs to start feeling around with her feet. She may find that her position is more precarious than she thought, and some action is quickly becoming necessary.

Behind her, the sea of her emotions is dashing itself to bits against the hard rocks of fate or past decisions. No matter how much she may wish this situation to just "go away," it's too late for that now. Ragged clouds race against the night sky, to show that her feelings are becoming ragged, and she may not be thinking as clearly as she needs to.

The moon is new; the situation is developing, and will continue, just as the moon will wax. You may feel it best to warn the Seeker to sit tight, or you may feel that she needs to find her way out now. Let your own intuition guide you, or work with the Seeker to find out what her intuition is saying. Remember, this is supposed to be a co-operative venture. If the Seeker just wants you to prove that cards work, I suggest that you not read for her. That's not what our gifts are for, and you don't need to prove anything!

Three of Swords

This card shows a bright red heart, being pierced by three daggers. Behind the heart, rain pours out of a grey, dismal sky. But at the top of the card, the clouds are lighter.

Key – **Tears and Woe**

This card means sorrow, loss, emotional pain, separation, heartbreak, grief, the end of a romance - basically exactly what it looks like; the feeling of being stabbed through the heart, and weeping.

This is perhaps the most obvious of all the cards in the deck.

Notice that the three daggers are coming from three different directions. It's possible that the pain the Seeker is feeling is coming from more than one source.

Also notice that although the hilts are all different, with three different colors, they are all dark. As always, dark colors in the Tarot show heavy, sorrowful emotions. Whatever the source, this hurts!

I made the swords on the right and left a matched set; but with opposites. Although they are the same basic shape and design, the one on the left is red and the one on the right is green. Red and green are opposite each other on the color wheel, so the combination is balanced. The guard on the red sword goes up, the one on the green sword goes down. Once again, there is balance. This is to show that even this pain is part of the balance, and the Seeker should not despair.

The dagger in the middle has a blue hilt, and the guard goes both up and down, to show this is balanced within itself. Blue shows spiritual stuff, the stuff of enlightenment. The entire suit of swords is also knowledge. So I intended this dagger to show the realization of a spiritual truth. Notice that the edge of this dagger is serrated. I did that because (at least for me) the discovery of a spiritual truth that shows that you have been wrong and have not learned your lessons the way that you might have liked to, and have either caused others harm or wasted years of your life, cuts far deeper than any other kind of pain. But on the top of the blade is a diamond shape, made of two intersecting jagged edges. I did that to remind me that this is the sort of thing that tempers us into diamond.

Liquid drips down the heart, and off the points of the daggers. While on the heart, it looks like blood. But as it drips off the daggers, it's apparent that it's really water. So this pain can feel like it's going to kill you. But farther along, you will notice that what was falling wasn't blood, but only the tears that wash pain away, and nourishing rain.

The sky is also grey, and full of rain. It feels like the very elements are weeping, and there will never be sunshine again. But if you look, the clouds are beginning to break up. The sky is lighter at the top of the card. So this, too, shall pass.

When this card comes up in a reading, it has always meant heartbreak of one kind or another. And the meaning is so plain that even someone who has never seen the Tarot before cannot miss it.

So I tell them a phrase that I heard somewhere. I wish I could remember where I heard it, because I'd like to credit the author. But it goes like this.

"Then she overheard the Gods talking, and the Lady said, "She broke her heart, and it never healed properly. So I had to rebreak it, so that it could heal right." This is very true, and often gives comfort to people who can't understand why this is happening to them.

As in all these "learning experience" cards, go gently, and listen for the little voice inside that tells you what to say.

Four of Swords

This card shows a tomb effigy; a sleeping figure carved from white stone, with a sword carved into the side of the bier. But the statue is entwined with ivy and roses; yellow, white, pink and red. Behind the figure, three scabbarded swords hang from an apple tree in bloom. Another tree stands in the distance. Farther away yet is a wood. Overhead, a single white star burns in the violet sky of dusk.

Key - **Restful Private Place**

The meaning of this card is rest, calm, peace, convalescence, recuperation, seclusion, suspension of activity, meditation. A return to the basics. A well-earned intermission. A period of repose. Solitude, retreat. The end of one phase of life, and the beginning of another. A still space to regroup before the battle continues. It does not mean physical death. It may also mean that the time of rest is over, and activity is about to begin again, depending on where it falls in a reading.

This card shows life surrounding the effigy of death.

The stone the figure is carved from is white, showing purity and beginnings. All endings are also beginnings. I made the figure out of stone to show a return to the earth, and the solidity and stillness which are there. This also shows a return to the Seeker's origins; back to the bedrock, as it were. (I've always assumed the bier is carved from the living rock.)

The carved semblance is richly dressed, with brocade and embroidery, to show that the last phase of the Seeker's life was completed successfully, with honor. A shield lies on top of the figure, showing that this person was a warrior in the phase of life just past. But a new phase is beginning; almost anything may happen now. A wing and a star are visible on the shield, as part of the device. Wings show spiritual growth and enlightenment, and stars do, too. So this person has reached a spiritual height that allows a period of respite.

On the side of the bier is a carved sword. This shows that knowledge is the base that the Seeker (or the person represented by this card) rests on.

All around the resting place grow a riot of roses, vigorous and blooming. This is to show the sweetness of this rest. But roses, as we all know, also have thorns. So even this may have a bit of a sting. The colors are white for purity; yellow for joy;

pink for love; red for passion. All the strong emotions are still present, even in this time of relative calm.

If you look closely, you will find that ivy is growing among the roses. Ivy is the plant of introspection. So this time should be used for introspection. Consolidating the lessons from the phase just past, and deciding what should come next. Don't forget to just rest, too, though. All things need rest at times!

Beyond the bier are fruit trees, heavy with blossom. These are for the fruitfulness of a life well spent, and also to show that this is a time of beginning, not of ending. Just as an apple tree doesn't bear fruit all the time, we can't always be producing things. We need a time of rest, of sleep, as the trees sleep through the winter. And then, when we do start to be active again, we need the time of sweetness and joy, of opening slowly in the sunlight and enjoying the bees, before we can produce more fruit. In this society, we tend not to give ourselves that necessary time. I heard a saying once: illness is the only acceptable form of Western meditation. So this card reminds us to take the time while we are well, so that we don't have to be sick in order to get it!

There are three swords hanging from the tree. They are in their scabbards. They, too, are at rest at the moment. Their knowledge is hidden, their edge is sheathed; they are present, but not dangerous. These may represent problems, situations, difficulties, etc. the Seeker has conquered. Things that have been taken care of, their menace stilled. Or they may represent the knowledge or help of friends that are ready and waiting for the Seeker to need them. As always, it depends on how you feel about it when the card comes up in a reading.

The shape of the two trees together forms an arch. This shows an opening into the next phase of the Seeker's life, a doorway into the future.

Beyond that is a wood, a place of verdant growth and life, but also a place of mystery, of unexpected paths and turnings. This is to show that although the present may be full of calm and peace, there is activity ahead, just waiting for the Seeker to be ready.

The sky is the violet of healing, because the time of rest is when we heal. There is a single star burning there. Stars, to me, mean hope and guidance, as well as beauty; so the Seeker is not abandoned. The guiding star is still shining.

Five of Swords

This card shows a young man, with flaming red hair and brown eyes. He holds two swords over his shoulder and another in his right hand, while he taunts two men who walk away, despondent and defeated. Two swords are pushed into the ground beside him. In the distance is the ocean. Ragged clouds race through the sky overhead.

Key – **Nyaa-nya-nya-nyaa-nya**

This card means failure caused by trickery, deceit, degradation. Winning by unfair means. Cowardice, manipulation, slyness, chicanery.

The figure on this card has red hair, brown eyes, and is dressed in the colors of smoke and fire. This is to show that if you play these games, you may win for a time, but you are likely to get burned in the end. In mythology, the fire Gods were often trickster gods, as well; fire may seem to be your friend, but if you don't watch it, it can quickly get out of hand, and burn you.

The sky is wild, and the wind is blowing hard. These are both signs of change, and of untamed power, untrammeled by the rules that the rest of society plays by.

This fellow has won; swords stand for knowledge and power, and he has them all. He has won all the knowledge, all the power, for himself. But he cheated. And, from the way he holds the sword, you get the distinct impression that he doesn't have the faintest idea what to do with it! It often seems to me, when I see this card, that the trickster has won simply to win. His whole goal is to defeat the others; not to gain the prize.

In his right hand, he holds a sword with gryphons on the hilt. This sword symbolizes knowledge, which he has taken. Gryphons symbolize the strength of a lion and the swiftness of an eagle, with the majesty of both. These things don't really belong to him; but he has them in his hand. They could easily be mistaken for his. If this card represents someone in the Seeker's life, not the Seeker, you might want to warn them about this.

The two swords next to him represent wealth and ability. He hasn't taken them up, because he hasn't earned them fairly, either, and really doesn't know how to handle them.

The one on the left is gold and purple, and set with gems. It clearly belonged to the richly dressed man who is walking away. (That's why he appears to be an extension of the hilt.) He has lost his wealth, because of the cunning trickery of the rascal in the foreground.

The other sword is plain; the tool of a soldier. its owner has also been defeated, and walks away bowed with loss. His armor didn't help against this.

Meanwhile, their opponent crows with pride in his conquest. I did this to underline his un-sportsman-like behavior. Taunting a defeated opponent is bad form; but that doesn't matter to this fellow.

In contrast to the wild sky and the jeering victor is the smooth grey pier and the calm sea. This shows that all of this trickery and chicanery is really only a play with this guy. It's all done in fun, in a feeling of mischievous diversion.

But that doesn't keep it from really hurting the defeated men. They have lost their wealth, and the tools to earn their bread.

This is the real problem with the person who has this card show up in the reading. If this card represents the Seeker, there is a good chance that she doesn't have any idea how badly she is hurting her victims. While she is being wild and greedy and arrogant and cheating all over the place, people are suffering because of her actions. And if she keeps it up, she will get burned.

If this card represents another, and not the Seeker himself, then he is having to deal with someone like this. In that case, he needs to guard his back, because this person doesn't play by the rules at all. They may not be being malicious; they just like to win. But that won't really make a difference, because they aren't at all likely to care about the consequences of their actions.

You will probably be able to tell from where this card lands in the spread whether it represents the Seeker or someone the Seeker has to deal with. But, as always, listen to your own instincts!

Six of Swords

This card shows a young man with a golden circlet, sitting in a swan boat. Six swords are thrust through the bows around him. An invisible boatman poles the boat across water that is glassy smooth on the left side, but troubled on the right. They approach a hill with a standing stone gate on the top of it, and a cavern underneath it. Inside the cavern a light is shining, as clear and bright as a star.

Key –**Rite of Passage**

This card means passing from one state of consciousness to another, higher one. It can also mean leaving troubles behind, going to a safer place, or finding understanding. Also a journey by water.

When I designed this card, I wanted it to have a fairy-tale quality, because so many of the old fairy tales, at their core, are allegories describing rites of passage. They deal with children, or people barely out of childhood, who come face to face with the hard lessons of life; death, cruelty, viciousness, betrayal; and yet learn, through their own actions, that if you remain true to the goodness and generosity within yourself you will win in the end, and "live happily ever after."

Many of them follow the archetypical journey of the hero; over water and under earth to win through to the light and victory.

That is the meaning at the core of this card. That soul-journey through hardships untold that leads to the discovery that you have, within yourself, all that you need to win through. All you have to do is remain true to the goodness inside.

So I made the young man in the boat a prince, to remind me of the fairy tales. He is blond, like the fool, because in the fairy tales it's always the fool, the youngest son, the one who doesn't know that he is supposed to take on the foul ways of those he encounters, who emerges as the victor.

His cloak is purple, to show his royalty. His trews are red, to show his courage. His shirt and the lining of his cloak are white to show his purity. His armband is black, to show that he has already passed through sorrow. A black arm band is a sign of mourning.

His boat is shaped like a swan, to show grace, tranquility, and beauty, and also to show transformation. In how many stories are royal children turned to swans, and have to go through dreadful trials to turn back? I also chose a swan to remind me of the story of the Ugly Duckling, which illustrates the concept that the most wonderful swan can be an outcast if he's trying to live in a barnyard. This, too, may be a part of life the Seeker is now leaving. Perhaps she is about to find out where she belongs, and to really hit her stride. The whole idea of a swan boat also conjures up the feeling of mystical journeys, of archetypical quests.

It is being ferried by an unseen boatman to show that even when we don't seem to be in control, we are not really drifting without guidance. Not, at any rate, while we are on a soul's journey. We are being watched out for, and guided. In fact, you might say that unseen forces are driving us! If you look carefully at the pole the boatman is using, you will notice that although most of it seems as insubstantial as air, the end that enters the water is as solid as the wood of the boat. I did that to remind myself that if we look carefully, we can see the business end of the forces that are guiding us.

In the boat are six swords, representing challenges that the prince has already answered successfully. All of the hilts are different colors, and different shapes, because all the challenges were different. He has learned from them all, and they are now his; knowledge and honor, without scabbards, ready for instant use.

The water on the left hand side of the boat is still and calm, to show that deep within himself, he knows he is doing exactly what his destiny demands. That on the right, the thinking, conscious side, is more troubled. It's possible that the Seeker is still worried about this whole thing. It's also clear, from the color of the water where it ripples, that this is very deep water, indeed. The intuitive, unseen forces are very much at work in this card.

Their destination is a set of smooth hills, or tors, in the distance. There are a few trees there, but mostly there is just smooth grass. This is reminiscent of the court cards, as are the piled clouds in the deep blue sky overhead. This shows, once again, that archetypal forces are at work here.

On top of the hill is an ancient stone gate or table, like the ones found at Stonehenge. These were seen as the doors to the Faery realms; to the worlds that lay under the hill. Once again, this shows the gate, the passage, to a more wonderfull place, and underlines the fairy tale theme.

Directly in their path is a mysterious cave. It's all dark in there, and unknown. But there is a light shining. This is to show the enlightenment that waits within. It also shows the "light at the end of the tunnel," the part of the story where the difficulties are finally past, and the hero wins through to his reward. He's not there yet, but he's getting there!

Once again, which part of the story this card is telling will be apparent in the reading; just relax and listen to your instincts.

Seven of Swords

This card shows a thief, dressed in black and brown, stealing over a low, overgrown wall. In his hands he has five swords. Two more are still standing in the earth behind him. Beyond the wall are regimental tents, showing an armed camp. Above him is a ragged, stormy sky, with only a bit of blue showing.

Key – **Thief**

This card means theft, robbery, unreliability, betrayal, spying, pilferage. The failure of a plan, or of a defense. A less than honorable action. Depending on the surrounding cards, it can also mean stealth, bravery, and care.

This card, unlike the five of swords, has nothing playful about it. This thief isn't involved in any kind of game, and he isn't doing this for amusement. He's out for those swords, and he's bound to get them.

He's not cheating because it's fun to run circles around those bound by rules. He's doing it this way because he doesn't think he can win any other way. He comes under cover of heavy clouds, and he is dressed in black and brown, so that no one will notice him.

Black also means sorrow in the deck; and his actions are going to cause quite a bit of sorrow.

The walls are low, and overgrown. They have obviously not been cared for as they should. There are also stones protruding that practically invite someone to step over them. And there isn't a guard in sight. I did this to show that there is a certain amount of carelessness involved in letting this person get away with this activity. If this card comes up in a position that shows something happening in the Seeker's life, you may want to advise him to be more careful.

When I drew this card, I also meant the wall to symbolize the thief's own ideals. They are badly neglected, and he is straddling them, trying to get away with something.

Once again, I made all of the swords different, to show that these are different things the bandit is making off with. Since it's a military camp behind him (implied by the similarity of the tents, and the regimented rows they stand in) what he is really taking is the tools of their trade; the things that are most important to them. In essence, because he is taking their weapons, he is trying to swipe their victory; to take the possibility of success away from them.

But there are still two swords standing upright behind them. He hasn't left them off-balance after all. If this card shows a situation that the Seeker is trying to deal with, you may want to point out those two swords, and remind her that she has not been left without defense or knowledge after all.

Also, if you look closely, the flap of the nearest tent is open, although it's too dark to see inside it. Perhaps there is a guard there after all, just waiting until the moment when he can catch the thief red handed!

Overhead, the sky is clouding up, with only a tiny bit of blue visible. Depending on the reading, and how you feel about that patch of blue, this could be the last hope of the thief to return to more ethical ways before the storm comes, or it could be the beginning of the light breaking through. As always trust your instincts as you are reading!

Eight of Swords

This card shows a young woman, blindfolded and dressed in white rags, her arms bound with red cloth, standing on a path through the surf. All around her stand great swords. In the background are rocks and cliffs, leading up to a fortress. Above her is a stormy sky, with the sun just about to break through the clouds.

Key – **I Just Can't!**

This card means fear, bondage, restriction through inaction, censure, illness, difficulties, paralysis due to indecision, the feeling that the task ahead is simply impossible. Traditionally, it can also mean prison.

This maid is the same as the one on card two; but now she is bound, as well as blindfolded, and she is no longer in control of the swords. Her position may seem worse, but at least this time she is on level ground!

I dressed her in white rags, to show that she still has a measure of purity; but she has been wrestling with this particular problem for so long that she feels all tattered and worn by it. Her eyes are covered, because she can't see any way out of her present difficulties.

She is bound with five turns of red cloth. The five symbolizes the five senses; all of those are bound up with this problem, and they are also what are binding her. She is afraid of being hurt, of having her senses abused in one way or another, and that's what's got her. I used red to show that her problems are those of this life, of the flesh. This is usually not a spiritual conundrum (although it can be.) In my experience when this card comes up, it's because of some very solid and material difficulty. For instance; a job that is hateful, in which the Seeker is expected to do things she dislikes herself for doing, and yet which she feels cannot leave because she needs the money too desperately.

She is surrounded by eight great swords, because the problems that beset her are very large, and very real. But if you look, the colors of the hilts range from white on the left, through red, orange, yellow, green, blue, and violet to black on the right. These make a rainbow! Hidden in the problems themselves are endless possibilities.

The swords stand in water. As in most other places where water appears in the Tarot, this stands for emotions. It makes the sand here treacherous, and yet the water is still, and deep with reflections. I did this to remind myself that the person in this situation has been reflecting on the problems quite a lot; but that hasn't made any difference.

And yet, she is on dry land, and her feet are free and bare. If she stops relying on the senses that she usually uses, and goes carefully, feeling her way with her toes, she can stay on the dry ground and avoid all of the swords. If she has great courage, she can even use the swords themselves to cut her bonds, and free herself. The solution to this problem lies within the problem itself. But in order to find it, she will have to take risks, and use resources that she isn't really aware that she has.

It's her own fear that really has her trapped here. If she can overcome that, she can get out.

Behind her, the sea of her emotions rages; she is very unhappy here! The rocks, once again, symbolize her past decisions, that have brought her to this place.

On the highest rock of all is a fortress. This can symbolize a number of things. Sometimes, it looks like the place that the problems are coming from; the people who have done this, and left her here. She needs to be aware of them, because they will be fighting against her freeing herself. Sometimes it looks like the walls she has built to keep those who would help her away from her, lest they interfere in this problem. Sometimes it looks like a safe place that she has left behind, and thinks of longingly. Sometimes it looks like it's merely a dream of safety, and not real at all. Sometimes it's a prison that she is trying to escape from.

As ever, go with what it looks like to you when you are actually doing the reading.

Above her, the sun is about to break out of the clouds. If she takes any action at all, this impasse will change. And, once again, if she is careful and uses her soul to find her way (I know, but you were warned about the visual puns) she will win free. There are no swords in front of her, even though she can't see that.

But she does need to act.

Nine of Swords

This card shows a young woman sitting up in bed, clutching the covers, and covering her face with her hand. Behind her, nine swords hand in the air. Or is it the same sword over and over again?

Key – **Night Terrors**

This card means suffering, desolation, doubt, suspicion, misery, dishonesty, slander; a vicious circle. Brooding on past injuries. Illness, anxiety, distress.

This card shows someone having what I refer to as "3 A.M.-sies," when you wake in the dead of the night, sure that everything is going wrong, and there is nothing you can do to stop it; that nothing will ever turn out alright again, that you are caught in a nightmare.

This young woman is dressed in white, to show her youth. Her blanket is covered with stars and planetary and zodiacal signs; but they are not in any kind of order, they are all just a jumble. I did this to show that she has some sense of the universe outside of herself; but not a clear one. She doesn't really understand it, and so she misinterprets much of what she sees. A little knowledge can be a dangerous thing, as they say.

The sigils that I chose to put on it are; Gemini, because she is beside herself (twins); Jupiter, because the problem keeps expanding; Mercury, because it's probably a problem with communication in the first place (this sort of thing often is;) Pisces, because she's probably in this fix because she cares too much what others think of her, anyway; Aquarius, because her idealism is involved; Mars, because she keeps hitting her head on a wall with this one; Cancer, because she can't let it go; and Neptune, because it's an emotional problem. Which of these stand out in a reading is important. Sometimes none of them do, and sometimes all I can see is the sigil for Mercury, and I know that miscommunication is at the root of this! Pay attention to what stands out when you are doing the reading, like always.

There is a blue lining to her comforter, though, because the universe is really working to help her learn and grow, as it is for all of us. And the central pattern is a crescent moon on a blue ground, as a reminder that the Lady is taking care of this, too, and has not deserted us, no matter how we may feel at the moment.

In fact, the reason that I gave her a comforter at all, and not a quilt or some other kind of blanket, was to show that comfort is there, if we can only open ourselves up to it.

The swords that hang over her are not really different swords at all. Unlike all of the other cards in this suit, these are all exactly the same, because this is the same sword, over and over again. In fact, if you look at them carefully, they don't have any shadows or any reflections on them. They aren't even real!

This poor soul has been brooding, and going over the same problem over and over, like a broken record, repeating the same phrases to herself until she has worked herself into this state. The actual problem isn't nearly this bad!

She needs to stop this, get some rest, and go out in the morning and actually face the situation so that she can gain real understanding of it, and overcome it.

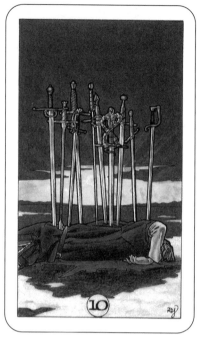

Ten of Swords

This card shows the twisted body of a man face down in a pool of his own blood, with ten swords sticking out of his back. He is all alone in a cold and barren wasteland. In the background, a pitch black sky breaks, and a bit of golden glory shines out.

Key – **No, It Really IS That Bad**

This card means misfortune, ruin, defeat, loss, failure, pain, desolation beyond tears, total betrayal. Or it may mean the end of these, and the beginning of hope.

This card was the hardest of all for me to draw, because for my money it's the worst card in the deck. In fact, it was so hard for me that I finished the card, and sprayed it with fixative, and then realized that he was lying in a pool of snow, not blood. I had forgotten to add the color to the area beneath him! So I had to go back and do it with acrylic paint, because the colored pencils I was using wouldn't stick on the fixative.

This card is the culmination of all the swords, the end of the strife that they suggest and also the conclusion of their deeper meaning of knowledge, sacrifice, and transformation. When this card comes up in a reading, remember that the end of one thing is always and inevitably the beginning of something else; and the best thing about being at rock bottom is that the only direction to go from here is up!

I dressed the body in gold and purple, to show that this was once a well-to-do man. He had all the things that people consider important, but none of them are important any more.

The ten swords are all different. If you look carefully at the one in the center, you will find that it's a representation of a man whose arms are serpents. This is an adaptation of a piece of jewelry made by Lalique at the turn of the last century, and it's haunted me for years. On the original piece, the arms are dragonfly wings. I made them serpents because of the tie between serpents and the old Goddess religions, where the serpent was sacred to the Lady, and a symbol of healing. It's here to remind me that it's possible that this card shows a death that is healing, as well as painful. Often things must be terribly hurt before they can begin to heal; like lancing a boil, or removing a cancer. So this pain, which seems to make one helpless, can be the first step in ultimate healing.

It may look very different to you, of course; and that's fine. What is important is how you react when you see it. What do your instincts say?

This is a card of questions; and how they are answered depends on the place that it has in a reading, and how you react to the card on an emotional, visceral level when it comes up.

Is he in this position because ten people hated him so much that they all got together and stabbed him in the back? Or was he a willing sacrifice?

Does the sky show the last fading glimmer of light before total darkness, or is that a new dawn breaking?

Is the dead man the Seeker, stabbed to the quick and suffering? Or is he an enemy, and this card signifies the end of the conflict?

In fact, is the fellow on the card actually dead? Or is he dying?

All in all, this is a difficult card; and although it may ultimately mean healing, and hope, it's still going to hurt. This is where you need to pay careful attention to the ethics of the situation (which I will discuss in a later chapter.)

Chapter 9
Wands

Once again, I'm going to begin by reminding you that, although I am about to tell you why I chose the symbols I did for each card, these are still just my interpretations and feelings. As we discussed in Chapter 5, Common Threads, everyone's symbol set is slightly different. An image that makes me feel relaxed and happy might have the opposite effect on you.

So, when you are reading the cards, go with your own symbol set! These cards, like any other deck, really mean what they seem to you to mean at the time you are doing the reading.

If you relax, and let it flow, your readings will be far more accurate than they will be if you try to force a traditional meaning onto each card, by looking it up or memorizing meanings.

Don't feel that you are somehow "wrong" if what you see in a card is not what I was thinking about when I put it there! That's perfectly alright, and is why a Reader is needed in the first place. Remember, all you are doing here is getting the information that your unconscious mind is already aware of, on a very subtle level. Relax, and see what your inner mind sees, and you'll be fine!

The Wands are one of the controversial suits in the Tarot deck. (The other one is Swords.) Some people are of the opinion that the Wands are ruled by fire, and the Swords by air, and some think the Swords are ruled by fire, and the Wands by air. I became aware of this when I began to work seriously on my deck. And after much debate, and reading, and discussion, I decided that in my deck air would rule Swords, and fire would rule Wands. There were many factors in reaching this decision. Partly I feel this way because, quite frankly, that was the way I was taught in the beginning, and so I am most comfortable with it. But partly I decided to do it this way because aligning Wands with fire meant that they also take on the other magical attributes of fire; that is, they become a symbol of the will. And since magic wands have been used forever to focus the will, and bring change to the universe, that seemed entirely appropriate and right to me. I also liked the fact that wands also mean growth, and the shape is reminiscent of a stem or wand growing tall from the earth.

When I was having the debates, though, a dear friend of mine was very insistent that I do it the other way round. His argument was that energy was fire, and a wooden wand would be burnt up in an instant. I thought that might be the point; that the wands provided energy for the fire, and that you had to be careful lest that very energy consume you. But the whole idea made him quite unhappy. And as I thought about it, I decided that if it was the fact that they were wood that made him so nervous, well, why not make them out of something other than wood? I decided that I really liked the idea of wands made of crystal and metal; materials that would conduct energy readily. And so that is what I did.

If I were drawing the deck now, almost ten years after I reached that decision, I might make more of them wood. I have found out why wood is so often used for wands. It maintains a link to the tree that it came from, and the spirit of the forest in general, and so using a wooden wand can link you to that endless and majestic spiral of life and growth. But I hadn't realized that then, so all of these wands are made of crystal and metal, which have their own cycle of growth, and their own links to something greater than themselves.

In my deck, then, the Wands are aligned with the element of Fire. Their direction is South, their time of day is Noon, and their time of life is young adulthood.

They stand for various stages in growth, and also will, negotiations, nimble speech, cleverness, and all aspects of life. Basically, everything that corresponds to fire also corresponds to this suit.

The lessons of this suit deal with focusing the will, and with self control, creativity, and using energy wisely.

King of Wands

This card shows a young king with a golden crown. His clothing is reminiscent of fire, and there is a lion embroidered on his chest. He stands with a crystal wand in his right hand, and his left stretched out, palm up. He is in a desert, with a bright yellow sky behind him. The only other living thing is a salamander, which crawls beneath his wand.

Key – **I Am**

The meaning of this card is a passionate man (or woman, or attitude) handsome, conscientious, noble, strong, individualistic, proud, but inclined to be hasty or willful.

This card was one of the hardest for me to figure out. I don't like to think of the court cards as simply people, because I find that too limiting. It seems to me that if you also think of them as character roles or archetypes, then you might find any of us playing any of these parts at one time or another. Looked at that way, they might also show us what our attitudes towards a situation are.

So, although all the books tended to say, "A man, with light hair and eyes.." or some such, that didn't cut it for me. I wasn't happy until I had figured out the attitude behind it. And then I had to remind myself of the attitude by how I drew the card!

So, I started by making him standing up. This is a card showing an attitude or person of action. I don't think he is capable of sitting still for long. This sort of person would much rather be up and doing.

His hair and beard are the color of marigolds to show his affiliation with fire, and also because this card can signify a gay man, and I had a very good friend who was gay, and dyed his hair and beard just this color!

I gave him fiery clothing with dagged edges that look like flames all in the colors of flame, because he is very much like fire itself. He is a good companion, and you want to have him around. He's fun to watch, and is generally the center of any group. And yet, at the same time, if you don't pay enough attention to him, he's likely to burn you!

I put a lion on the center of his shirt, to show that he shares many attributes with the lion, too. He's beautiful, and noble, and strong. He's also proud, and tends to be just. But he is certain that his rightful place is at the center, and it's hard to deny him. For one thing, he burns through a room, and every eye tends to follow him. And he has all of the communication gifts of the fire, so it's easy to just let him have all of any conversation. But if you deny him that, he can be very aggressive or hurt.

The lining and hem of his overtunic are brilliant blue, because that is the color at the heart of the hottest flame, and also the color of a cloudless sky.

This attitude can bring a whole new dimension to the term "sunny personality," if so inclined, and I wanted to remember that.

He has white fur on the bottom of his sleeves to show the pure, soft, fuzzy feelings that he can project. This guy can make you feel warm faster than nearly anyone else, if he wants to.

His crown is gold spikes, to show the radiance that he projects.

He is standing with one hand out for two reasons. Depending on how it looks in a reading, he is either offering his hand, and willing to give anything that is needed, or he is looking for a handout.

One of the problems with a personality like this is that often people give these folk things just so they will stick around, or to placate them if their feelings get hurt. And then they tend to grow to expect such gifts as a matter of course. I've known several people who were playing this role who couldn't understand why anyone would expect them to earn their own livings. They simply wanted to be "kept" men, and they usually managed it, at least while they were young.

He is smiling, because that is the way he greets the world.

In his right hand he holds a wand made of crystal wrapped with gold. It has two more crystals, at the top and bottom. The one on top is glowing. This is his staff of office, and also shows his magical ability, which is considerable. It's clear crystal, because this fellow has no deception in him at all. What you see is exactly what you get. He may be immature at times, and too hasty at others, but you will figure that out very quickly, and he will never pretend to be anything else. And, mostly, he is as generous and good hearted as they come. The crystal on the top is radiant to show his brilliance, and that he really shines when he is on top.

He is standing in a desert to show his affiliation with fire, and heat. The sky is yellow for the same reason, and also because he is a very joyous person.

The only other living creature on this card is a salamander. I put it there to show his affiliation with fire again, as salamanders are a very old symbol of that element. And I wanted him to have some company on the card, because although this guy is very individualistic, he really thrives in company. But after the card was done, a friend looked at it, and said, "It looks like he's getting ready to squish that lizard!" I looked again, and he was right! But I decided not to change it, because that is another thing about this attitude, or this person. He won't usually be aggressive, because he'd rather have admirers than enemies. But if he decides that you are an enemy, he'll simply squish you.

Queen of Wands

Queen of Wands

This card shows a young queen with flowing blond hair, and a fiery dress with suns on the hem. She holds a crystal wand in her right hand, and her left is stretched out, palm down. A black cat stretches at her feet, and sunflowers bloom behind her. She stands in a desert, with a yellow sky overhead.

Key – **Welcome**

This card means a person, or attitude that shows considerable energy, warmth, and passion. Fond of nature, generous, energetic, and yet practical.

In many ways, this card is the feminine phase of the King of Wands. And so, as the feminine nature is more circular and nurturing, as opposed to the male nature which is linear and "fixing," she is just as bright, passionate, erudite, voluble, and charming as her male counterpart, but uses this energy in different ways.

Like the king, she is standing, because she can't sit around very well. She needs to be doing things, and tends to champion causes, as you may be able to tell from her general stance and attitude.

I gave her light blond hair, to show her youth and energy, and the brightness of her spirit. It's untrammeled and free, flowing in wild abandon down her back, to show that she is wild, in the sense of being untamed. She allows nothing to bind her! To her very roots, she is free!

She is smiling, because that is how she greets the world. Like the king, this personality type tends to move brightly, like a comet, attracting attention everywhere she goes. The main difference is that she is slightly mellower, and much more likely to be pragmatic.

Her golden crown has waves like fire licking upward, to show the crackling energy that leaps from her mind.

Her clothes, like those of all the court cards in this suit, are reminiscent of fire, because of the alliance of this suit with that element. Her sleeves are long and her skirt flowing because she is graceful. There are suns appliqued on the hem, because her disposition is usually sunny. But when she bends the full energy of her brilliant, unswerving attention into the dark places in a person or institution, someone is going to get burned. Then it's like the fire of several suns, for she makes a formidable enemy.

The suns themselves have silver centers, and golden rays, to show that at her heart she is completely pure, and everything around her has a certain richness.

The lining of her dress and the hem of her overdress are blue to show the color at the heart of a flame, and also the color of the cloudless sky.

She, too, has a lion on her chest; and if you look carefully, you will notice that it's a male lion, not a lioness. I did that because when she takes on the attributes of a lion, she also tends to go for the male attributes of being linear and problem solving.

Her left hand is stretched out, but the palm is down. She almost never asks for a handout, being far more likely to offer a "pat on the head."

In her right hand she holds a crystal wand, wrapped with gold and with a crystal at either end. The wand shows the suit of this card, the clear crystal shows the utter clarity of her character. The gold wrappings show the attributes of fire and the sun. The crystals are for clarity, again. The one on the top is glowing, to show the radiance of her nature.

A black cat is playing and stretching right behind her feet. She has a cat to show that she shares in the hedonistic, passionate, sensual nature of a cat, as well as the grace and agility. Also, the cat shares many characteristics with the lion, but is more domestic (although not necessarily tamer!) So the Queen of Wands has many of the same characteristics as her counterpart, but in a more practical, useful, and domestic fashion.

I made the cat black because that is the color of soot, and this cat has been playing around the fire, and also because I had a black cat named Phoenix while I was drawing this card; and so, for me, this brings in some of the Phoenix energy. I made him stretching to underline the sensuous nature of this personality.

Behind her are sunflowers. Although she may seem exotic, she has a really sensible, down-to-earth, homey side to her. I put the sunflowers in to show that part of her personality. You can't get much more homey and sensible than sunflowers. And, at the same time, they show once again her alignment with the sun, and the whole fire thing.

She is standing in a desert, because of the attunement with the south, and fire. That is also the reason that the sky is yellow. And it shows her boundless joy and enthusiasm, as well.

Knight of Wands

Knight of Wands

This card shows a young man dressed in golden armor, astride a chestnut steed with mane and tail made of fire. His helmet is shaped like a lion's head, and his clothing and saddle blanket are the colors of flame. He holds a wand in his right hand, as though it was a spear. They are in a desert, with a bright yellow sky overhead.

Key – **Where Angels Fear to Tread!**

This card means overwhelming passion and bravery. Action taken in spite of distractions. Courage, daring, spirit. Someone just looking for a cause to champion, preferably a lost one. Traditionally, it also means a journey, or change of residence.

This card is the same essence as the other court cards in this suit, but made more active yet!

I gave him golden armor to show his affiliation with the sun, and with fire. His helmet is shaped like a lion's head, to show that he has all the qualities of the lion; bravery, strength, loyalty, fearlessness, beauty, nobility, etc. Of course, he also shares in the pride and occasional violence of the lion, as well.

His breastplate is made to show off his muscles, because he is athletic, and also proud. In the center and on his shoulders are more lion's heads, to underline the connection.

He is wearing very little armor. leaving his arms and legs bare, because he doesn't tend to be well armored He relies on his swiftness and agility to keep from getting hurt; but with pride like his he's likely to get hurt quite a bit, all the same.

His clothing (what you can see of it) and his cloak are the same fire colors as those of the other court cards in the suit, and for the same reasons. They burn like flame because he has the attributes of fire; he is joyful, and willful, brilliant, and strong. He is usually the center of attention, and if you don't watch him, he can get out of hand! In his case, though, it's usually through being over enthusiastic! Once again, they are lined and hemmed with bright blue, because that is the color of the hottest part of the fire, and because that is also the color of the bright and cloudless sky. The disposition of this character is also naturally sunny and cloudless. But when it isn't, watch out!

His saddle blanket is these same colors, for these same reasons, with the addition of bright yellow tassels and fringe to make it look even more like flame.

His saddle is yellow, as well, and decorated with a motif of fire and salamanders. The salamanders are traditionally the creatures of fire and the south.

His mount is a bright chestnut, with flaming mane and tail, to show that this Knight is in control of his fiery nature, and his will. (If he were not, this would be a dangerous card indeed.) His horse is rearing, to show the readiness of this attitude to leap up, and charge into action! Yet he is looking back at his rider, to show once again that all of this fiery energy is under control.

His chamfron (the armor on his face) is gold, for fire and the sun, and decorated with a pattern of red and blue, once again for the fire and the cloudless blue sky of noon. At the top is a red fire sigil, in case you missed all the other references to fire!

His harness is of golden leather, to show that affiliation again.

The decorations hanging from his reins are gold, once again to show the fire aspect, and have five points. I originally meant these to stand for the five senses, but have found that sometimes they look more like the five elements (earth, air, fire, water, and spirit) or five as a round number, or even five days!

The center point is larger, to show that there is still balance, even with all of the activity going on in this card.

The Knight holds his wand like a lance, as though he were about to joust. And, indeed, that is the sort of thing he likes best! He enjoys battle, and championing causes. His wand is crystal again, wrapped in gold, to show the clarity of his personality, and the affiliation with fire and the sun (just in case you have somehow overlooked it in the rest of this card!) Once again, the crystal on the tip is glowing, to show his inner radiance, and his considerable energy.

He rides through a desert, to show the affiliation with the south and fire, and the sky is bright yellow again to accentuate that affiliation and also to show his boundless joy.

Page of Wands

Page of Wands

This card shows a young girl, dressed in a tunic the colors of flame, standing in a desert under a yellow sky. Her red-gold hair is bound at her neck, and she has a bunch of firecrackers hanging from her belt. She holds a crystal wand aloft with outstretched arms. There are three rings at the top of the wand, and they chime like bells as she shakes it, shooting eight beams of light into the air. At the bottom of the wand a crystal burns like a fire, and at the top another crystal glows white.

Key – **Hearken!**

This card means a child with too much energy. An announcement, loyalty, devotion, faithfulness. A good employee. A great idea that leads to success. A stranger who is about to explode into the seeker's life.

Like all the pages, I made this one a young girl, so the deck would be balanced. In this case, she is standing still; but she still manages to look energetic. Like all the other court cards in this suit she has bright hair to show the association with fire, and her clothing echoes that connection. In her case, though, I gave her long sleeves to remind me that this character frequently has something up them! She is as loyal and trustworthy as they come; but she is also a little too full of energy for her own good, and likes to play tricks.

She has dark blue cuffs on her tunic, unlike the bright blue that the other court cards sport, because she is likely to get farther out into space. For the same reason she has moons and stars on her cuffs. For her, the sky is not the limit. She is quite willing to go farther! These also show the magical side of her personality.

Her hem, however, does have the bright blue to show her connection to the brightest, hottest part of a flame, and also to a cloudless sky.

Her belt is of red and yellow triangles, to show the fire once more, and also to show that even so, she is balanced, as a tripod is about the most stable platform that you can find.

From it hangs a bundle of firecrackers as a reminder that her personality is a little explosive, and that she likes the sharp, bright sound of fireworks, and the excitement and joyous fervor of a bang-up celebration. I gave all the pages mnemonic devices like this, because when I was learning to read it was hard for me to remember what they meant.

Her hair is bound behind her, to show that she is trying to curb her natural enthusiasm. But it is also escaping in curls, because that's a very difficult thing for her to manage.

Her red and yellow boots repeat the whole fire imagery thing.

She faces into the sun, grinning, because that is her nature; to face the light squarely, and to take joy in everything that happens.

She is holding her wand in both hands, and shaking it vigorously so that the rings chime. (At least, that was my intention. I hope you can see this.)

This is because that is her job; she is a herald, and makes announcements. So she is standing on the edge of a sand dune, ringing her chimes to get everyone's attention.

The wand itself is crystal wrapped in gold, like those of all the other court cards in this suit, to show the clarity of her nature, and the alignment with the element of fire.

When I was designing this particular wand, I first drew a bunch of little bells on the end to ring for attention. And then I decided that I liked the image of actual rings, instead, because the circular shape brings to mind all the infinite, circular patterns in the world. That is also why I gave her three of them. In my experience, this card often signifies a "wake up call," a reminder from the universe that there are consequences for our actions, and we may want to pay attention to them! So there are three to stand for the "Rule of Three," which states that everything we do comes back to us three times, and they are rings to show that "what goes around comes around." I made them gold to show the value of remembering this.

As they chime, eight beams of light flare out from them. There are eight for the eight spokes on the Wheel of the Year, or the eight corners of the compass. This is to show that the announcement is going to affect all parts of the Seeker's life, or perhaps all of the next year. It may also look like it's covering all quadrants of an area of influence, or any other eight. If it does, go with it! That is the purpose of having a Reader read the cards, after all.

At the bottom of her wand, the stone glows with the color of fire, and at the top with pure white light. I did that to show the transformation that this person or attitude can bring into the Seeker's life; changing the ordinary into the extraordinary, amplifying the energy present to an amazing degree!

She stands in a desert, with a yellow sky overhead, to show the affiliation of the suit of wands with fire, and noon, and heat; and also to show her own boundless joy, as deep as the sky!

Ace of Wands

This card shows a clear wand, with a double helix inside, upright and burning. The flames start out yellow-green near the wand, and go through white and yellow to orange at the tip. There is a clear crystal bound with gold at the top, and a deep blue one wrapped in silver at the bottom. Beams of rainbow light radiate from the whole length of the wand. At the base of the card are two sunflowers. Behind them all, the sky is blue and cloudless.

Key – **Creation and Power, New Life**

This card means creation, creative energy, beginning of growth or life, increase, inheritance, birth, adventure, virility, fertility, evolution, unfolding possibilities.

Like the other aces, this one is both the beginning and the end of the suit; in this case the suit of wands. It is at the same time the symbol from which all the others spring, and which they are all based on, and the culmination or most perfect expression of that symbol.

In this case, wands mean life, and growth, and energy; change and evolution. So for this symbol I chose to use a single wand, crackling and burning and glowing with energy, floating without regard to gravity in front of two sunflowers. Together they form a phallic object, which is intentional, because part of the meaning is virility and joy in creation.

I made the wand itself absolutely clear, to show the extreme clarity inherent in this suit. Inside I put a double helix, the shape of DNA, the stuff that all the animal and plant life on this planet is based on, to show the endless variety and possibilities of life that we are talking about here. It also shows the beginning of life, since life starts with a handful of these strands, and very little more. And it shows the potential for evolution, for life changing into something greater and better, which also happens at this level. In a reading, this usually signifies spiritual evolution; but it could also mean the Seeker's job or dreams are evolving into something else.

At the top of the wand I put a quartz crystal filled with rainbows, to show the brilliance of the daytime, active, productive part of life, wrapped with gold to show the sun, and the masculine energies.

At the bottom is a deep blue sapphire to show the depth of the night time, resting, regenerative part of life, wrapped with silver to show the moon, and the feminine energies.

Both of these are necessary to make a wand that works; to be able to use this much energy in a creative, joyous way, without burning oneself up or sinking into despair. Intellect and emotions, rational thought and dreams, activity and rest. All of these balance each other. If you try to limit yourself to one half or the other you lose perspective; you cripple yourself. It's no accident that many of the greatest scientific discoveries came from dreams.

When you have these two parts of your life in balance, then you have energy and to spare, as shown here.

The flame that leaps and crackles along the whole length of the wand starts out green, for the vegetative, plant energy, and runs through white, and yellow to the red of animal energy. This is to show that all life uses the same kind of creative life energy, just as all of our patterns use the same basic building blocks in our DNA. Only the different combinations make me a reasonable facsimile of a human, and the blue spruce in front of my house a tree. At a very deep level, we are all related; and we can share energy with each other, and help each other whenever we wish.

The white flames show the essential purity of this creative energy, and the yellow/gold shows that it's fundamentally incorruptible.

Beyond the fire, a brilliant light shines the length of the wand, to show the illumination that the acknowledgement of such a relationship, and such energy can bring. The myriad rainbows that spring from the wand show the endless possibilities and beauty of this kind of pure, joyful, quintessentially creative, life affirming force.

The two sunflowers show the affiliation of this suit with the south, and with fire, and also show once again the double spiral of life, in the arrangement of seeds. They also remind me of the radiance shown here, because they face the wand, and not the sun.

In the background, the sky is a very deep blue. This contrasts with the light from the wand, so it's visible. But it's also to give a deep, cloudless, sky-is-the-limit kind of feeling.

Two of Wands

This card shows a blond man in rich clothing, standing by a wall and looking out to sea. In his right hand he holds a globe. In his left is a silver wand with a crystal on the top. Another wand is fastened to the wall at his right. Beyond him, is a rocky shore, and a hill with a lighthouse. The sky is full of clouds, and there is nothing to be seen on all the surface of the ocean.

Key – **Watch and Wait**

This card means the wait before plans bear fruit. Also kindness, generosity, intellect. A well-balanced, creative person. Ingenuity, fulfillment, good things coming.

This man is a merchant or scholar. His hair is blond to show the affiliation of this suit with fire. His tunic and hat are deep blue to show his deep spirituality, with red trim to show his courage. Sometimes, waiting takes more courage than anything else that you can do! (Especially when you can't see anything happening.)

In his hat, he has a gem. It's gold for fire and the sun, with a blue-green stone for the sea. If you can combine these two, and find the balance between them, that's wisdom. (Or maybe it's just steam! But steam is power, too, and if you harness it, you can run anything.) Anyway, I intended this to remind me that perhaps he is waiting for a gem of wisdom.

His tabard is patterned with red roses and golden squares. The red roses are for passion, desire, and activity; while the golden squares are for stability. The roses have five petals, which is the old pattern of a rose, and shows his deference to tradition. They also form the basic shape of the pentagram, so they show his balance with the creative forces in nature, as well. Each rose is on a light blue ground, for the boundless sky, and circled with gold, which shows the cycle and harmony that are the themes of this card. A good part of any cycle is often spent waiting. The deep blue ground signifies his spiritual development, again.

All of this is balanced by the border, which shows pure white lilies on a bright blue ground. The lilies stand for purity, and also for intellect and chastity. The light blue stands for bright skies.

So the whole garment shows passion and activity balanced by intellect and chastity. He is more than willing to act, provided that the time is correct. He won't do anything rashly. And that means that he waits.

There is also white fur along the edge, to show that his purity is warm, not cold. It's not that he doesn't care; it's just not the right time.

I made him just a little heavy, to show that he is well fed. This isn't a hungry, desperate man, who can't afford the time it may take. This fellow has learned to plan, and to budget his resources. He's willing and able to take whatever time is needed to do the job right.

In his right hand, he holds a globe. This shows how far ranging his interests and ideals are; they cover the world, and include everything on the planet. It also shows how far his fortunes and ideals have brought him. The world is his.

In his left hand, the hand of the unconscious, he holds a silver wand. The wand is a symbol of growth and energy, as accentuated by the silver leaves that grow around the tip of it. But those are ivy leaves, the sign of introspection, and the wand is silver, the color of the unseen and unconscious self, and held in his left hand, also showing the deep, hidden side. So what you have here is activity and growth, but its inner growth and activity. In other words, he is taking this time of waiting to learn and grow.

This is what I call "active waiting." Not sitting and doing nothing, and looking only to the future and what you expect to happen, but using the time of enforced inactivity to recuperate and develop within.

This is what I think is meant by "living in the moment." It doesn't mean ignoring the past or the future. We have the past to learn from, and the future to plan for, and that's as it should be. It means that, whatever you are doing, you should be doing that thing actively, even if that thing is waiting. Otherwise, you miss most of what is going on, and you hardly ever get to enjoy yourself. When you are remembering and learning, then focus on that. When you are planning for the future, then focus on that. But don't plan for the future when you are looking for your ship, or you are likely to miss it! Instead, really look at the ocean, enjoy the feeling of the wind in your hair, discover that you like the way the sun sparkles on the water. All of these things contribute to your inner growth; so take the time to do them.

The crystal at the top of the wand shows the clarity of his vision.

Combining the inner growth and the clarity of vision, you get the creativity and ingenuity that are some of the meanings of this card.

And, as all the "twos" stand for some kind of balance, this one stands for the balance between stillness and activity.

Next to him, there is another wand, bolted to the wall. This is to show that sometimes the activity is forced to be still, and emphasizes the principle of active waiting. When it's necessary to wait, as it sometimes is, then rein in your desire for activity, and enjoy the waiting, instead of being impatient. See this as a part of your life, instead of a boring bit between two parts! It makes all kinds of difference if you do.

He is standing behind a wall made of light grey stone. Walls are the things we use to get distance between us and everything else. So the fact that he is behind a wall here shows that he is still separating himself from the thing he is waiting for. He thinks of it as being "out there." Sometimes, in a reading, the wall just jumps out at me, and sometimes it's not important at all. As always, when you read, pay attention to the parts that look important, and read from those.

Beyond him is the shoreline, with beaches and grass in the foreground, giving way to hard rocks in the middle ground. This shows the various kinds of reception that conditions or ideas might have. Sometimes, you are really ready for the thing you have been waiting for, and accept it easily. Sometimes, you don't actually want it at all, and it's harder.

On top of the hill is a lighthouse, to show once again that although he is waiting, he isn't "merely" waiting. He has made the preparations necessary for success.

The ocean reaches to the distant horizon, to show that his prospects are unlimited. The sky above him is cloudy, though, because look as he might, there is nothing there yet, and he still must wait.

Three of Wands

This card shows a man with red hair and a white beard, grasping a silver wand in his right hand, and shading his eyes with his left as he looks out at three ships sailing on a sunset sea. He is richly dressed, in gold and crimson velvet. To his left is another wand, and behind him is a third, with a vine growing up it. In the far background are hills, and brilliant sunset clouds.

Key – **Ships Coming In**

This card means good business, successful completion of business, strength, good grasp of the future, good grasp of what is needed for future growth, etc.

This man is not young, but he isn't old, either. I wanted him to look like someone in the prime of life; and so I gave him red hair, but a beard that has already turned white. (The colors reflect my husband's coloring at the time.)

He is dressed richly, because he is a successful merchant. The gold represents the gold that he has reinvested or put away for the future, and also his general richness and prosperity. His tunic is of red and gold brocade, because I wanted to show his courage, as well. It takes quite a bit of bravery to take the risks necessary for this kind of venture.

His cloak is red, for the same reason, and he has a red feather of bravery in his cap.

On his cloak, you can see the partially hidden figure of a gryphon flying through a ring. I used this for two reasons. First, it was the design that I painted on a dear friend's wedding tunic. As such, for me (and the other people who know Jim and Tay) it symbolizes hope for the future, and a willingness to invest and commit to that future. But the reason that was the design that went on the tunic was to show the strength, majesty, and fearlessness of a lion paired with the grace, speed, intelligence, and vision of an eagle. Combined like this, they can reach new spiritual heights, and new dimensions of nobility. The gryphon is flying through a ring, which symbolizes eternity and the endless circle of life. This encompasses him, and he is free within it.

The gryphon is partially hidden to show that all of this greatness is not revealed yet. But it will be soon.

The design of laurel leaves on the hem of his cloak are for victory. He has triumphed this time; his ships are returning safely.

The three rods which stand around him stand for the past, the present, and the future. The rod of the past is clear, because you can see clearly what is in your past. Hindsight is 20/20 and all that. This man can learn from his past. It has a golden crystal set in the top, because he remembers the past as golden. It's wound with silver, to show that he was using his intuition then. If you look carefully at the top, you may notice that there is a crescent moon in the design at the top of this staff. I put it there, and made it the waning moon, to show that this is the past. This is over, and waning.

The wand directly behind him is the present. This is where he is now. It's solid silver, because it's frequently difficult to figure out what is really going on while it's happening. But it has a pink crystal at the top, because the present looks rosy. It also has a vine growing up it, because the present is the only place where actual growth, or activity, can happen. I used a vine, to show introspection, and also because it wrapped around the staff nicely! This staff has a full moon, because these are the things that are currently in their fullness.

The third staff represents the future. It's also silver, with an indigo blue stone, because the future is unknown, except through the psychic senses. But the stone is glowing, because the future looks bright. It has a new moon on it, because these are the influences that are waxing, or just beginning to come to pass.

He has a good grip on this staff, to show that he has a good grasp of the future; he knows what he's doing!

Below him, three ships sail in on a smooth, golden sea. The color, of course, implies the richness of the ships and their cargo. There are three of them, because this is a three card, and also to show past, present, and future; or the three stages of life, or any other three that looks right at the time you are reading the card. You may also notice that each ship has three sails, as well, for the same reasons.

Farther in the distance are three ranks of hills. Hills and mountains in the Tarot stand for enlightenment; and that's what these are. The Seeker is learning from this experience, as well; although these hills are softer than one sometimes finds, so it can be extrapolated that these learning experiences are easier, too!

The sun is setting on this card, in fiery shades of gold and orange, to show that he has been waiting for some time for this, and also to show the alignment with fire, which all of the wands have.

If you are reading, and it looks like a sunrise, not a sunset, by the way, go with it. Remember that the most important thing is what the cards look like to you when you see them in an actual reading.

Four of Wands

This card shows a couple dancing on a platform under a canopy held up with four silver wands that sparkle with light. At the top of the wands glow red and green crystals. Their platform is draped with flower garlands, and they wear flowers in their hair as well. Behind them, harvested fields become hills, which fade out to a soft sky.

Key – **Romance and Tranquility**

The meaning of this card is harmony, romance, a wedding. Newly acquired prosperity. Harvest home, rest, enjoying the fruits of labor. Safe haven. Festivities and celebrations.

I first began to formulate the design for this card when I was asked to make a card for the wedding of two friends of mine. Because it was an orthodox Jewish wedding, it took place under a canopy. Since one of the meanings of this card is the consolidation of a relationship, which may mean a wedding, it seemed natural to go ahead and put the canopy on the card!

The canopy itself, of course, also stands for shelter. This is a sheltered moment in the Seeker's life, a time to rest, and also to celebrate a job well done, or a relationship well begun. The lace on the canopy is to symbolize the careful work that has gone before this moment. Without all the care taken with courtship and wooing, there would be no wedding. Without careful planting and reaping, there would be no harvest home. Without work, there is no cause for celebration! This is a reminder of that.

The wands that hold up the canopy are made of silver, as are most of the wands in this suit, because of the intuition and magic that goes into the growth shown here. But these also sparkle with many tiny lights, to show that there is a lot of energy present in this card. They also remind me of Yule lights, and so of celebration.

On the top of the wands that we can see are two crystals, also radiant. One is green, and one is red. These are for the two halves of nature, vegetable and animal, or for male and female, or for any two opposites. They are here to show that these opposing forces are working together, and creating harmony and shelter.

The whole arrangement stands on a wooden platform that is raised above the surrounding land. That shows that this time and place are lifted above the ordinary, and exalted. You can't stay on this plane forever, but it's fun to be here now.

All around the platform are garlands of flowers. These emphasize the celebratory feeling, and show the great joy that is present here. If you look carefully at them, you will find the white lilies of purity, and the red roses of passion, as well as violets for love and sweetness, and blue forget-me-nots. There are a lot of green leaves, because this is a living, growing thing. And there are a lot of buds, because there is a lot of flowering yet to come.

A couple is dancing on the platform, to show celebration and joy once more, and to show that this is active celebration. This is not simply a rest, but a festival!

Their steps match, because they are moving together, in harmony. They have light hair to bring to mind the colors of fire, and the harvest in a golden autumn.

They have garlands of flowers in their hair, once again, in keeping with the general holiday mood.

Their clothing reflects the colors of the crystals that top the wands, and for the same reasons. But if you look carefully, you will notice that he is dressed in red, dancing under the green stone, and she is dressed in green, dancing under the red stone. This is to underline the balance, harmony, and accord of this card.

The trim on their clothing is gold, to show the richness that this position brings.

At the base of their platform burn seven candles. I put them there to show the perfection of the balance, and also to show how holy it is, since we use seven candles in our circles. (One for each of the four directions, and one each for the God, the Goddess, and the Maiden.)

All around them, the harvest has been gathered, and the grain has been stacked. I actually found a picture of grain that had been bundled like this in a field, and decided to use it on this card for two reasons. First, the shape is the same as that for the sigil of fire, and wands are associated with fire in my deck. They also reminded me of Tepees, and so it called to mind the whole concept of starting a home again. In fact, if you look at the far right of the card, you will notice that a couple of the stacks have had a cloth pulled over them, which echoes the canopy, and also looks like a dome tent.

If you count, there are seven hills, counting the one they are on. Seven is for perfection, again. The first one is completely harvested, and the second is mostly in.

But there is still a third hill that seems to be covered in ripe, uncut grain. Most of the time, this isn't noticeable. When it pops out at me, I know to tell the Seeker that there is still some work left to do. The harvest is mostly home, but after the party it will be time to go back to work again.

Beyond that hill, four more fade back into the blue distance. As always, hills in the Tarot mean enlightenment, or learning. This whole experience contains lessons to be learned, but they are gentle ones.

The sky is hazy, to show that everything is gentle and soft right now. Autumn rains will fall, but the dancers are under the canopy, and the harvested grain is stacked, so the rains won't be a problem to anyone.

Five of Wands

This card shows five young men, fighting (or perhaps dancing) with five long wands in an excess of energy. They are raising so much dust that any surroundings are completely obscured.

Key – **Unfulfilled Struggle**

This card means conflict, obstacles, unsatisfied desires, strife, indecision, internal dissonance. Or perhaps striving for order.

This card shows what may either be a fight or a dance. You will know which when you see it as part of a reading. In either case, these young men have almost made a pentagram out of their wands. All of them are at the right angles, but they haven't quite come together yet.

There is a lot of energy in this card; the question is what use it's being put to.

An interesting note is that these positions were all posed for by a single man, who is a friend of mine, and also a martial artist. So sometimes it seems apparent to me that this is really an inner conflict. This is the Seeker fighting with himself.

They all have fairly light hair, because I was trying to keep that theme for the wands, since they are aligned with fire. But they range from light blonde, to red, to brown to show the range of the conflict (unless it's a dance) here.

This range is also shown in their clothing which is all different colors and ranges from fairly simple, everyday wear to rich brocades, and encompasses several styles, as well. But if you look, the colors do go round the color wheel, with blue at the top, and then green, yellow (on the trim; I didn't like the aesthetics when I tried to make the whole shirt yellow,) red, and purple. I did that to show the buried harmony, that is just waiting to reveal itself in this situation. These colors are shown, as well, in the crystals that adorn the ends of their wands.

According to my notes, I was going to make the wands copper, to show the vast amount of energy that was available here. I no longer remember why I didn't. Michael (my husband) says that as he remembers it, I misplaced some of my notes during the move we had at the same time; and since my deadline was fast approaching, I just finished the coloring without them. At any rate, I seem to have decided that I would make all of the wands in the whole suit silver. So, if I may admit to a mistake right here in print, I'm sorry. These should be copper, and if I ever get a chance to fix them, I will.

These guys are raising such a lot of dust that you can't tell where they are. This is to show that if you are struggling like this, you are likely to lose sight of what is actually happening around you.

In fact, there is some evidence that until these folks get their act together, this is just struggle for the sake of struggle.

They are engaging in furious activity, but accomplishing little or nothing. There is more than a bit of chaos in this exercise, but the balance that would bring the pattern to the forefront is nearly there.

When this card comes up in a reading, you will also be able to tell if the pattern is just coming into focus, or if it is in the process of disintegrating. Is something about to be built here, or is it all just falling apart? As always, let your instincts guide you and listen to your inner voice; then you'll be alright.

Six of Wands

This card shows a blond man on a white charger, wearing a wreath of victory, and riding past cheering throngs. He holds a wand wrapped with laurel leaves, and flying a standard showing a brilliant sun on a pure white ground. Behind him, children throw flower petals into the air in front of a brilliant blue sky.

Key – **Triumph**

This card means public acclamation, gain, or achievement. Good or important news. Reward after hard work. Great expectations. Public vindication. Triumph in some area of life.

I gave this young man blonde hair, because I wanted to express the concept of the "fair-haired" man, the one for whom everything works out well.

He has a laurel wreath on his head to show that he has been victorious in whatever endeavor is being celebrated here. His clothes are white and yellow, to show his purity and joy. His trews are red to show his courage. He has a sun on his chest, his gloves, and his flag to show his brilliance, and his activity, and how others look up to him. The sun also shows his glory, and the joy he brings to others. And, finally, it's there because in some readings it gives the overtones of a sun-king; a man who enjoys power and homage for a moment, and then becomes a willing sacrifice. As always, you will know which meaning applies when you are actually doing a reading. Simply listen to your instincts.

His clothing in banded in gold, to show his richness, and his majesty. It also echoes the whole fire/sun alignment shown throughout this card. He is wearing gloves, to show that he was gentle in the conflict. He never "took the gloves off."

His wand is twined with laurel leaves, to show his victory once again, and the flag has the same sun symbol that I put on his clothing for the same reasons. That makes three repetitions of the sun, by the way, and so shows that the three-fold law is working here, as well. This victory is well deserved.

The crystal on the top of his wand is clear to show his purity and clarity, and blazes with a brilliant light to show his brilliance.

His horse has no saddle, and there are no weapons present, because this is not a military victory; this is a victory of the spirit or intellect. He doesn't need a saddle, either, because he has absolute control of his horse.

The horse itself symbolizes all kinds of powerful, animal instincts and forces, all of which he has firmly under control. It's white, because of his purity. It wears a golden bridle to show once more the relationship the rider bears to the sun, and to glory, majesty, and honor. The decorations on its reins are red and yellow flame shapes, to show the fire aspects and the strength of will with which he controls his mount. They also have little golden jingle bells on them, to show his laughter and joy. I firmly believe that you should rejoice in your victories!

Behind him, children dance and laugh, flinging flowers into the air. They are there to show the exuberant, joyful side of this card once more. They are dressed in red, for courage, and blue for spirituality. The blue tunic also has pockets, to show that there is also a practical side to all of this. The flowers are white, red, and yellow to show his purity, courage, and joy.

Behind them are rows of adults, mostly blocked from view, who are standing and holding their own wands upright. These wands are also topped with jewels, and they are of many colors, to show that many different people are joining in this very public acclamation. They are mostly hidden to show that the Seeker might not even know that he is being so hailed, or by whom; or perhaps because he is being cheered by total strangers. But you can see a bit of a face peeping out here and there, because they are willing to let themselves be known.

The crowd is dressed in their finest, as can be seen from the bits and pieces visible; brocades, purple, gold trim, etc., are all apparent. This is to show that right now, everyone is presenting their finest appearance to him. There is even one guy who is waving a branch of laurel! If you notice that hand at all, it's probably a pretty good indication that he had help to get to this position.

Overhead, the sky is a glorious cloudless blue. I chose this color to show that there are no dark clouds on his horizon right now. At this moment, he is basking in the sun!

Seven of Wands

This card shows a man dressed in a kilt, wielding a wand as a quarterstaff. He stands on green grass on a stony cliff, facing six wands plied by unseen opponents. Behind him are hills, wreathed in mist. Above him clouds fill the sky.

Key – Take a Stand

This card means success against obstacles, problems solved or turned aside. Bravery, resolution, valor, righteousness, tenacity; being unwilling to let go of a problem. Continuing to fight when all seems lost. Dogged determination and will. Winning against impossible odds.

This card stands for someone who is willing to fight to the finish, who won't give up just because the odds are against him or he's badly outnumbered.

I made him a Celt, because this is my own heritage, and in my family we never give up, even if it's obvious that there is no way to win. In fact, my father says that we sometimes ask the question, "Is this a private fight, or can anyone join?" I was raised to believe that this entire attitude is a racial/cultural bias.

I gave him a kilt to show that heritage, and also to show that he is a non-conformist. What others are doing is actually of little concern to him. The colors in his kilt are white for purity, blue for spirituality, red for courage, and yellow for joy, and to show his affinity for the fire signs, reflected in all the wands, and therefor the strength of his will.

The plaid also shows that he combines all of these characteristics, and from them makes more; such as the green of growth made from the yellow and blue.

His wand is perfectly balanced, to show that although he is engaging in a struggle, he is not, himself, out of balance at all. The crystal finial on the right is white, and the wand is wrapped in a deosil (clockwise) increasing direction. The crystal on the left is black, and the silver wire wraps around in a widdershins (counterclockwise) decreasing direction. They meet in a knot in the middle, showing that they are intertwined with each other. Both crystals are glowing, because he is giving energy equally to each.

He is barefoot, to show that he is in touch with the earth, and grounded; and he is on a cliff above the others to show that he has the advantageous position, or the high moral ground.

The grass grows richly beneath his feet, to show that this is a position that he can grow through and with. The rock is almost black, to show contrast with the light sky above him. Sometimes, it also looks like the people holding the other wands are in the dark!

Facing him are six wands, with crystals of various colors. I made the people invisible, because they aren't always people! Sometimes they can be ideas or institutions. They all aim their wands at the fighter, to show that he is beset with many problems. The wands are all topped with crystals, but none of them are glowing, because they lack the sort of spiritual energy and life that he has. They are also not arranged in any order, because I didn't want the opposition to look that organized!

Behind him are hills wreathed in mist. This is to show the enlightenment that is possible; and yet it's still veiled in uncertainty and mystery.

The sky is overcast, to show that there is struggle here, and all is not clear. This isn't a bright and sunny place; it's ready for incipient storms.

There is a story that goes with this card.

No one told me ahead of time, but when you decide to make a Tarot deck, you get to live through each of the situations shown on the card. (Talk about learning experiences!)

I was working on this card when my mother called me, to tell me that a dear family friend, the father of the family that had been like a second family to mine when I was growing up, had just been diagnosed with pancreatic cancer. They were giving him only a few weeks to live. I was so upset that I couldn't work on this card anymore, and I put it aside. But because of deadline pressure, I had to keep working. And eventually I had to go back to this card, even though I felt like crying all over again as I picked up my pencils to finish it. But while I was working on it once more, the phone rang. And it was my mom, again, calling to tell me that they had done experimental surgery. The tumor was benign, although it was large enough that it would have killed him if they hadn't operated, and he was going to be alright.

So this card, which can mean victory over impossible odds, was made extremely real and potent to me.

All of the cards have stories like this, although this is the most striking.

Just shows to go you what you can get into if you decide to actually make a deck yourself!

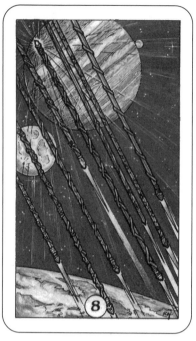

Eight of Wands

This card shows eight jet propelled wands, breaking out of earth orbit and shooting past Jupiter. On the way they pass our Moon, and also one of the moons of Jupiter. Beyond them is the sky, rich with stars.

Key – **Sudden Advancement**

This card means swift activity, the path of activity, hope. Freedom of action after a period of inactivity. Things moving just a little too swiftly. Decisions made too hastily. Travel.

This card shows expansion, especially expansion that has gotten a little out of hand. When I thought about that, I decided that merely earth-bound expansion didn't really fit in with the feeling that I wanted to show in this card. So I decided to take it to a whole new level.

I made the wands spacefaring. And that also means that I made the expansion extraordinary. (The rest of the cards don't seem to show a spacefaring culture!) This isn't just moving quickly. It goes far beyond that. This is things happening at exponential speed!

All of the wands are different, to show that there may very well be a range of things going on here. For the same reason, the crystal finials are all different shapes and colors, arranged in no particular order.

The designs on some of the wands are symmetrical, and those on others are mirrored from top to bottom, or are pretty much random. If any of these designs seem significant in a reading, I explain to the Seeker what seems important and why. This is part of what I designed into the cards, because I've always felt that being open to your intuition was what reading was all about. So it made sense to give myself something to play with!

The one wand that is entirely visible has clear white crystals at both the top and the bottom. I did that to show the clarity of this movement. The one at the top is blazing like a star, as well, because sometimes when a person is willing to move with this kind of alacrity, it gives other people a star to follow. Of course, with this card, it may also mean that the Seeker is going too fast, and is out of control. In that case, it usually strikes me that this crystal is a headlight, but this wand is actually behind the others. Running faster than your headlight is not usually a good idea!

The flames shooting from the ends of the wands not only shows how fast they are actually moving, but also tie in with the idea of fire, as shown in all the other wands.

They also show beyond a shadow of a doubt that the wands are moving upward and outward. This is because this card is supposed to be showing expansion.

And to emphasize that point, I've also put Jupiter, the planet of expansion, on this card.

The stars and moon are there to show that not only is the sky not the limit, but things have already progressed 'way beyond that point! We are talking space, here. The "phase" is not quite full, to show that although things are going like crazy, it hasn't peaked yet; there is still a bit to go before there will be any hope of slowing down.

It may also strike you, when you are reading the cards, that the two moons (one of which is supposed to be Luna, while the other was meant as Io) show some balance left even in this situation. Or they could show how far the Seeker is going to travel before it's all over. As always, feel free to read anything into the cards that seems right at the time!

Nine of Wands

This card shows a young man, battered but unbowed, leaning on a wand with a glowing tip. He is barefoot and shirtless, and there is a bandage around his forehead. Behind him, eight other wands are standing upright. Although the sun is shining brightly on him, the sky behind him is grey with clouds.

Key – **Wait For It**

This card means waiting for difficulties, changes or new challenges. Hidden foes, subterfuge, duplicity. A temporary cease-fire in hostilities. The calm in the eye of the storm.

This young man has obviously been through a fight. I made him bare-chested, because it often looks to me like he's lost his shirt in the battle. He's wearing a bloody bandage to prove it. I made the bandage white, to show purity; and there is blood on it so that there is no mistake that it's a bandage. In a lot of the decks that I encountered during my research, he has the bandage around his head, like this. I toyed with the idea of moving it to another part of his anatomy; but I finally decided to keep it on his head because so many of the battles that are fought right now are intellectual. I decided that if I left the bandage there, it would pop out at me if this was mostly a battle of mind and will. And, at least for me, this is how it's been working.

I made his pants brown, to show that he isn't in this position because of his wealth. He's just an ordinary guy. There is blood on his pants, too; but he doesn't seem to be wounded. I did this to show that he gave as good as he got in the struggle.

His feet are bare, because he is in touch with the ground below him.

I gave him a belt, but no belt loops, to show that this position can be dangerous and tenuous. My husband is fond of calling himself a "belt and suspenders man." This is the exact opposite of that. He obviously needs help to keep his pants up (that's why I made them gathered at the top,) but that help may not be all that he expects of it. This also underlines the deception that this card may show. It's possible that the Seeker's help will fail at a most inopportune time. Of course, often I don't even see his belt; but if it's important to notice, it's there!

Around his neck, he wears a medallion with the rune of protection and defense, Eolh, on it. This is to show that even in this position, he is not without protection from the powers that be.

He leans on a wand that has the glowing white crystal of clear vision on the top, and the purple sphere of healing on the bottom. The staff itself is wrapped with two strands, one going deosil (clockwise) for increase, and the other going widdershins (counterclockwise) for decrease. This is to show that he has balance, and that he knows when to build things up and when to tear them down. There are also little spheres all over it, to show wholeness and oneness with the universe.

The sun shines full on him, to show that he is in the eye of the storm at the moment. There was a fight before, and he is waiting with grim anticipation for another. But right now, there is peace.

He stands on a platform, to show that he is in the position of look-out. It's made of a solid piece of brown stone to show that there is warmth, strength, and solidity here. It's also fairly high, as shown by the fact that no other landscape is visible.

Behind him stand eight more wands. Sometimes they look as if they are ready for use, sometimes they look as though they belong to his allies. I drew them so that they could be either, depending on what it felt like during the reading (as always.)

Each of them has a crystal on the top, and these crystals are arranged in spectral order, to show that there is no confusion here; just apprehension. All of them have different designs on them, to allow them to represent different things. I even put a live vine on one, in case this problem was growing and changing. As always, if one "pops out" at you, then go with whatever feeling you are getting.

The sky is grim and foreboding, promising more storm to come. In fact, I did my best to make it look just like the sky in the three of swords, because it presages the same sort of pain and sorrow.

When this card comes up in a reading, I usually encourage the Seeker to use this time of uneasy peace to regroup and make sure of the merit of his position (it would be tragic to go through all of this if you were fighting for a mistake!) It wouldn't hurt to be certain that his allies were still willing to fight on his side, as well. Because the rest of the fight is sure to come, unless he decides to surrender instead.

As always, though, when you are reading, let your own instincts guide you, and say what you feel you should say in kindness and gentleness, being aware of the probable effect on the Seeker.

Ten of Wands

This card shows a man in peasant clothing, bowed under a heavy load of ten wands, trudging down a road. In the distance is a town dominated by a castle, toward which the path leads. All around are hills. His shadow stretches long before him.

Key – **Overload**

This card means too much success becoming oppressive. Heavy burdens. Martyr complex. Too much willingness to take on too much; especially of other people's burdens. Tackling a job that is just too big.

Wands represent the fiery attributes of willpower, energy, passion, and growth. All of these are considered good things, at least in this society. But, as this card shows, you can have too much of good things too! All of the tens represent an abundance of the attributes of the suit. And too much of these things will wear you out, because you will just be trying to do too much!

Too much power is too much! Extremes of power when power is seen as privilege will corrupt. Extremes of power when power is seen as responsibility will break a person. Either one is not a good thing at all.

That is the deep meaning behind this card.

This man is going to have to struggle to make it home with all those lovely wands that he is trying to manage. But he's still trying, even though he can't even see past them. He certainly can't use any of them in this state; but that doesn't stop him from trying to "do his duty."

I made him blond, to show that he is the fair haired boy from the six of wands again; but now time has passed. He is older, and his beard has grown.

All his fine clothes are gone, and he is dressed like a peasant. There are no cheering crowds now; there is just the hard work that he has set out to accomplish.

His shirt is red, to show his great courage. I gave him grey pants, to show that he still has some balance. (Although sometimes, when I'm reading, they just show that it's all become colorless drudgery to him. Remember, the cards are supposed to show different things at different times. That's part of how they work!)

His legs are wrapped in homespun, not quite as white and pure as he might hope. Sometimes, a Seeker has gone through many compromises, and sometimes they have compromised things that they wish they hadn't, to get into this position. If so, this will let you see that.

He's wearing a twisted length of cloth as a belt, to show that to some extent he has things all twisted up in his middle. If you look carefully, you can also see a wallet on his belt. I gave him that to show that he is carrying other baggage, as well. Once again, it's one of those things that I don't always notice when I'm reading; so when I do, it's likely to be important.

The wands have all kinds of decorations on them, and all colors and shapes of stones as their finials, once again to show the great variety of things the Seeker is working with, here. But they are all jumbled up, because by the time the Seeker is in this position, there is a great possibility that much of the job has really lost meaning for her.

His face is buried in the wands, to show that he has become so buried in the job he is trying to do that he has no energy to spare to look around him. Or maybe it's just showing that he doesn't care about anything else anymore; that the job has become everything in the universe to him. Once more, you will know which when the card actually comes up in a reading.

His shadow stretches long on the ground in front of him, to show that the sun is sinking; it's getting late. And there are still miles more to go before he can rest.

The grass grows on both sides of the path, but it's no longer a vibrant green. This is grass that has done most of its growing. It's getting ready to enter a dormant phase. This shows that the time to end all the work is approaching, as the setting sun does, as well.

But it's not time yet. The sky is still blue, although it's getting pale.

The village, which is the fellow's destination, is tiny in the distance. This is to show how much farther he still has to go. The central building looks like a castle sometimes, and like a cathedral at others. I purposely gave it some qualities of both buildings so that it would do this. If the overload is mainly spiritual or otherwise non-material, then it looks like a cathedral. If it's primarily a physical, material problem, or one dealing with some kind of power struggle, then it looks like a castle.

All around are hills. This is to show that there is potential for learning in this situation, as well. Sometimes what the Seeker needs to learn is that it's alright to put a few of the wands down. Sometimes she needs to learn that she can handle all of them after all. As ever, depend on your own instincts while you are reading the cards, always remembering to pay attention to the other cards in the spread, and to the Seeker. Don't be afraid to ask the Seeker if any of this looks familiar to her, and to draw her out. We aren't doing this to prove that we are psychic, after all; we are doing it to help the Seeker to make sense of the situation that she finds herself in, and to make the best decisions that she can.

Chapter 10
Cups

I am going to start this chapter, as I have started all the chapters on why I chose the symbols that I did, with the warning that these are my personal interpretations and feelings.

As you are reading the cards, you are likely to have your own. These are not "wrong," even if they are not at all what I saw while I was making them! As I have said before, if I have done my job right, you are bound to see things that I didn't even know I was putting in there!

I recommend that you go over each card much like this, and write down what you see, and why you think it's meaningful. This doesn't mean that you won't see completely different things in some other reading. But it will help you to get into the habit of really looking at the cards.

I'm providing this material because a lot of people have asked for it, and because you might find it interesting to see what was going through my mind while I was designing the deck.

The suit of cups is attuned to the element of water. In our tradition of Wicca, water corresponds to the emotions; from very shallow ones to those with great depth. This suit deals largely with emotional matters; love, friendship, contentment, and discontent. There isn't any violence here (although you will find some pretty heavy duty sulking!)

They also deal with imagination, dreams, and healing.

Since they are aligned with water, they also share the other correspondences of water in our tradition. So their direction is west, their time of day is evening, and their time of life is maturity.

The lessons of this suit deal mainly with emotions; how to handle them all, from healing friendship and love to disillusionment and despair. They also teach about aspirations, longings, ideals and fantasies. Everything that comes from the heart, and flows like the tides.

King of Cups

The card shows a blond king with a golden crown in the shape of a trident, sitting on a lotus throne carved from grey stone, with waves crashing all around it. Around his neck he wears a golden fish. In his hand he holds a golden cup with a silver band showing a yin/yang symbol. Behind him, a dolphin leaps from the ocean under the violet skies of evening.

Key - **Gentle Father**

This card means a kind, considerate man. A father figure. Someone who is interested in the arts, and gentle things. A deep man, with a quiet demeanor, but none the less powerful and well balanced.

Some Readers will tell you that a court card symbolizes a person with the attributes shown on the card; sometimes only the physical ones (in this case a mature man with light hair and hazel eyes,) sometimes more of the personality shown. I don't think this is always the case.

I think that the court cards can also mean that the attributes of the person shown on the card are manifesting in the Seeker's life. Please keep this in mind as you read the descriptions of these cards.

I began by drawing a man who had a kindly look on his face. Smiling slightly, with crinkles at the corners of his eyes. I gave him light hair, because that is traditional with the cups, and I wanted the folks who do traditional stuff to be able to use these cards. I also figured that someone with brown hair who spends a lot of time outdoors near the ocean is going to wind up with light hair. (At least, that's how it works in my family.) I gave him a beard to show his maturity.

He's seated on a stone in the middle of the water, with waves crashing against it. The stone shows his great inner strength and steadiness. The waves are for the restless turmoil of emotions (water) around him. His throne rises above the waves; he is calm and steady even though he's surrounded by constant motion and turmoil. This balance is part of what gives him his strength.

The bottom of his throne is rough, dark, natural rock. (In fact, it is one of my favorite rocks, and actually exists on a beach in Okinawa, Japan.) It is volcanic; it once was a liquid, like the water itself, thrusting up with molten violence through the earth's crust. Now it is solid, and weathered by the water, but it still shows its fundamental nature, now transformed by time and gentler emotions. This is to show that the once volatile nature of this man has been tempered and changed by the action of emotions, so it is at once firmer and gentler. I see this transformation as showing his kind nature, built on knowledge of rougher things.

The top of his throne has been carved into the shape of a lotus blossom. This is a symbol of wisdom, as well as being another indicator of water. It is a pearly grey, and slightly polished, to show further transformation from the rough volcanic rock. A sort of flowering into refined wisdom. But it's still rock; the strength is still there. Also, the juxtaposition of dark and light rock show balance again.

His crown is a trident, with waves cresting toward the middle. This shows that he is one of the manifestations of Neptune, God of the Ocean.

All of his ornaments are gold, to show the richness of his emotions.

Around his neck I put a fish on a necklace hung with sea-stars. This shows several things, depending on how you look at it. At the simplest level, the fish and the sea-stars are water animals, which reinforce the watery imagery of the card. Also, in just the way a fish is completely at home in the ocean the King is completely at home with his emotions. Sea-stars, of course, open shellfish easily. The kind of soft tenacity found in a person like this can also open the hardest shells. This may be something you want to be wary of; I don't know. And also "fish" is ancient slang for "penis." (Honest. I'm not making this up. You should see some of the Athenian sculpture and stuff.) This shows his masculinity and fathering side (in the biological, not nurturing, sense.) The masculinity is always there, in spite of the strong feminine influences in this card.

I made his belt a simple gold band, clasped with a seashell, both to carry the ocean motif along, and to show that he isn't ostentatious. The shellfish shows that he knows how to control himself (when to "clam up.")

I put him in a robe the color of the sea near the shore on a sunny day to show the quiet, sunny side of his disposition. If you notice, the robe gets lighter near the bottom. The sea, of course, gets lighter near the top. I did that to show that sometimes this fellow can behave in a manner opposite to what you might expect; or that these emotions and attributes may lead to the opposite of what you expect in the situation shown by the other cards.

Around his hem is a picture of a tranquil sea, with puffy clouds and shorebirds flying. This shows his inner calm, especially calm in the face of turmoil, as shown by the real ocean around him.

His robe is lined with purple, like the depths of the ocean, to show the depths of emotion and wisdom he is capable of.

His cloak is a full circle; what we call a "moon cloak." The dark is the dark moon, the silver the full moon, of course.

I gave it to this king (even if he is a man) to show his balance. Also, as the moon controls the tides, so he controls his emotions.

I gave him sandals, not boots, because I wanted to show that he is not afraid to touch his emotions. He under-stands them, if you'll pardon the pun. (I know, but that's how my brain works.)

He is sitting in a relaxed position, because he is at ease here, completely comfortable in this environment. His balance, wisdom, kindness, and generosity are so deep that he would be comfortable nearly anywhere.

In his right hand, the side of his intellect, he holds a golden cup. He accepts and understands his feminine, intuitive side. This gives him balance, as shown by the yin/yang symbol on the cup. The cup also has a silver rim. Silver is the metal of magic, intuition, and the moon. Putting it on a golden cup reinforces the idea of balance. (Gold, as you remember, is the sun and the visible world.)

Around him the ocean surges and foams. As I have mentioned, this shows how turbulent emotions can be. The froth and bubbles also show how much fun they sometimes are. I tried to emphasize that aspect by showing a pod of dolphins playing behind him. (OK, I know it looks like there is just one. But look again, really carefully. The others are there.) Dolphins are considered to be highly intelligent and wise. So, by using dolphins, I meant to show free, spontaneous, playful intellect.

The sky is one that I once photographed after an ocean storm. On this card, it not only shows evening, which is the time of the west (water,) it also shows the calm after the storm. Once again, this symbolizes the transformation of turbulence into calm through the balance, maturity, and wisdom personified in this card.

When reading this card, the salient, important stuff will seem to "jump out" at you. For example, the thing on the card that seems the most important may be the smiling, relaxed figure of the king himself. In such a case, it might be appropriate to say, "You seem very at ease and relaxed in this situation, with your emotions well in hand."

At another time, what strikes you may be the fact that the rock is really volcanic, and the lotus blossom may seem to be just sort of stuck on. Then you might want to say, "This situation looks attractive and welcoming. But be careful, because it's really volatile at the root, and may erupt into violence at any moment."

Give yourself and your subconscious mind room to look and interpret. Don't be a slave to any one meaning, and you will find your readings become more accurate. Remember, the truest way to read is simply to interpret your visceral reactions to the cards.

Queen of Cups

Queen of Cups

The card shows a woman with light hair and a golden crown seated on the seashore in a throne made of seashells. She is dressed in a soft, flowing robe of sea greens with an exuberant border of curling waves in which fish and waterbabies play. In her right hand she holds a covered cup. Behind her otters, seagulls, and whales frolic in the ocean, under the evening sky.

Key – **Loving Mother**

This card represents a soft, nurturing mother figure; perhaps a little overprotective. Kind, but usually passive. Someone who will help if it's not too difficult. A person with insight, love, and gentleness, or a situation where these qualities manifest in or around the Seeker.

The first thing I did when I began to design this card was to choose the pose for the character. Since she is kind, but not energetic, I had her sitting with her legs crossed, and one hand on her chest. This may be because she is out of breath. It also may be because she is showing that her heart (feeling) is her strongest part.

She is looking into the cup, with an almost neutral expression on her face, because she may actually be more aware of her own feelings than of yours. She loves you a lot; she is very nurturing. In fact, she may be so very nurturing that she nearly suffocates you. And then again, she may really know just what you need, because she is very intuitive.

Her crown is gold, with waves cresting into a pearl held high above her face. This is because her intuition (water) can uncover and raise the pearls of wisdom that are normally hidden. And, just as a pearl takes a long time to form inside the hidden shell of an oyster, so her insights may take form over time deep inside her mind, to be revealed only at the right moment.

Her hair is fixed to resemble a sea-shell, because of the ocean motif of the whole card, and also to show the sometimes convoluted working of her mind. She has two small white star shaped flowers in it, though, to show the purity and brilliance of its workings.

Around her neck, she wears a choker. I did this to show that if she isn't careful, this kind of overprotective loving can choke people. She only wants what is best for her children, and she never wants them to be hurt. But sometimes they can only learn and grow through being allowed to take risks. (The trick is learning when to protect them, and when to let them get hurt, if they have to. Speaking as a mother, if you have mastered this trick, please let me know how to tell for sure.)

Her robe is very soft satin, to show her general softness, beauty, and suppleness. It is the greens of the ocean; but if you look closely the light green is on the bottom. In the real ocean, the lighter colors are on top. This is to hint that she may behave in the exact opposite of the way you would expect.

It is lined with purple like the deepest ocean to show the depth of her intuition, love, and understanding.

The hem is a rollicking picture of tumbling waves, bright fish, and happy waterbabies. I did this to show that although she is more dreamy than active, she has a lighter side, and really enjoys it when those around her enjoy themselves. The fish are to show that she has sexual passion, too (if you don't understand why fish mean that, read the King of Cups.) The babies are because she really enjoys babies and young children. They really do need lots of cuddles and protection, so she is perhaps happiest with them.

If you look carefully, there is also an octopus in the hem (it's right by her foot.) That is to show that she can hold a bit too tightly, even here.

An alternate meaning of the whole hem, with the rolling, turbulent waves, is that although her exterior may be calm and placid, underneath she is full of passion and rolling, suppressed emotions. It all depends on what hits you when you see this card in a reading. (I often put things in that could mean two different things, because I always read the card by visceral reaction, and this gives me something to relate several reactions to.)

In her right hand, the hand of the intellect, she is holding a golden cup with an almost transparent cloth over it. The cup, as always, represents her feminine, intuitive side. The cloth simply emphasizes that we are speaking of her subconscious. It also represents women's mysteries, which she is intimately familiar with. I gave it a lace hem to further spotlight that aspect, but I made it sheer to show that she understands it, and can convey that understanding to us. Not uncovering, but still revealing those hidden things.

From the cup come rays of light, showing the brilliance of the mysteries held within. Maybe it's a good thing we can't look directly at them! They might be a bit blinding. Then too, this light shows the luminosity and purity of her emotions and intuition. It can also show enlightenment.

She is sitting on a throne made of sea-shells to show her fragility, and also her slow and patient growth. Only half of the shell is there; she is no longer likely to simply clam up - and yet it still protects her from many things. Inside it's pink, to show her softness and femininity.

She is on the shore, where the waves lap at her hem, because she is between the worlds of the conscious (dry land) and the subconscious (water.) At her foot is a sea star, to show the reflection of the heavens, and also to show her soft tenacity. (Sea stars, as you probably know, open shellfish by simply being more tenacious than bivalves.)

She is in a cove to show how she wishes to shelter everyone and everything. On the other side of the rocks, waves break and hurl themselves to destruction. But in here, the water is calm and placidly ripples up onto the beach. The rocks are black, by the way, because they are volcanic. There is really a lot of heat deep inside this one.

A mother sea otter plays with her babies in the cove, to show the protective mothering thing again, and also to show the playfulness that is a (sometimes hidden) part of her character. Sea gulls fly above the waves at the break point, to show that sometimes she courts those tumultuous waves; but she tends not to venture out into them.

Far out, a whale dives into the deeper water. Whales represent mystery, wisdom and ancient knowledge. All of these things are represented by this card, as well.

The sky is the same as that in the King of Cups, and is one I once photographed in Okinawa after a storm. It represents the calm after turmoil, and the shades of evening. (In my tradition of Wicca, the west corresponds to water and evening, among other things.) This is a time of completion, of the beginning of rest, of winding down. I wanted all of these to be shown in this card, too.

The pink in the sky is the same as the pink in her shell throne. This is to show that those attributes are echoed back and forth. The calm with the protection of the shell, the protection of the shell with the calm beauty of the sky.

As always, you may find other things in the card that I didn't put there (at least, not on purpose.) This doesn't make you "wrong," and me "right." It simply shows that the unconscious is more fertile than you might think, and we all speak to it in slightly different languages.

I drew these cards for me, really, and they use my language. If they speak yours, too, that's great; even if the words don't mean exactly the same things.

Knight of Cups

This card shows a young, beardless man riding a grey sea horse, (an animal part horse and part fish, with a mane of sea foam) through a rolling sea. He is dressed in silver mail made of fishes scales. His silver helmet is shaped like a nautilus shell with golden fins. In his right hand he holds a silver cup.

Key – **The Lover Arrives**

This card signifies the arrival of opportunity, or a lover. Something coming that has appeal, creativity, and inspiration. It may also show that the Seeker wears his heart on his sleeve!

Knight of Cups

The knight has light hair, like the rest of the cup court cards, and a smile. He sits at his ease on the horse, idly swinging his legs, and riding confidently without spilling a drop from his cup. This is to show that he is perfectly in control of his emotions, and enjoys and understands them. They don't frighten him a bit!

His helm is a silver nautilus shell, with golden fins. Spirals show introspection and awareness of self. So the nautilus shell shows this, with slow growth and beauty. It's silver to show intuition, the unconscious, and hidden things. I put golden spines on it to show that he is reaching out intellectually, as well. A combination of active, inquiring intellect with intuition and contemplation. This balance is one that yields a great deal of creativity, and also flashes of inspiration.

He is wearing scale mail, because I wanted to put him in armor (he is a knight, after all) and this seemed appropriate. It's also fairly light and flexible. This fellow is flexible in his approach to things.

If you look very carefully, the scale on the middle of his sleeve looks pink. If you look even more closely, you will see that it has a heart on it. He is wearing his heart on his sleeve. His emotions are right out there, for anyone to see. This can be dangerous for him.

His under tunic is lavender, to show the soft, feminine side of him, along with the depth. In all of the cup court cards, I use purples to show depth of understanding and emotions, because deep water looks purple (just before it looks black; but black has another meaning in the Tarot, so I stuck with the purple!)

His tabard (the sleeveless shirt over his armor) is sea green, with a trident on it. The color is the color of sea water with the sun shining through it, to show the basic sunniness of his disposition. The trident is to show he is related to the king; some of the same attributes without as much maturity. Around the hem are silver and gold fishes, to show his masculinity (See King of Cups) and to show the balance between the seen and unseen again; how he can manage both the material and hidden parts of himself.

His cloak is blue, to show the depths of the ocean. It is fastened to his tabard with a round silver brooch, like the moon.* I did this to show the feminine influence here, and to show how he can control his emotions, like the moon controls the tides.

His boots are really sandals, because he is not afraid of his emotions; not afraid to get his feet wet. The diamond pattern is reminiscent of fish scales, again. They are gold to show that he can walk in the material world, but have silver bands around the top to show the unseen, too.

In his right hand, the hand of the intellect, he holds a silver cup of intuition, with a heart right on it. He is a lover, offering his heart to the Seeker in an intuitive gesture, with nothing of calculation in it. This is genuine. The cup does have a golden rim though; he doesn't mean for it to be all spiritual!

In his left hand, the hand of intuition, he holds the reins. He controls his emotions intuitively. These are decorated with a motif of sea shells and fish tails. The shells are gold, to show the richness that is coming. The fish tails are sea green, to match his tunic, and reinforce the idea of the sunniness.

The same holds true for the color of his saddle blanket. It also has the silver band of intuition, and the purple lining of depth. Notice that he doesn't have a saddle. Except for the blanket, he is bareback. I did that to show that he is closely connected to his mount. He doesn't need the separation of a saddle and stirrups to stay on, or to control him. In some ways, their joining simply makes a single animal of the two of them.

All of the knights are seated on a mount that shows the basic elemental correspondence of the card. In this case, I put him on an animal that is part horse and part fish to show his alignment with the ocean, water, and the emotions. I made the beastie grey with silver fish scales to show the balance (as in the balance between white and black) and also to show that he can ride his intuition. (Silver means intuitive things, the "unseen" world, etc.) This animal is completely at home in its watery environment, but would be helpless on dry land. In much the same way, this fellow is much better at the emotional, poetic, dreamy stuff than he is with practical matters. (Remember, the card might not be a literal man. It might be anything else with these same attributes, or even these attributes showing up in the Seeker.)

*It was supposed to be silver. Please be kind, and don't notice that it didn't get colored in at all. Small imperfections are the mark of hand-made goods. And too-tight deadlines. While you are at it, please don't notice the other bit of this card that I didn't color, either. (I never claimed that I don't ever make mistakes.)

On the other hand, it might not look like that to you. In another reading, you may see this as an animal that partakes of the nature of both the sea and the land, and is perfectly balanced between them. That is the beauty of the cards. They can have different meanings at different times; so the combinations are virtually infinite.

I gave him sea green eyes, a blue bridle, and a purple lining on his chamfron (a horse's faceplate) to show that he is at home in all levels of the ocean. And so, of course, is his rider. The chamfron itself is of silver, with a gold band, to show the balance of seen and unseen. It has the alchemical symbol for water on it, to show the correspondence with the element, in case you missed it in the rest of the card!

In the background, I put a simple evening gradient, to show the alignment with the time of evening. Ordinarily, though, an evening gradient would have the pink at the bottom and the blue at the top. I purposely reversed this, to show that the things in this card may behave in a manner opposite to what you might expect. Water has always had that unexpected, sudden reversal feeling to it, at least for me. For you, it may look more like that means that the appearance of this guy is going to turn your life upside down. That's fine too, of course. Remember, the important thing is to read 'em like you see 'em.

Page of Cups

Page of Cups

This card shows a young girl with light hair, standing on a grey stone dock. She is dressed in a white tunic with a pattern of water lilies at the hem, belted with three strands of pearls. From her belt hangs an artist's palette. In her right hand she holds an ornate cup, with a flying fish just starting out of it amid streams of light. Behind her, the ocean foams and froths under an evening sky.

Key - **Developing Talent**

The card means a helpful youngster, with an artistic temperament. A trusting and trustworthy employee. The Seeker finds that a child brings joy to her. It can also mean a birth.

I made the pages in my deck young women, because I thought there should be more balance. Two males and two females among the court cards felt better than one female and three males! So here we have a young woman, just out of girlhood. I gave her a slight smile, and a dreamy expression because I wanted her to look gentle, sweet, kind, and thoughtful; all attributes that are associated with this card.

I gave her unbound hair, to show that she is not yet bound by the conventions that will catch her up later in life; she is still a free spirit. But the crown of her hair is caught up in strands of pearls. She is not entirely uncivilized. I used pearls to show her affinity with the ocean, and also to show the precious luminosity of her thoughts. Her hair is light, of course, because of the family resemblance among all the cup court cards.

Her undertunic is a very light lavender. She is just beginning to touch the depths she is capable of.

Her overtunic is pure white, to show her purity, with a border of pink water lilies and still water. I gave her this border because I wanted to show her affinity with the bright beginning of the Ace of Cups, and also to show the sweetness of her nature. It is lit from behind, with the light shining through it, to show her natural radiance. This is a person who brings a sort of innocent, quiet joy everywhere she goes. Or it could be the entrance of that sort of joy from some other source.

I gave her a belt made of three twisted strands of pearls. Pearls are interesting jewels. They are made in hidden, dark shellfish, by an organic process; so they correspond to things of great, gleaming beauty coming out of hidden, dark places.

You never know, when you open an oyster, if you are going to find one; so they correspond to joyful, unexpected surprises. And there is a legend that if a person who is impure tries to wear one, it will lose its luster; so they also correspond to purity. I meant all of these things when I gave her this belt.

It has three strands because of the three phases of the moon, which is itself closely allied with water, and because of the three faces of the Lady (Maiden, Mother, and Crone.) It could also stand for any three which you are happiest with, or for a different three every time you read the cards. It might even look like there will be three little girls coming to visit!

I gave her an artist's palette because when I first started to read the cards all the court cards were difficult for me, and pages were the worst. I had no idea what they were supposed to mean. So in my deck, I gave each page a device to make it very clear, and hung it from her belt. In this case, the card also means artistic accomplishments or temperament. So she gets an artist's tool – a palette. It has seven blobs of paint on it to cover the entire color wheel plus white. With these, all other colors are possible. So her artistic possibilities are limitless.

She has sandals, like the other cup court cards, because she is not afraid of her emotions in the least. They are gold, like everyone else's, to show the inherent richness of this position.

In her right hand, the hand of the intellect, she holds an ornate cup. The cup, of course, is the feminine symbol, and also stands for the emotions. In her case, it's gold, with a silver mermaid on it. (Honest. Look closely.) The mermaid is silver to show that she is completely at home with her emotions and her intuitive side. This comes across both in the silver (intuitions and the "unseen.") and in the form of the mermaid herself. How much more at home in the water can you get while still retaining your humanity? I made the cup itself gold, to balance the silver mermaid. Gold, of course, represents the sun and the "seen" world.

From it jumps a flying fish. Now, in the decks I used to use, there was always a fish jumping out of the cup in the Page of Cups. It took me a while to really figure that out. Eden Gray said it was "a symbol of an idea in the imagination.*" which was nice, but didn't seem to go far enough. And then I realized that this card also means the birth of a child. A fish in the cup could certainly mean that! Even if you overlook the fish meaning penis connection (see the King of Cups) I understand from friends of mine who have been pregnant that a fetus feels a lot like a fish when it first begins to move. I mean, after all, it even has gills and everything! And since we know that the cup, or chalice, symbolizes the womb this makes perfect sense.

So, the fish means the birth of either an idea or a child. And with the other influences in this card, I decided to make it bursting forth with joy! So I put wings on the fish to show its freedom and uplifting jubilation, and made it shining with light as well, just in case I missed the point. The light has eight rays, to show the eight spokes in the Wheel of the Year.* I did this to show that the joy of this goes on and on, and that it may appear at any time.

The young woman is looking at the cup, because that is the important thing in this card. (Besides, if you were holding a cup, and it suddenly exploded with brilliant light and a flying fish, wouldn't you look at it?) From the way she is looking at it, it may seem that she has caused this effect. She certainly isn't surprised by it.

Like all the other pages, she is standing. Youth is an active time of life for most people. In this case, she is standing on a grey dock, apart from the water itself. I kept that aspect of the traditional cards, because I liked the balance implied by the color grey, and I wanted to show that she is still a little apart from her emotions. They are there, and she understands them, and isn't afraid of them; but she is also not yet swimming in them, not surrounded by them. They foam and froth in all of their rambunctious, turbulent energy; but behind her, not around her. They are also uninhabited. She has only the barest experience of their depth and promise at this point. Hers is the serenity of inexperience, not of wisdom.

Behind her, as behind the knight, is a gradient that suggests the evening sky; but in reverse. Although the evening sky does sometimes do this, it's far more ordinary for the pink to be at the bottom. So this person may stand your expectations on end.

All in all, though, expect something delightful and unexpected when you see this card.

*In the Wiccan calendar, there are eight major holidays; the Solstices, the Equinoxes, and the Cross Quarter days midway between each one. These make up the Wheel of the Year. If you want more information about this, it's in Appendix C.

Ace of Cups

This card shows a silver cup, sus-pended in the air, ornamented with gold and jewels. The bowl has a mermaid embracing a ruby heart. Water bubbles and flows from the cup, forming five rivulets that fall into the water beneath. Also rising from the cup is pure light, shining out with five rays. Below it grow lotus flowers at the edge of endless water. Behind it is an evening sky, with purple clouds piled high just above the horizon.

Key – **Bounty**

This card means joy, abundance, per-fection, fulfillment, fertility, consolation, ease; every good emotion you can think of, overflowing. All brought about by an abun-dant love and compassion.

The aces in the tarot deck stand for the beginning of that portion of the whole; the aspects, feelings and ideas corresponding to that suit. And, in the circu-lar reasoning of the intuition and the Tarot, they also stand for the most complete and pure aspect of those attributes.

The cups are the suit of water, emotions, the feminine and intuitive side of nature or individuals, things felt more than seen, and the hidden mysterious work-ings of the universe. In my opinion, these all come down to love. So the principle symbol on the cup, the one that leaps out at you, is the heart.

When I began to design this card, (and this was the first ace that I designed,) I decided first that the symbol of the suit should stand on its own. I thought that hands, or clouds, or other things holding it felt hokey to me. If the symbol is strong enough to stand alone, and I think they all are, then that's how I would draw them. So I did.

The cup, then, is free floating in the air. I made it silver because that is the color of the moon, and intuition, and the hidden "unseen" things. All of them are strongly symbolized in this suit, so there they are. I gave it gold trim, though, to show the richness of these emotions, and also to balance it. These things are meant to shine out in the light of day, not remain sequestered in dreams and unspoken feelings.

On the cup, I put mermaids. One you can clearly see, the others are hidden on the other sides of the cup, and you can only see the tips of their tails, and their flowing hair. I used mermaids because they are completely at home in the water; that is with their emotional, intuitive natures.

The mermaid is smiling, to show the joy and tenderness inherent in this card. Her eyes are closed because this is also the dream nature. Then, too, people often close their eyes in moments of passion; and I wanted to convey something of that as well.

She is holding a great heart made of a single translucent ruby. The choice of ruby was fairly obvious. It has been associated with love for centuries, and has that rich glowing color. I made it translucent to show that such love is clear and transparent. There are no secret agendas or hidden goals.

She is swimming among fishes to show that these waters are alive. This isn't some distant, sterile idea of love. This is the real, and fertile, stuff. It may be messy at times, but it's full of life.

Around the rim, I put an enameled design in blue and lavender to show the depths of this emotion. Water gets darker as it gets deeper, and purple has always meant very deep water to me. So this isn't some shallow thing, either. This runs deep.

I put wings and blue stones on the border because wings mean freedom and uplifting joy. This comes with this sort of love. They are gold because that is the seen part of the unseen emotion. The emotion translated into action, if you will. If you love someone with this sort of purity, then it elevates both of you to a higher plane. This kind of love never "puts down." It "raises up."

I used a blue stone because that's the color of the Lady. (The Goddess in my religion.) At the heart of this kind of love, and this kind of freedom and joy, I always find Her.

The shape of the cup, with the broad bowl, the stem, and the cone-shaped bottom, was chosen for a couple of reasons. To begin with, it's a fairly old Celtic shape; and the Celtic influence is strong in all these cards (and, indeed, in my life.) Additionally, this means that the bottom is a sort of cup, as well. And that leads to the "As above, so below," correlations. That is, the giving nature of this kind of love is reflected in all things. It also shows the same basic shape as that of a woman in the "Goddess Position," which we use in my religion for Drawing Down the Moon, when the woman becomes a chalice, and welcomes the Goddess into her. So this kind of love is the kind the Goddess shows; warm, passionate, and very empathic.

The stem of the cup is golden, again, to show the manifestation in the physical, without which we wouldn't be able to get to "Below" from "Above." It is decorated with a cross-hatched pattern resembling fish scales to further emphasize the watery connections of the card.

Crystal clear water, or pure emotions, are bubbling and flowing out of this cup. This is to show all of the good things of life in such abundance that they simply overflow. Bubbles always seem to mean lightness and gaiety to me. The tingly sort of effervescent happiness that you get when you are small, and it's Christmas morning, and everyone is glad and singing, and there is a box under the tree from your favorite grandfather. You know the feeling. That is what I was trying to convey here.

That is why enlightenment is also coming out of this cup.

This visual symbol, of a ball of pure light rising from a chalice, has been with me for a very long time. I have made several attempts to show it, from a doctored photograph that I made in the darkroom in Okinawa years ago, to an animation on my computer a few weeks ago. One of them is this card. To me, this symbolizes enlightenment in its purest form. Simple brilliance rising from within the intuition. Perfect knowledge coming directly from the Lady.

In this instance, I meant it to mean complete and utter love and compassion, arising from within.

There are five rays of light shining out, for the five points of the pentagram, to show that this kind of love is very magical, and makes everyone complete. (The pentagram, as well as being a symbol of magic, shows the five elements that go to make a complete person (earth, air, fire, water, and spirit.) It also stands for a person, with the four limbs and the head.) This completeness is a natural outgrowth of this love.

For the same reason, the water flowing out of and over the cup divides into five streams at the bottom. There it adds its effervescent nature to the endless water that covers the rest of the card. The love and enlightenment shown in this card stretch to the horizon, and enter into all facets of life. The water flowing endlessly from this cup, and going as far as the eye can see, also shows that this kind of love is endless.

The lotus blossoms stand for enlightenment and wisdom. And I put some buds in, to show that this is just the beginning. The full flowering is still to come.

The sky is the sky of evening, because in my tradition of Wicca, the element of water corresponds to the west, and the evening. The sky there is pink to show tenderness and femininity, glowing toward yellow to show the beauty and sheer brilliance of this sort of emotional clarity.

There is a bank of purple clouds just above the horizon, to show that the presence of this love and blessing doesn't mean that nothing will ever go wrong again; just that you can get through it. The purple color stands for depth, as well as being the color you would get in the evening, and the color traditionally associated with healing. And clouds are also where new water comes from. Even the sad, messy bits can yield even more of this love, if you allow them to.

All of the aces are the cards of beginning. So this card, taken as a whole, means that a pure, joyous love is entering this person's life, and will change everything.

Two of Cups

This card shows a man and a woman, standing beneath two trees. Between them, they are holding two cups, with one hand on each. Around these cups shines a rainbow, and radiant light that forms a caduceus with a winged lion's head.

Key – **Balance and Friendship**

This card means a healing relationship, a contented and satisfying love, platonic relationships, harmony, cooperation. Two opposing forces blending and yielding a glorious whole.

When I began to design this card, I knew I wanted to show two people who were as "opposite" as I could. So I made one a man, and one a woman. But each is standing beneath a tree, to show the strength and viability of their own position.

He is dressed all in red and gold; the colors of the sun, the will, and the conscious mind. His clothing is trimmed in dark fur, and he has lions embroidered on the front and sleeve of his tunic. His hair is blond, and wreathed in blood-red roses, symbolizing his passion and vitality. His cup is gold, with red stones, and the bowl of it is long. But the rim is silver, to show that he is reaching toward some balance here. He symbolizes the hot emotions, carnal desires, passion, the physical plane.

She is dressed all in blue and silver; the colors of the moon, intuition and the unconscious. Her tunic is covered with a motif of green leaves and white flowers, to show her gentle purity. Her skirt is light blue, with fish all over it, to show that she is at home with her deep emotions. But the fish themselves are palest gold, to show that she is also aware of the passionate, vibrant side of things. Her tunic is trimmed in white fur, to show her purity again. She has black hair, and wears a blue ribbon with white violets twined in it. This shows her delicate, shy, gentle nature. On her shoulder is a caduceus, to show that she is a healer. Her silver cup has a round bowl, and is trimmed with green stones. But it has a golden border, because she, too, is reaching toward balance. She symbolizes cool reason, mind, spirituality, the unknown.

They both have purple on their clothing, to show the depths of the emotions and states of being they each bring to this partnership.

Each holds their own cup in their left hand, the hand of the unconscious, of inborn things. This is what they are. Each reaches towards their partner's cup with their right hand, the hand of choice and conscious will. This is what they need in order to balance what they are. This is what they are choosing in order to become complete. Both cups have hearts on them, to show that they are both willing to love the other.

As their cups and hands meet, a wonderful transformation takes place. Light (enlightenment) flows out of them, and shoots off in all directions. A perfect rainbow, showing completeness (all colors, all states of being manifest), perfect balance (a circle) and beauty appears. And from their joining, his symbol, the lion of virility, pride, and physical action comes together with her symbol, the caduceus of healing with the snakes of wisdom and flexibility. Through this, they are both transformed, becoming a single symbol, and gaining the wings of spirituality and joy.

So this joining, this partnership, heals and balances both; with a whole that is much greater than the sum of its parts. Two complete opposites, meeting in friendship, love, and cooperation - agreeing to disagree, and not to fight - can balance and heal each other, and bring this transformative power and experience to the world!

In the background is a blue sky, to show the glorious nature of this joining. There is also a green lawn to show how smooth this path may be. The trees at the foot of the lawn show the growth and strength that comes from this joining. The hills beyond show gentle enlightenment.

The whole card, then, should give the feeling of two opposites meeting in a spirit of love to bring transformative healing.

Three of Cups

The card shows three young women dancing. Each holds a golden cup. At their feet is spread a wealth of fruits and musical instruments. Above their heads are grapevines. Behind them is a bright blue sky in which three birds fly free.

Key – **Good Luck**

It means good fortune, artistic ability, sensitivity, fulfillment, healing, and harmony. The fates are feeling good, and having a party!

I used dancers on this card to show the arts, and also to get a feeling of total joy and abandon; but joy and abandon based on the discipline of working toward a goal. A dancer may look graceful and carefree on stage, but we know that expression is based on hours of practice and dedication. In the same way, the instruments and palette spread on the ground can only be mastered through commitment and practice, and the fruits take a while to get to harvest.

So there is a lot of unseen, focused work behind the great abundance and good fortune in this card. It's not unearned.

The three maidens represent the past, present, and future. Here they all come together, and all is fortunate. They are merry with the wine of life, the "milk of human kindness" and they dance, united in their joy; concurring in good fortune.

The one on the left is the past. Her cup has the new moon, and she is all gold and rosy with remembrance. In her blonde hair are the lilies of innocence and purity. Her head is tilted back, she is more exuberant and her dress briefer, to show her youth. Her sash is silver, because she lives in the realm of the unseen. We don't see the past, we just remember it; and no one remembers it as being quite the same as anyone else. At the same time, her eyes are wide open, because hindsight is 20/20. If we are wise, we look carefully at the past, and learn from it.

In the front is the maid of the present. Her colors are the red and green of vibrant life (animal and vegetable.) On her cup is the full moon of fulfillment. In her bright red hair she wears blood red poppies. They symbolize both her passion and vibrancy, and her willingness to dream. Her sash is gold, because she is in the now, and is seen. She looks at her cup, because she is most aware of what is going on right now.

In back is the maid of the future. She is holding hands with the present, to show that at this point the present is leading the future. She is dressed in the deep blue that represents the spirit. Her hair is black, because she is the unknown. In her hair are white roses of change. On her cup is the new moon, and she holds it high above her head to show that you have to reach for the future. Her sash is the silver of the unseen, magic, and moon energy. Her eyes are closed, because although we may sense much about the future, we cannot see it clearly.

They are dancing on deep green grass, to convey a feeling of luxury and beauty, and also a feeling of spring. (The grass is seldom like this except in spring, before it's been cut.) Behind them is a line of trees to show the growth and strength here. The sky is brilliant blue to show the spring time feelings, and to give an impression of perfect, cloudless days.

The three birds echo the three maids, but translated into a higher plane. They now have the wings of the spirit, and clear bright voices, and they have left the bonds of gravity and are flying free.

Above them you can see the corners of what must be a grape arbor; but it's outside the edges of the picture. At any rate, the ripe grapes are growing there in abundance. Grapes in all the cards are symbols of richness and plenty, and these are no exception.

At their feet are containers of fruit and veggies. One of them is a silver bowl, one is made of wooden staves, and one is woven withy. These, too, show three states of being. The silver is precious, but not flexible; and it has all the connotations of silver (magic, the unseen, mystery, etc.) It holds a variety of fruits. This shows the magical nature these maids are ushering into the life of the Seeker.

The second is made of wooden staves, and is a plain, utilitarian vessel of the kind that farmers have used for centuries. It's full of vegetables. It symbolizes the practical nature of the things that are coming; the part that is good for you.

The third is woven of flexible withy, and holds only grapes, apricots, and green leaves. It shows the flexible, artistic nature of whatever things the card seems to represent.

In the same way, a flute, an artist's palette, and a drum are also lying on the ground. The flute is for harmony, the palette is to show artistic nature, and the drum is for balance, as a drumbeat keeps all the instruments in the group in time. Drums also show a shamanistic leaning.

All of these things being laid out at their feet shows that they have mastered all of these, and also that all of these are in plentiful supply. There are also overtones of offering in this. And, of course, the implication that there is lots more, it's just not quite in the picture at the moment.

Taken together, it's a card that fills one with the feeling of joy and plenty, and the fates smiling as the past, present, and future meet to give the Seeker abundance.

Four of Cups

This card shows a man with a disgruntled expression sitting with his back against a tree. In front of him three cups are lined up on the ground. To his right, another is floating in the air, in the act of either appearing or disappearing. But he doesn't seem to see it.

Key – **Introspection and Discontent**

This card means discontent with the present order, or with materialism in general. A time of introspection and contemplation. The beginning of self-awareness or of self-involvement. A search for understanding. Solitude. Disregarding or simply not noticing offered gifts or other things approaching.

The young man in this card is wearing a white shirt and grey pants. These colors often show purity and balance; but here they usually show his lack of passion or depth. He is barefooted, because he is in touch with the forces of the earth. The earth corresponds to stillness and wisdom. So, although he isn't happy with things as they are, he is at least being still, and listening to his inner wisdom. He's trying to get to the root of his problem, instead of distracting himself with other concerns.

The tree he is leaning against is an oak. I chose that because it symbolizes strength, and in the Celtic tree alphabet it's also a doorway into the mysteries. Around it grows ivy, which means a search for the self; introspection. It's also always green, which shows hope.

The tree is just beginning to bud out, which shows early spring. This is the beginning of this path for the Seeker, or the person this card represents.

The grass around grows thick and green, to show vibrancy, growth, and newness. But under him there is no grass growing. I did this to show that this kind of attitude can keep things from growing, if it's carried to the extreme.

In front of him are three golden cups, gold for richness and things seen, covered with spirals of introspection. He has already done quite a bit of work to bring that which is hidden inside of him to light. But, as you can see from his face, this doesn't begin to satisfy him.

Next to him another cup is appearing, as beautifully decorated as any of the others, but with the added addition of a blue stone, showing the tranquility and spiritual gifts that could be his. But it isn't quite real yet. It's just beginning to manifest in a glow of light. Below it, a single white flower is blooming in its radiance, hinting at the wealth of beauty that could come from this.

He isn't paying any attention to any of this. I doubt that he even knows it's there.

Behind him clouds are beginning to fill the sky, showing his general uncertainty and possible stormy weather ahead.

When I drew this card, I meant the cup to be manifesting. But at one of the Tarot panels that I did, someone pointed out that it could also be disappearing, because he isn't paying attention and doesn't care. A sort of "use it or lose it" feeling. And that's very true. It's what I mean when I say that reading is what you see when you lay out the cards. Sometimes it might be coming, and sometimes it might be going. Listen to your own instincts, and you will know.

But this card, at its simplest, shows someone who is beginning to get in touch with her inner self, and has done some work in that area; but she discounts all that she has done, and isn't aware that more is happening. She may need to look around, see the value of the work already finished, and reach out to grasp that which is coming!

Five of cups

This card shows a person in a black cloak, staring in despair at three cups spilled on the ground. She doesn't see, or doesn't care, about the two intact cups standing behind her. In the background is a stream with a stone bridge across it, misty grey hills, a standing stone gateway, and a castle on an escarpment. The sky is filled with heavy grey clouds.

Key – **Despair**

This card symbolizes sorrow, loss, disillusionment, bitterness, the end of a relationship, loss of work …you get the idea. But it also shows that in spite of what the Seeker may feel he should look around. He hasn't lost everything yet.

It has always seemed to me that there are people who enjoy feeling miserable, contradictory as that may seem. I think this card shows someone in that mood.

So I gave the central figure a long black cloak: black, in this case, to symbolize despair. And I showed her wrapping herself tightly in it; clinging to it. She is finding some sort of comfort in this feeling, clasping it tightly to herself. It's precious to her, for some reason, and she doesn't really want to let it go.

You can hardly see anything of this person. Not even enough to tell if it's a man or a woman. (For those of you who really want to know - it's a woman, Pat Grey, who posed for a great many of these cards on one bitterly cold afternoon. The photograph for this one was taken outside in the snow. At least here I let her wear sufficient clothing! This wasn't true of all of them. All I can say in my own defense is that I was barefoot and coatless myself.)

One lock of hair hangs lankly from her hood, to show this person isn't taking care of herself. Other than that, all you can really see is that she is staring at the spilled cups, and cares nothing for the others.

The cups themselves are all golden. This is all manifest stuff. And they have different colors on the rims. Blue, white, and yellow are spilled; but green and red remain. These colors can mean different things at different times. I thought about it for a long time, and then decided to spill the white for innocence, because most of us lose that sooner or later, and the deep blue for spiritual stuff, because I am most apt to despair when I have made some mistake in that arena. The yellow I spilled because that color is one that corresponds to air in my tradition, and that also means knowledge and communication. So this person has forgotten something crucial, or broken her lines of communication. She is brooding, and not open to the advice of others. Yellow is also the color of joy in the Tarot, and when your joy is spilled and gone, it's true that it often seems that nothing is worthwhile any more.

The red and green that remain, however, stand for all of life, or for growth and will. So this person isn't as badly off as they think!

It took me some time to decide what color to make the spilled liquid, as well. I thought about making it clear, like water. But no one gets that upset over spilled water. Then I thought about making it white, to drive home the "don't cry over spilled milk" idea. But I finally decided to make it bright red, like wine or blood, because the person at least feels that she has lost something vital. Something important and necessary poured out on the ground and wasted.

The ground where the figure is standing is bare, because I wanted to show the feeling that all was waste. But beyond the figure things are green, although faded by the mists of uncertainty and despair to almost grey.

The running water is the Stream of Consciousness. As water almost always does in the Tarot, it symbolizes reflection, depth, and things mysterious and not quite known.

This person can cross it if she wants to; there is a bridge, and the path she is on leads to it, if she just turns around. And beyond it the path continues through hills of enlightenment and a ridge of trees (growth) to the standing stones and eventually to the castle.

I put the standing stones in to show the ancient wisdom that is there; available but often ignored. The castle represents the current pinnacle of human achievement. Both of these things are accessible from this point, although the trip won't be easy.

The lone bird flying in the sky shows spirituality, although from here it's a long way away. Still, it's there!

All in all, this card shows a person who is clinging to despair; brooding about what she has lost, instead of looking at what she still has. The losses are real, but so are the things that remain. If she wants to grow, she will have to give up her melancholy, turn around, and begin the journey.

Six of Cups

This card shows two young children, a boy and a girl, standing in the road in front of a cottage. Arranged around them are five cups full of bright flowers, and the boy is handing another to the girl. The children have wreaths of flowers in their hair, and the sun is rising behind the thatched roof of their home, giving an impression of warmth and delight.

Key – **Home and Childhood**

This card means the past, memories, nostalgia, innocence, youthful idealism. Giving out of pure generosity or love, with no thought of getting anything in return.

This card doesn't show childhood as much as it shows a dream of childhood. Real children are often selfish and dirty, and every tiny little thing is fraught with enormous meaning. I can remember being a child quite clearly, and being more upset by misplacing a toy than I am by anything today. Now I have perspective; then I had none. I never felt innocent, either, although I was. I felt like no one was explaining the rules to me!

So, this card shows all the good parts of being small, with none of the bad. That's why it's really nostalgia. It's also the sense of wonder you can have when everything is new, and you are still exploring the world for the very first time.

The children in this card are on a path; but it's still not far from home.

The little boy is dressed in a blue tunic, showing spirituality; but his stockings and sash are red, showing his courage and passion. His sleeves are trimmed with white for his purity, and gold knotwork. The knotwork is a series of designs made from a single line that loops around on itself to make a three pointed design. I chose this because it's the simplest form of knotwork I know, and so symbolizes the simplicity shown in this card. It also has the three points, which stand for the past, present, and future; or the Maid, Mother, and Crone; or the unconscious, conscious, and super conscious mind; or any other "three" that strikes you during the reading. They are gold to show that this is precious.

On his sash are embroidered white lilies for purity.

Around his head he wears a wreath of white lilies, pink rosebuds, and violets. The lilies are for purity, again. The pink rosebuds symbolize love. The violets are for friendship, and also to show that it's spring; the time of childhood and beginnings.

The little girl is dressed in pink and green; the colors of life, but muted as they begin for a child. Her vest is laced with blue for spirituality, and she wears a spotless apron to show that her innocence is protected. She, too, wears flowers in her hair, but hers are pink poppies and daisies. The daisies are for freshness. The poppies show the childish passions. She feels quite strongly about things, but there is nothing carnal there yet. Her wreath is open in the front, to symbolize that she is open to the gift she is receiving.

She has not yet reached out for it, though, because she is at a very passive stage. Receptive, but not grasping.

The cups themselves are very reminiscent of the cup shown on the ace card, and colored the same way for the same reasons. But these have no mermaids and no hearts. Instead, they are decorated with a motif of various shields. I did this to show the inherent nobility of this sort of idealistic card. The feeling of giving because that is what you do, and expecting nothing in return. The feeling of protecting those who are weaker than you, instead of exploiting them. The dream of nobility, as this card is the dream of childhood.

They are filled to overflowing with white lilies, yellow daffodils, pink rosebuds, violets, and starflowers. The lilies are for purity, as always. The pink roses are for love and affection again. The daffodils and violets are to show that this is spring. The starflowers are to show that sort of "starry" feeling, and to symbolize the pentagram, a very magical and hopeful symbol in my religion.

The cup the boy is offering to the girl is smaller than the others, because it is something just beginning, that will grow.

Behind the children are two walls, which are between them and the house. This is to show that although there is still a path "home," there is some separation beginning, too. The wall behind the boy is tall, to show his beginning independence, and has a carving of a knight in shining armor. This is to show his youthful idealism. The wall behind the girl is shorter, because she is younger and therefore closer to her home. It has a carving of the Celtic Tree of Life, to show that she is part of life, and will grow into much more than this, herself.

The home is the sort of thatched roof, white washed cottage found in fairy tales. I did that to show the idealism of this card once more. It has vines growing on it, to show the introspection and to show clinging to home. We can see two sets of windows. The ones on the ground floor are a set of three arched windows, to show grace, beauty, and your favorite three again. They are all lit up, to show the warm, welcoming sort of place this home is.

The upstairs window is dark, with a curtain half drawn over it. This is to show that the seen and the unseen are there, too. This window is the unseen, or only partially seen. The friendly mystery of presents unopened, or clean white curtains half drawn in your very own home.

A white dove perches on the roof, to show the peace in this home.

Between the road and the cottage, the grass is the vibrant green of spring. There are plenty of trees, too, behind the house. They show strength and growth, and are also the brilliant green of spring.

The sun is just coming up in a perfect robin's-egg-blue sky. This is to show the beginning of a new day, as well as a new season, and the perfection and clean scrubbed purity and newness symbolized by this card.

The whole thing, then, shows the innocence, purity, nobility and generosity of an idealized childhood. All the good things; all the feelings of rightness and sparkling newness. All the wonder and comfort, and the giving without expecting anything back. All that is best and brightest about the dream. It's an emotion, as all the cup cards are; the pure joy and delight of giving, from my home to yours.

By the way, the boy on this card is my stepson Tim, when he was only six.

Seven of Cups

This card shows a richly dressed person, head in hand, dreaming. The dreams manifest as seven cups, each holding a different symbol and with a different design around the rim, suspended in golden clouds.

Key – **Dreams**

The meaning is overactive imagination, illusion, dreaming in place of doing. A choice of paths or goals. A mystical experience. Positive visualization, goals, or ideals. Introspection.

This is one of those cards that taught me a lot while I was drawing it!

I began with deciding to show that all of this was dreams, imagination, or visualization by letting the dreamer appear face forward. Her curls become clouds, to show that all of this is in her mind.

I began by thinking of this as mostly wish-fulfillment; but as I drew this card I realized that it was much more. I came to understand that it was dreams from which all our goals and aspirations come, and this card represents the beginning of that journey. The seed from which they all spring, and the choice about which path to take.

Starting from the top left, then, the first cup has a silver band, representing magic and mystery, with a bright red heart and engraved flowers on it, representing love. From it spring fireworks and stars. This cup represents the tingly, starry-eyed "falling in love" kind of love. The sort that sweeps all other cares aside. The kind that young girls dream of. (I don't know if young boys dream of it too – I haven't been one recently!)

The second cup has a deep blue band, for spirituality and the Goddess, decorated with the triple moon sign of the Lady. From it rises a snake, which also symbolizes flexibility and wisdom, and has meant the Goddess and feminine power and energy for ages. (That's why the early Jews, and the Christians after them, were so opposed to snakes!) This cup represents the spiritual path, and the life of a Priest or Priestess.

The third cup has a black band, with a skull and cross-bones on it. Resting in the cup is a victory wreath. When I first began to work on this card, I was surprised to find some death symbol connected to this cup in all the material I could find. I didn't understand it. In fact, I have some early notes where I ask "crush your enemies?" But that didn't feel right. One evening, I finally said to my husband, "I don't get this 'Victory over Death' stuff! ...Oh." And it became clear that this is what this cup represents. Victory over death! That's the reason that the wreath is made of green leaves, and the ribbon on it is red. Those are the colors of life!

The fourth cup has a red band with chains on it, and a red dragon rising from it. Chains, of course, are for binding. They are also found on the Major Arcana "Devil" card, which stands for greed. And that's what I meant when I put them here. Greed. The dragon, however, stands for sovereignty in Celtic mythology. So having a dragon in this context symbolizes the ability to rule your own greed. Having power over that part of yourself that wants everything. The dragon is red to show its vitality and passion. It looks a bit worn about the wings to show that it isn't always an easy fight; but it's one the Seeker dreams about winning.

The fifth cup is decorated with a green band with a motif of dollar signs. In it are heaped all kinds of jewels, from pearls to jewelry of silver and gold set with sapphires and rubies. This cup stands for wealth, of course. Depending on how it strikes you, it could also stand for wealth of the spirit, because pearls, in legend, could only be worn by a woman who was pure in spirit. Any other kind would make them grow dull, and eventually they would turn to dust. But usually it looks like pure material wealth to me.

The sixth cup has a rich purple band, with a silver crown on it. Inside it is a castle. This cup may stand for power, or it may stand for home. (A man's home is his castle.) It all depends on how it looks in any particular reading. I made the crown silver, by the way, to show the magic inherent in the dream.

In the center, surrounded by all the other cups, is a cup with a silver band decorated with spirals. The silver is for mystery, magic, and the unseen, of course. The spirals stand for introspection, the search for self. Sitting in this cup is a mask, with the blue ribbons of spirituality on it. When the Seeker reaches this cup, and begins to know herself, she will realize that this is the mask she has been wearing; that's the inside of the mask that we are looking at! From here, it's white, but that is the white of a piece of paper that hasn't been drawn on yet. Who knows what is on the other side?

So when you understand this whole card, you see the dreams which start you on a path. Which one appeals the most? Which should you choose? Which does the Seeker focus on? For it would be very hard to go down all of these roads at the same time. Each of these things requires quite a bit of time and energy, if the Seeker is going to do anything more than just dream.

Eight of Cups

This card shows a figure robed in crimson, walking into rugged, misty mountains under the moon at night. In his left hand, he holds a staff with a feather, a willow branch, and a horse tail on it. Behind him is a glassy stream. On the near bank sit eight golden cups, each with a jewel on the rim. Eight wild geese fly across the face of the moon.

Key – **Enough of This!**

This card means leaving this phase of life behind; rejection of the material to turn towards the spiritual. Disappointment in love. A search for a new path. Leaving the familiar to "find yourself."

This card is dominated by the eight golden cups that are left behind, sitting on the grassy riverbank. I did this, because sometimes the things left behind are more obvious than what is ahead. They are all gold, because they are all part of the seen world. They are things that the Seeker is well familiar with, and ready to part from. They are plain, except for a colored stone in each. These colors are all the colors of the rainbow; crimson, red, orange, yellow, green, blue, indigo, and violet. This is to show that all facets of this part of life have been thoroughly explored by the Seeker, and she is ready for something new. They also show that the Seeker is leaving behind a full spectrum of possibilities in their search for a new, different path. Or you might see them as the colors of the chakras, or the stages of life, or anything that springs to mind in a particular reading.

They are sitting on the grass to show the pleasure and ease of the life that is being left behind, as compared to the rugged landscape that the Seeker has chosen now.

Between the cups and the Seeker is a stream, showing the mystery of the unconscious. In this case, it also shows that a definite landmark has been crossed; that the old way is left completely behind. There are many legends about running water and what may or may not cross it; and there are also tales in which once the water is crossed there is no turning back. I meant to evoke that sort of feeling.

It's also glassy and reflective, but behind the Seeker. The time for reflection is past. Now is the time for action.

The figure is dressed in leather boots with fringe, such as the pioneers wore. I did that to show his pioneering spirit. He is also wearing the red cloak of courage.

It takes quite a bit of courage to leave what is known and comfortable and strike out into the unknown.

He carries a staff to help him on his way, and to give him sure feet and a steady path. He can use it to test the road ahead, or to meet challenges. On it are bound an eagle feather for bravery, white horsehair to speed him in his search, and green willow in mourning for what is past and gone. He knows what he has left behind, but can't turn back, because it is no longer what he needs.

He walks into the mountains of enlightenment, the mountains of the spirit, still shrouded in the mists of uncertainty; but they are now his goal.

The sky is dark to show the mystery and uncertainty of this path. This is done by faith, not with clear vision.

Above him eight wild geese fly above the moon, to show that this path is as inevitable, and as necessary, as the migration of the geese. The moon itself is both full and waning - the full moon held in the arms of the old. I did this to show that the completion of this phase is upon the Seeker. The time for the ending of this part of his life has come.

All in all, then, this card shows the Seeker, armed with courage and steadfastness, leaving behind that which is familiar and comfortable and beginning an inevitable trek into the mountains of enlightenment. Basically leaving what he has known, and striking out anew.

Nine of Cups

This card shows a well dressed man, jolly and well fed, holding out his arms to embrace the universe. Behind him, nine golden cups are arranged on a golden horseshoe-shaped shelf.

Key – **Party Hearty**

This card means satisfaction, plenty, well-being, success, security, sensual pleasures, wishes fulfilled, and so on.

I decided to show this man close up so it would be easy to see the expression on his face, even though that means it's harder to tell that his arms are outspread in welcome.

He is dressed very richly, showing that he has enough and to spare of everything. His tunic is red, for richness, passion, and ebullience., with brocade of gold, to show wealth and material stuff. The design is of exuberant flowers, vines, and fruits to show plenty, bountiful growth, and thriving. (It also reminds me of the sort of clothing that a friend of mine, who has very much this sort of personality and attitude, wears to the Science Fiction Conventions that we both attend.)

His collar is purple, to show the depth of these feelings, and the richness. On each part of it are nine gold coins, to show wealth again.

He is wearing the sort of hat a wealthy merchant or burgher might wear, to show that he has earned the richness he is so willing to share with all.

He himself is obviously happy and well fed. He clearly has plenty of everything, and shows great emotional and physical well-being.

Behind him are nine identical golden cups, to show abundance - more than enough of all that he wants. They have silver rims, to show balance. On each is a design of gold coins, again showing abundance. But the fact that they are identical may imply that this fellow doesn't have much variety in his life. As always, it depends on how the card strikes you in the reading.

The shelf they are arranged on is shaped like a horseshoe to show good luck. It's also the shape of a rainbow, to show that sort of beauty and promise; and it may actually be the shape of a circle, to show completion. It all depends on how it looks when it turns up.

Behind the cups is simply warm golden light.

There is great contentment shown in this card. All the colors are warm, and the man himself seems very warm and friendly. Perhaps he is a host, welcoming the Seeker into his bounty. Or he may be the Seeker, finally having so much of everything that he can give unreservedly.

In either case, it's a card of plenty, of contentment, of deep joy and every wish fulfilled. It shows deep emotional wealth, and a giving spirit that makes everyone welcome, and invites everyone in to bask in the warmth.

Ten of Cups

This card shows a family dancing for joy and embracing. Behind them is their home, with a heart on the rooftree, and the sun just breaking from among the clouds. Around them is a border made from a rainbow which flows from one cup to another, spanning all ten in its journey, and making an oval reminiscent of the wreath on the World card. Beyond that are white clouds, with a pair of bluebirds flying among them.

Key – **Welcome Home**

This card means home, joy, familial bliss, peace, plenty, love, contentment of the heart, respect from your neighbors.

This card shows great emotional joy and love, although not a lot of material wealth. The man and woman here are happy, and rosy cheeked, and obviously love each other and their two children. The man is wearing a blue tunic, for spirit, with a large star and four hearts appliqued onto it. The hearts are for love, of course. The star is for fulfillment and joy, faith and idealism. It has five points, too, so it also stands for magic and spiritual awareness. The blue ring around it shows spiritual completion and continuity. The silver leaves show his spiritual growth and vitality.

His wife wears a blue vest as well, to show her spirituality, with red edging for passion, and white hearts for her pure love. Her skirt is green to show her growth and vitality, and her association with the Goddess. In her hair she wears white flowers, for purity and gentleness.

Their daughter is dressed in blue and green as well, for growth and spirituality, and has pink hearts on her vest to show her own affection and love. Their son is dressed in purple and red, to show his passion and joy in life. On his sleeves are tiny red hearts for he, too, has a loving nature.

Behind them is their modest home. They aren't wealthy in material things, just in joy and love. It has a heart on it, in case you weren't clear on the concept. Behind them are trees, for strength and growth.

The light is just breaking free of the clouds. The storm is over, and the sun is coming out. The promise of happiness has arrived.

The rainbow that surrounds them goes from the cup on the left, which has a white gem to show spiritual fulfillment, to the one on the right, which has a deep purple gem, for healing.

The cups themselves form the other half of the circle. They are all made of gold, to show their richness; but they have silver rims. This is spiritual and emotional wealth. Each also has a single gem, a different color for each cup.

The purple gem shows protection and healing. The indigo is for spiritual growth and second sight. The blue is for tranquility, understanding, and patience. The deep green is for growth and peace. The leaf green is for fertility, luck, and hearts ease. The yellow is for strength, joy, and warmth. The orange is for adaptability, attraction, and kindness. The bright red is for courage, strength, and vigor. The deep red is for passion and comfort. The white is for purity, truth, and spiritual fulfillment.

Together, they show all things good and pleasant, strong and protective, completing and complimenting the rainbow.

Around this whole happy picture are clouds, to show that it is a spiritual state, with the bluebirds of happiness flying through them.

The whole card, then, shows a family united in love and joy. This makes them spiritually strong, and able to withstand the storms that may come their way. It also gives them much happiness, and the ability to heal each other.

This may not be a birth family, but it is a group in which the Seeker can finally feel loved, and "at home."

As all the cups show emotions, this one shows emotions completely fulfilled.

One final note on this card, though. At one of the Tarot panels I did, I had a participant say that it didn't look at all like a real home to him. It looked like a dream of home; an idealization. It was all "in the clouds," and didn't actually exist. If it looks like that while you are reading, then read 'em the way you see 'em.

Don't be limited by what I was thinking when I drew these cards. That was a long time ago, and even I am not the same person now that I was then! So let your own mind and experience color your readings, and give them that unique depth that only you can provide.

Chapter 11
How Does it Work?

No one knows for sure how the Tarot works. But there is plenty of speculation.

This ranges from "It doesn't," to "It's Magick!" Both of these, of course, are really non-explanations. All they do is negate the need for any real explanation at all!

Some people go into Jungian philosophy and archetypes. If you are interested, there are plenty of books about that. But this book is already way too long to try to go into that now.

Some think it works because all of the universe is really ordered. Somehow, the Tarot taps into that order, and reveals it to us. This gets into Quantum Mechanics and all sorts of other things that I simply don't have room for. Once again, there are books that do explore this.

Some think that Angels, or Spirits, or other non-corporeal forms of life are busily arranging the cards as we shuffle, and that's why they reveal what they do.

Some think it's all a matter of chance and self-fulfilled prophecy. If you are sure that something is going to happen, then, at some level, you see that it does. Also, they believe, the pictures on the cards are vague enough that the Reader, working from clues she gets from the Seeker or information that she has learned ahead of time, can read into the cards anything she wants, and she tailors the reading to what she already knows. I disagree with this one, because I've seen readings that were very accurate too many times when the Reader had no knowledge of the Seeker at all.

But to answer the actual question …well, your guess is as good as mine! But I'll tell you what mine is (at least until further notice.)

My favorite theory is that it works because it's really a focus.

According to this theory, all of us really know all kinds of things about what's going on all around us, but we keep this knowledge at a unconscious level. At that level, too, we are able to communicate with the people around us, so we can absorb the knowledge that they have.

Let me try to explain.

I had a dream once. In it, I was going to see a play with a friend of mine. We were sitting in the balcony, waiting for the play to begin, when an announcement came over the PA, telling us that the format of the play was not what we were expecting. It wasn't going to be held on the stage; it was in the bleachers in back. The voice went on to explain that we were all to leave the theater, find our way to the back, and sit wherever we wished. Then the play would begin.

So my friend and I, along with a whole crowd of other people, left our seats and streamed through a doorway into the bleacher section. In the confusion, we became separated.

The bleacher section had bleachers, all painted black, arranged around a circular, raised platform. In the middle of the platform was a circular wall, shaped like a cog wheel lying on its side; about ten feet tall and made of glass. There were speakers in all the inset portions of the wall, and behind the glass were a number of actors.

I thought that I saw my friend sitting on the platform, leaning against the glass wall. It startled me for a moment, but then I decided that they *had* said to sit anywhere; so I climbed down the bleachers and joined her. But when I got there, it wasn't her at all, it was a stranger. However, the play was beginning, and I was too embarrassed to move at that point.

As the play progressed, it became apparent that it was a play about the mind. The actors behind the glass were the ones playing the part of the conscious mind. All of us on the outside, all around them, were the unconscious.

We could hear everything they said, because of the speakers. But there were no microphones. In order to try to communicate with them, we had to use semaphore, and charades, and drawing with our fingers on the glass. And to make matters worse, they tended to ignore us completely, and we had to bang on the glass to try to get their attention.

Those of us who were actually part of the cast were the unconscious of the Person whose mind it was. Those of us who were part of the audience, and had wandered in, were from the unconscious minds of other people. We could talk easily to the unconscious mind of the Person, and even help with the communication effort.

But communicating anything to the Person was difficult, to put it mildly.

Which was frustrating, because we also had the voice from the PA, playing the part of the Universe, giving us information that the Person needed to keep from making a horrible mistake. But getting that information across to the actors who were the Person's conscious mind was well nigh impossible.

When I woke, I realized that it would explain a lot if that is how it really is. Think about it. Makes sense, doesn't it?

When we think of our unconscious mind as the subconscious, a part of us that's buried beneath our conscious mind and walled away where it seldom sees the light of day, I think we have it backwards.

It's not our unconscious that is barricaded and difficult to communicate with. It's our conscious. Our unconscious can talk to the unconscious minds of everyone on the planet! (And perhaps beyond.)

The only trick is to get the knowledge from the unconscious to the conscious. We do that in dreams, and in flashes of insight, and in vague feelings. But we have often been taught to ignore our insight and feelings, and many of us forget our dreams.

The Tarot, though, is physical. There it is. So we are more likely to be able to pay attention to it. When a Reader looks at a Tarot card, she can allow the feelings and insight to come out. And because there is a card to point to, it's easier to express them, and easier for the Seeker to listen.

Our unconscious minds, and the universe, are desperate to communicate. Just as, in the dream, we were trying like mad to get the actors behind the wall to listen to us. In fact, at this point in my life I think that communication is so deeply desired that we could probably do divination with bottle caps and paperclips! If we gave the unconscious a code, by deciding first what the various bits meant, I'm sure that it would use them to try to talk to us.

All of us can be Readers, just as all of us have dreams. The trick is just to relax and let it come.

The correct cards show up, I think, because those are the cards we really know we need. The universe is very accommodating about giving us what we need (not to be confused with what we think we need, or what we want!)

So the more in touch you become with your feelings and intuitions, the less you fight your unconscious mind, the better your readings will be. Try it!

Chapter 12
Beginning Reading

When you sit down to begin reading the Tarot, there are a few things I think you should do first.

Number one is to establish a space free from interruptions and distractions. If you have an altar, or sacred space of some sort already established, you may want to use that. If you don't, make sure that no one is expected. Then go into whatever room you are most comfortable and secure in, close the door, disconnect the phone, and get ready to begin.

This is necessary, because you are about to make contact with a side of yourself, or of the universe, that is not part of your normal, waking conscious. As you become more used to this kind of connection, it will become easier to establish, and more tolerant of disturbance. But at least at first, why not make it as easy on yourself as possible?

The next step, and one that is absolutely essential, is to Ground and Center.

Centering means aligning your energy body with your physical body, so that they are both in exactly the same spot. We all have physical bodies, which occupy this physical plane, and which we can touch, and feel, and see. We also all have non-physical bodies, which enfold our physical bodies like the skin of an onion. They are harder to see and touch, although they are as real as anything. As we go about our daily lives, our non-physical bodies, or energy bodies, can become misaligned from our physical bodies.

Have you ever had a day when you felt disoriented somehow, as if you weren't really there? Have you felt as if you were standing slightly to one side of your body, working it by remote control? Have you felt as if there were layers of glass or gauze between you and the world? If you have, then you have experienced being misaligned from your physical body. That's what happens (usually due to emotional or physical stress of some kind) and that's what it feels like when you are grossly uncentered.

You can be subtly uncentered, too; but there are techniques to fix it. And that's Centering.

Grounding is tapping the energy of the Earth, so you don't deplete your own supply when you are working with energy. Something like Tarot reading uses energy at a ferocious pace. If you aren't Grounded, you may find yourself feeling drained and exhausted after a few readings. You are also likely to get headachy, with a feeling ranging from tension and weariness behind your eyes to pain so severe that you expect an imminent head explosion! You don't want that. (At least, I assume you don't. I don't know. Maybe you like pain!)

These are symptoms of energy depletion. They can be cured by rest, proper breathing, plenty of water, nutritious food, and time. Or they can be avoided by Grounding in the first place.

Although Grounding and Centering is a wonderful ability that can help in every facet of your life, not just Tarot reading, it is seldom taught in the schools. Which is too bad, because besides being important for good health, it's really easy to do!

If you don't know how already, try this. Close your eyes. OK, open them, and read the rest of this description. Then close them again, and remember what I said. Or read it to yourself on a tape recorder, and play it back. Or have someone else read it out loud to you. It's probably best to do this while sitting comfortably in a chair, legs uncrossed, and feet flat on the floor. Try not to have any part of your body resting on any other part.

Close your eyes, relax, and take three deep breaths, in through your nose and out through your mouth. Count 1, 2, 3, 4 as you inhale, and 5, 6, 7, 8 as you exhale. Again, 1, 2, 3, 4, and 5, 6, 7, 8. And one more time 1, 2, 3, 4, and 5, 6, 7, 8. Relax your body. Feel all your muscles relax.

Now feel your energy, your essence, lining up in the center of your body.

At the base of your spine, at the bottom of your body, there is a red spot, a spot glowing red like the most beautiful of red Christmas lights. Line the red spot of your energy body up with the red spot of your physical body. If you can't feel it, just imagine you can. See them coming together perfectly in your mind's eye. When they are perfectly aligned, front to back and side to side, imagine you hear a tone in your mind's ear. Imagine a middle C, a clear chime sounding do *(doe.)*

In the middle of your belly, about the width of your hand down from your navel, there is an orange spot, glowing orange like the rising sun. Line the orange spot of your energy body with the orange spot of your physical body. Imagine them coming together perfectly, glowing orange. As they merge, front to back and side to side, and become one glowing orange spot, you hear a clear D tone. Imagine you hear a chime sounding re *(ray.)*

Above your navel, at the level of your diaphragm, is your solar plexus. There is a spot there, glowing yellow, a clear, bright yellow like the summer sun. Line the yellow spot of your energy body with the yellow spot of your physical body. Let them flow together to become one glowing yellow spot. And as they join, and become one spot, front to back and side to side, imagine you hear a chime, a clear note sounding E. A silver chime singing mi *(me.)*

At your heart there is a green spot, a spot glowing green like the sun through the leaves in early June. Feel the green spot of your energy body lining up with the green spot of your physical body. Feel them coming together, and becoming a single spot. Merging into a single spot, glowing green. And as they merge into one spot, front to back and side to side, hear a tone, a chime, sounding F. A clear chime singing fa *(fa.)*

In the middle of your throat, at your adam's apple, there is a blue spot. A clear bright blue spot like the sky by the ocean on a cloudless May morning. A beautiful spot, glowing blue. Bring the blue spot of your energy body into alignment with the blue spot of your physical body. Coax them together until they become one spot, from front to back, and from side to side. And as they flow into a single spot, a single spot glowing beautiful blue, hear a G. A clear, beautiful tone, singing* so *(so.)*

In the middle of your forehead, where your "third eye" is, there is an indigo spot. A spot glowing with a deep blue-violet color, like a summer sky after the sunset has faded, but before the stars come out. Glowing a serene blue-violet, a beautiful indigo. Imagine you are bringing the indigo spot of your energy body into perfect alignment with the indigo spot of your physical body. In your mind's eye, see them lining up perfectly front to back and side to side so that they become one spot; one brilliant glowing indigo spot. And as they come together perfectly, you hear a chime, a note. You hear the note A. Singing out brilliant and beautiful, the tone* la *(la.)*

On the very top of your head, on the middle of your crown, there is a violet spot. A beautiful, glowing violet spot, like the most perfect of violets growing in April. Glowing and lovely, a violet spot. Now match the violet spot of your energy body with the violet spot of your physical body. Bring them together, let them merge into each other, front to back and side to side, until there is only one spot. One beautiful glowing violet spot. And as they become one, hear a note, sounding clearly, hear a B. Hear a crystal chime, singing the note* ti *(tea.)*

Now imagine your spots all lined up; all the beautiful colors glowing, and perfectly aligned. Your energy body and your physical body occupy exactly the same space. This is easy, because it's how you are meant to be. It feels good, it feels right, it feels strong. As you see your bodies perfectly aligned, as you see the spots of light forming a single straight line from your tailbone to the top of your head, imagine the whole thing wrapped in a white light. As you do so, imagine you hear the final tone. You hear high C,* do *again, completing the scale, and completely balancing the energy of the spots.*

Now you are Centered. See what it feels like? You should do this every day, whether you are reading cards or not, just to keep in practice and keep all the energies of your bodies flowing easily. As you do it, you will find that it becomes even easier to do, until you will be able to just take a deep breath, and zip yourself into line like a zipper!

By the way, if you have somehow become way far out of alignment (and if you have, don't be ashamed. You can't expect yourself to do something no one ever taught you to do; and you could hardly be farther out than I used to be, before I learned how to do this) you may find it easier to go the other direction; from your head down to your tailbone. If you do, then do it that way. Eventually, though, I would recommend learning to go this direction. It makes it easier to do other things later.

And, in case you haven't caught it, the spots of color that I've been talking about are the energy vortexes commonly called "chakras." There is a wealth of information available about them, so I'm not going to go into any of that here. Suffice it to say that if you visualize them as bright and glowing every day, it will go far toward keeping them "open" and in good health. Which means to say, the energy will flow properly, which is what we are after, after all.

And now that you are all Centered, it's time to Ground. Once again, I'm going to talk you through it. It will be easiest to tape this, or have a friend read it aloud to you.

Relax, Center yourself, and then take three deep, long breaths, in through your nose, and out through your mouth. Count 1, 2, 3, 4 as you inhale, and 5, 6, 7, 8 as you exhale. Again, 1, 2, 3, 4, and 5, 6, 7, 8. And one more time 1, 2, 3, 4, and 5, 6, 7, 8. Relax your body.

Now imagine that you have a root, that grows from the base of your spine. Imagine the white light you wrapped around all of your spots becoming a cord that connects all the beautiful spots of light, so they can all communicate with one another. All of your glowing spots are connected by a white cord of energy, and the cord grows out of the base of your spine.

As it grows, it becomes whatever color you are most comfortable with.

And this glowing root leaves your body, and stretches down into the earth. Feel it penetrating the chair you are sitting on. It easily penetrates the chair, because that is the nature of this root. It is strong and subtle, and can slip through physical matter as if it wasn't there.

Now feel it continuing to reach down, down, down through the floor, and the foundation of the building you are in. All the way down, down, down until it reaches the earth the building stands on.

Feel your root growing into the good, rich earth. Smell the smell of the soil, and taste the water that lies beneath. Taste the taste of rock, and hear the heartbeat of the Earth.

And you can feel your root growing deeper and deeper, down, down, down into the earth, toward the heartbeat of the Earth.

And as you feel your root growing downward, you sense that there is a wonderful, limitless, glowing pool of pure energy down there. And you know that the Earth is alive, and full of energy; more energy than you have ever imagined, more than you could ever need. And the Earth loves you, and wants to share this energy with you. You are Her child, and this energy is there for you to use.

Now grow your root down into this energy. Feel the clean, pure, boundless, limitless energy of the Earth. And as you touch this energy, and taste its light and pureness, your root will automatically begin to draw the energy up into your body, because that's what roots do.

Now feel the energy. Feel the bright, true, beautiful glowing energy of the Earth flowing up your root. Feel it flow into your body, filling it with wholeness and love, and softly glowing light. Feel yourself become full of energy, the clean energy of the Earth.

This wonderful energy moves easily up your root. And now it's in your body, and flowing up the cord between your own energy pools, cleaning, renewing, and revitalizing them as it goes.

And when it reaches the top of your head, let it flow out of the top of your head, out of the violet spot on the top of your head, flowing up like a fountain, like a bubbling spring, like the trunk of a tree. Flowing up, and carrying all the old, tired energy out of your body with it.

And as it reaches the top of the flow, let it fall back down to the Earth all around you. Let it return to the Earth, like a fountain arching down to its basin, like the branches of a beautiful weeping willow sweeping the earth. Let the energy flow all through you, and up, and out of you, and back down.

Pull the energy up, and let it flow through and back down, up and through and down, up and through and down to return to the Earth. Let it flow so that you are the middle of a circle, a circuit, a fountain of energy, flowing easily up and through and down into the Earth.

And when you are finished using the energy of the Earth, when you no longer wish to maintain the circuit, see your root pulling back up into your body, into the base of your spine. Kiss the energy goodbye, and thank it, and pull your root back up into your body. You are left with exactly the right amount of energy. You are balanced, and have exactly the right amount of energy, not a single drop too little or too much. Keep every bit that you need, and return any excess energy safely and gratefully to the ground, leaving you perfectly balanced, with just the amount of energy that you are used to having, just the perfect amount. The only difference is that this energy is pure, and clean, and fresh. And you feel good. Not high, and not tired, just good. Calm and peaceful and serene and balanced.

And that's Grounding. The two most important things to remember about it are to Center first, and to always, always, always balance the energy at the end, so you have the same amount you started with. I can't emphasize this too much.

When you first start doing this, you may be tempted to quit when you are still too full of energy. After all, it feels really good. You feel charged, and strong, and ready for anything. Who wouldn't want to keep that feeling?

Or perhaps you have the opposite problem. You may be so afraid of keeping extra, that you let too much drain after you have withdrawn your root, and end up with too little.

You will want to avoid either of these. Any unbalance in energy will eventually get you. If you try to hold more energy than is normal for you, or give too much back to the earth, it has an effect, just the way the eating too much or too little has an effect.

If you eat too much you will feel bloated and uncomfortable. If you hold too much energy, you will get a severe headache, and feel out of sorts, groggy, and uncomfortable. Not right away, but within a few hours.

If you eat too little, you will feel empty and grumpy. If you keep too little energy, you will get a headache again, and feel drained, tired, and lethargic. Once again, it may not hit you for a little while, but it will hit you.

If you find yourself feeling either way, or even a little headachy, after Grounding and Centering, then Ground and Center again. But this time, make sure that you retain *exactly* as much energy as you are used to. If you tell yourself that you are going to keep exactly as much as is normal for you, and return to a perfectly balanced state, you will. You don't need to worry about how much that is; your various bodies will take care of that for you. They know. Trust them.

As with Centering, Grounding becomes easier as you get used to it. With practice, you can walk around Grounded and Centered most or all of the time. Until you are used to it, you may find yourself falling out of it not because it's tiring, or difficult, but because it does take some concentration. Remember when driving took all of your brain cells, and you had to consciously think about how to put your feet on the pedals, and how to hold your hands on the wheel, and when to turn the indicators on, and watch the traffic, and watch the road for potholes, and try to stay in the middle of your lane, oh and don't forget, don't get lost or miss your turn!? But now it's all just second nature (at least it is if you've been driving for several years) and all you really have to worry about is the suicidal maniacs and missing your turn. Grounding and Centering becomes second nature, too. Eventually you simply do it when you do it!

Like Centering, it's a good idea to do this for at least a few moments every day. You might find that the combination, Grounding and Centering, is a wonderful resource to have when facing the stresses we all face. It's marvelously calming, and nothing restores your equilibrium better.

So, to get back to the topic of reading the Tarot cards, first find a nice, quiet place free of interruptions, and then Ground and Center.

The third step is to figure out your question. This is perhaps the hardest part of reading the cards, since the usefulness of your answer is totally dependent on how you ask the question.

There are basically three kinds of questions. The first can be summed up as "What do I need to know about this?" That is simple and straightforward, and can be asked exactly like that. In fact, I find that this is the best way of using the cards, since they will tell you what you *should* know, and not confine themselves to what you *want* to know!

The second type is a plain yes or no. "Should I do this?" In my experience, this is a little light for the cards. They tend to give you more information than you need if you ask a question like this (after all, they are designed to do that) and sometimes it's difficult to sort out the simple answer. Sometimes, of course, it's glaringly obvious; but this is often not the best kind of question to ask unless you are doing a very simple two or three card spread. It has always seemed to me that if all you want is yes or no, with no information about why or why not, you are better off with a simpler system. In such a case, the real question seems to me to be, "If I do this, what will happen?" This gives the cards the scope to answer the way they do best; by telling you all about the past, present, and future of the situation, and basically giving you insight about it.

The third type of question can be summarized as "Should I do A or B?" If you ask it like that, once again, the answer you get is likely to be foggy at best. You may wind up with a reading that clearly shows that it will be difficult at first, but things will work themselves out, and you will achieve the final outcome you want. But is it talking about A or B? How can you tell? Or the reading may come up as so much conflicting stuff, with no clear answer anywhere. This isn't surprising. If you knew the answer to someone's question, and couldn't say a single word, but had to convey the answer by lying out a handful of cards from a deck of only 78, how would you do with a foggy question?

If I need to know an A or B question, I find that I get much better results by first asking, "If I do A, what will be the outcome?" and then doing another reading, asking about B. It's usually pretty easy to choose between the two outcomes. And on those occasions when it isn't, I either decide that it doesn't really matter that much, or I do another reading to get further insight.

Because that's what it's all about, I think. The whole point of using the cards is to gain insight into a problem when all the normal "mundane" means of telling which direction to leap don't seem clear enough.

While we are on the topic, there are two different viewpoints about having the Seeker tell you what their question is.

I usually do, because I think it helps the Seeker to focus.

Some don't, because they find that if no question is verbalized, the cards will answer what the Seeker needs to know. I have a friend who says that, for her, nine times out of ten the answer has nothing to do with the question anyway.

Whether you wish to have the Seeker ask aloud or not, of course, is up to you.

Alright. You are in a quiet place, free of distractions. You have Grounded and Centered, and figured out how to ask your question.

The next thing I suggest you do is mentally state your purpose and intent, dedicate the reading to the God or Gods of your choice, bless the cards, and ensure the truth will manifest in the reading for the good of all and by the free will of all.

Something like this. "Lovely Lady, Laughing Lord; I, (Name,) intend to use these cards, to find out (question) for (Seeker's name.) I dedicate this reading and these cards to you. Lend me your power, as I will that this reading reflect only truth, wisdom, and harmony with the universe. Teach us what we need to learn. Enlighten me. Give me the wisdom to understand and the words to explain that truth, wisdom, and harmony. Bless this reading and these cards, and give me the courage and compassion to give good counsel, that this situation may be resolved for the ultimate good, in accordance with that harmony. This I do will for the good of all, and by the free will of all.* So mote it be."

This makes sure the reading will be accurate and in accord with the harmony of the universe. It also makes sure that nothing baneful can use the reading for its own purposes. Not that anything baneful is likely to want to; but it never hurts to be careful and sure. And it helps you to focus your intent and will on just exactly what you want, and communicates this to your subconscious mind.

So, now you are in a quiet place, Grounded and Centered, your question in mind, and the cards dedicated and blessed. You are ready to roll.

This is where things like shuffling and cutting come in. Some people prefer to let the person who is going to ask the question, who I call the Seeker, to shuffle the cards. Other people don't feel comfortable letting anyone but themselves touch their cards, ever. In this, as in any other question about the care and treatment of your cards, do what you feel is best. Don't let anyone else tell you that your method is wrong. There are no wrong methods! All of this is very personal, and what you personally feel is the right way to handle it *is* the right way for you personally!

So, do what you feel most comfortable with.

What I do is begin shuffling as soon as I have Grounded and Centered, as I begin figuring out the question. I continue to shuffle all through that process, and during the dedication and blessing. I do all the shuffling myself. When I feel that I have shuffled long enough, I put the cards down, and lay my left hand on them, to unveil the hidden things. While I do this, I will the truth to be revealed once again, for the good of all and by the free will of all. Sort of giving the cards an extra oomph.

Then I cut the deck into three piles. If I am reading for someone else, I ask them to choose a pile. When they pick one, I use the old slight-of-hand trick, and

---

*It's a good idea when doing any kind of magical working to include this phrase, just in case you aren't all knowing. It keeps you from accidentally stepping where you shouldn't and picking up the bad karma associated with that. A sort of magically covering your heinie.

either put that pile on the top, or on the bottom, depending on what I feel is the right way at that time. If I'm reading for myself, I still stack the three piles up in whatever order I feel is correct; I just don't say anything while I'm doing it.

Then I begin to lay out the cards.

The important thing to remember when you are doing a reading is that it will be as valuable and accurate as you allow it to be. What makes you a Reader, and makes you more valuable than a computer generated reading, is *you*.

In my opinion, which is entirely mine, we all have psychic ability. There is nothing supernatural about it; it's as natural as breathing. And like breathing, we usually don't think about it at all. We use it for everything from talking to our loved ones to deciding not to get on that particular train. (Ever do any research into just how many fewer people than normal are on a train that is going to crash? Look into it sometime. It's fascinating.)

The problem arises when we become conscious of it; when we think of it as something unnatural, that we can use for some things. Then, just like we can hold our breath, we suppress our natural psychic abilities.

Sometimes we do this because we are all rationalists, due to societal training. If we can't think of any really good, rational reason not to get on the train, then we do, against all our better instincts. And when it crashes, we say, "I knew I shouldn't have boarded this one!" But we do, because we don't want to appear superstitious or irrational.

Only if we are labeled "psychic" do we seem able to relax and go with it.

So I'm telling you now, you are a Psychic. There. Now relax and go with it.

You don't really need the books to tell you what the cards say, as I've said before. Your wonderful mind, and your inborn, normal, natural psychic abilities will do that. All you have to do is look at the pictures, relax, and tell the story that you see there.

I denied for years that I'm psychic, even when I realized that everyone is. I have come to understand that was mostly because I was afraid of two things. The first was that if I was seen as psychic, then people would want to put me in some position of responsibility. Since I hate telling people what to do, or being responsible for anyone (or anything) but myself, I didn't want that. The second was that people would hate me, or fear me, or hurt me. Well, they might. People hate, fear, and hurt other people all the time. But that's no reason to cripple or limit myself.

Your reasons are your own, and you will have to find them yourself. But I suggest that you do so. There is no reason for you to be crippled or limited either!

So when you are settling down to read, find a quiet place, Ground and Center, find the question, dedicate and bless the cards, shuffle, and relax and read, listening to your instincts and feelings as you go, so your inborn psychic talent can manifest.

What spread you use isn't really that important. I'll be discussing a few spreads later; but for right now assume that you are using one that you like, and that feels appropriate to you in this situation. (Notice I said "feels" again.)

If you are reading for yourself, then all you have to do at this point is be honest with yourself, and take advantage of the knowledge that the cards can bring you.

A brief caveat here; some folk find that they cannot read for themselves at all. They get too wound up in what they want or fear, find it too hard to be objective, and get into a sort of feedback loop, where their desires or fears are magnified in the cards; but it has no bearing on life in the consensual universe (the world as we all know it.)

If this is you, don't fret. You are in plenty of good company. An awful lot of people can't heal themselves, or scratch the middle of their own backs, either. Some can. It doesn't really reflect on your value or worthwhileness as a person, or your degree of evolution, or any other buzzword at all. You can try learning to be more objective. It probably won't hurt you. But you may find it better to just get someone else to do your readings for you.

It's when you are reading for someone else, though, that all kinds of other issues pop up.

We call these the ethics of reading, and I'll cover them in the next chapter.

Chapter 13
Tarot Ethics

You may be wondering what ethics could possibly have to do with reading the Tarot. I mean, you just lay out the cards, and what you see is what you say, right?

Ah yes. But how do you say it? And when should you say things, and when should you keep silent? And what do you do if the reading distinctly shows that the Seeker is doing something she shouldn't oughta be doing?

And is trying to find out the future ethical in the first place? I was raised to believe that the future is the province of the Lord, and He would tell us what we needed to know in His own good time.

I'm going to address the last point first. In my opinion, which is only mine, the Tarot is about a whole lot more than predicting the future. It's about where you are on the path you are following, and what shape that path is taking. Where it comes from and where it's going. That's why at least as many of the cards in most spreads deal with the past and the present as deal with the future.

As such, it can cast some light for our steps (visions of the Hermit card.) And I think it is far better to be aware of what you are doing and where your path is taking you than to wander blindfolded and simply hope for the best. I don't think it's the Gods' job to watch our every footstep. I think we need to grow up a little and start watching our own feet!

So what happens when that light reveals something that the Seeker might rather keep hidden?

I think that, as Readers, we have a responsibility to those who come to us, seeking for the truth.

It's not our place to decide that they don't need the bit of truth that is all over the table, staring us in the face, simply because it might be unpleasant to deal with.

Truth often is.

But if the Seeker doesn't know the truth, they can't possibly do anything about it. If you don't warn the blind fellow about the truck barreling down on him, he is unlikely to get out of the way.

I don't think this is a popularity contest. Sure, people might like you better if all of your readings were sunny and bright, and only a few things were accurate.

Truth is often scary, especially when you know things you couldn't possibly have any way to know. People like to think that their secrets are safe, and that the things their own unconscious minds are screaming about are just nightmares. Too much spicy food, or that movie they watched on TV last night. Not something really, seriously wrong in their lives.

But they suspect something, or some part of them really wants to know, or they wouldn't be coming to you.

And that is the first thing you should do, I think. Make sure that the Seeker is there of his own free will. Not because of peer pressure, or because someone gave him the reading as a gift.

I don't ever take money for a reading. Part of this is because of religious considerations (I don't take money for practicing my Art, and that's what reading is.) Part is because never taking money effectively removes the temptation to read when I am too tired or ill to do it right. Part is because if no money changed hands, the Seeker also feels that she can leave, or discount the reading, if she finds she isn't really comfortable with it. And part is because no one can coerce someone else to get a reading from me by paying for it.

Like other forms of counseling, it does little good if the Seeker doesn't want it, and isn't interested in hearing about where they are, or where they're going. And if the Seeker doesn't want to change, no change is going to happen!

So, first I ask if the Seeker is sure they want this. I ask them how familiar they are with the Tarot, and if they say they have never had a reading before, but it looks like fun, I warn them that it isn't a party game, and I don't do it for kicks. If they still think it's all in fun, I usually don't read for them. I don't do this for entertainment. I'll talk to them about the cards, and answer any questions they might have about them; and sometimes as we talk they realize that it's not just a game. But if they are busy playing Hide and Seek in the dusk, they probably won't appreciate having the spotlight turned on.

The other thing I think vitally important is to realize that the Reader cannot abrogate her responsibility. I had someone during one of my Tarot discussions at a convention say that she nevers remembers what she says during a reading, because she is channeling all of it, and that people tend to bolt screaming from her table.

Please listen to me. If you are channeling an entity that leaves you no memories, and that frightens people that badly, I suggest that you seriously reconsider what you are doing.

Harming other people is a bad idea for a lot of reasons, and frightening someone that severely can do them harm.

We aren't in this for thrills or self aggrandizement. Please don't intentionally try to frighten your Seekers, just to make yourself look more powerful.

Remember the Strength card.

Real power doesn't need to show off.

We are in this to help people, and badly frightened people aren't usually paying much attention. A bad scare triggers something called the "Flight or Fight" reaction. The system is flooded with adrenaline, the thinking part of the brain goes "off line," and the animal part is left behind to run away or fight to the death. This is a recipe for overreaction. And what people fear, they must eliminate. Scare enough people badly enough, and you will be shocked at the kind of reaction you eventually get.

Besides, they won't listen to a thing you say.

When I was a kid, I couldn't see very well; so I was constantly running into things, or knocking things over and breaking them. When I think back on my childhood, sometimes it seems like a long string of broken china and crystal. But my mother learned fairly early that if she saw me standing with my elbows out right next to her prize pitcher she shouldn't become alarmed and shout, "Look out! Right next to your elbow!" That was sure to make me whirl around and send it crashing to the ground. If, instead, she calmly asked me to come to her, I would, and the pitcher would be safe.

Do you see what I'm getting at here? Frightened people act impulsively and abruptly, without thought. Since our goal is to help people, we should try not to frighten them.

I'm not talking about them finding our accuracy scary. I haven't found any way to avoid that, although it, too, can be helped by being super calm about it; or grinning and saying, "Yeah. It spooked me too, at first."

I'm talking about you, as the Reader, reacting to a reading as if it were frightening. Even if it is, keep calm. And whatever you do, don't try to deliberately scare the pants off a Seeker, even if you think a good scare might be good for them. That's not your place.

Next, remember that the cards don't show physical death. The Death card is change, not physical death. The Tarot ignores physical death entirely. I think that may be because death is just another step along the path, and sometimes it's not a very important one. All I know for sure is that the Tarot doesn't seem to care.

So if you think you see death in the cards, examine them more closely. It's more likely to be a sudden, involuntary change; or the ending of a friendship, a business relationship, or an attitude.

Now, what do you do when you lay out the cards, and see that something unpleasant is going to happen?

The first thing you should do, before you say anything to your Seeker or react at all, is to determine why this thing looks likely, and if there is anything that can be done about it at this point.

If the unpleasantness is in the past, the Seeker already knows about it. Don't worry. Just use it to establish timelines and accuracy.

If it's in the present or the future, look at the significator and the past cards and see if a pattern emerges that explains why this is going on.

I begin broaching the subject by asking the Seeker if there is something in particular they are worried about right now. Watch carefully for non-verbal cues as you do this. Be sensitive to the mood and attitude of the Seeker.

If she is forthcoming, and says, "Yes. I'm having some problems with ___," and that's what you saw, then you can begin to talk about it. Explain how the things in the past affected this, and what she needs to be careful about. If you know something about the subject under discussion, you may want to share your knowledge. For instance, if she feels like she has the flu all the time, and you know that sounds like Fibromyalgia because your sister has it, you may want to tell her what you know about the syndrome, and suggest that she see a rheumatologist. If she tells you that she is depressed all the time, because it's winter, you may want to recommend that she see a psychiatrist about that. If she tells you she doesn't know what to do, because her boyfriend is beating her, explain where she can go for help. Don't make a diagnosis (unless you are a doctor, of course) but don't be afraid to recommend a professional if that seems like the wisest course.

Most people, of course, will have problems they just want to talk about. This is when it might be helpful for you to have a course in counseling under your belt. If you are interested in getting one, try volunteering for your local hot line – they usually provide some training, and can almost always use the help. Or check your local area's religious network (for your religion, or for another.) They often provide lay counseling training.

If you have to go it alone, remember that most people know the answers to their problems. They just need the chance to let their mouths run until the answer comes out! And when it does, mostly what they are looking for is validation. They don't want to hear about your problems, although short anecdotes may make them feel less alone. And if you have a good strategy for dealing with a particular problem, by all means share it. But let the Seeker do most of the talking.

As an example, if they are worried because they don't have any money, don't tell them all about the time you were dead broke. Say, "I know what you mean. I've always found it helps to budget a few luxuries that don't really cost much. A good chocolate truffle, for instance, is less than a dollar, really. But if you treat yourself to one once a month or so, you feel like you couldn't possibly really be this broke. At least, it always helped me." Then listen, really listen, to what they are saying.

Don't be judgmental. If you tell someone, "Well, it's your own fault, really. What do you expect trying to live with two men at once?" they will instantly stop listening to you. How they live, or who they live with, is their own choice. This is their path, and their life; not yours. As long as they aren't harming anyone, their choice is valid for them. As long as they aren't trying to make you live your life their way, it's none of your business, really!

Don't be critical. Once again, telling someone off will ensure that their ears, at least, turn off! That's not what they are there for.

Don't tell someone what to do. Even if they ask you, I think this puts you on really shaky ethical ground. Before you do it, ask yourself why they are trying to get you to take the responsibility here. By all means tell them what you might do in their place, or what a friend of yours did. But what they do is entirely up to them. Make that crystal clear; or they may be back on your doorstep in a few weeks or months, blaming you for their troubles.

In my experience, people who ask someone else to just tell them what to do with their lives are trying to duck the responsibility themselves.

Remember that everyone already knows the best path for themselves. They just need room to acknowledge that wisdom, and perhaps emotional (or material) support in order to take the step.

Be gentle, be understanding, be supportive if you can. You are really acting as a counselor here; so be the best counselor you can be. And always remember that anything they tell you, or anything you discover, is privileged information. It should never be discussed with anyone else.

Chapter 14
Spreads

When I originally planned this book, I was going to put a whole chapter about spreads in here. But, as you may have noticed, the book got very long. So, after thinking about it for quite a while, I've decided to touch on them briefly, and then really explore the topic in a workbook that will be a companion for this one.

There are thousands of ways of laying the cards down to do a reading. We refer to these as *spreads*.

Some people use the same spread all of the time. Some use different kinds of spreads for different kinds of readings or questions. One reader I know uses a different spread every time that she reads. (They come to her spontaneously, straight from the unconscious. If you want to do this, just invent them as you go along. It works the same way!)

Most spreads are composed of three parts. One part describes the past, and is a good way to see how things the Seeker has already experienced foreshadow what is going on now, or provide strengths to lean on or weaknesses to overcome in the present situation. If you think of life as a school, with lessons to be learned, then the cards that describe the past show an earlier part of the same lessons. They are also a good way to test for the accuracy of the reading. If the Seeker can't remember anything like that happening, then you may wonder about your accuracy at this particular time. (Even a very good Reader can have an "off" day, due to illness, exhaustion, distraction, etc.)

The cards that show the past also give some idea of the time involved in a reading. If you can pinpoint an event shown here, then the cards that show the future (we'll get to them in a moment!) are usually about the same amount of time ahead. In other words, if The Lovers comes up in the past, and you get the immediate impression that that marks a time when the Seeker found her life mate, and she knows that happened a year ago, then you can be pretty sure that the cards which show the future will be about a year from now.

The second part usually found in a spread describes the present situation; what is going on in the Seeker's life right now. This part usually has cards that describe what the Seeker fears, what she hopes for, what the environment is like, and what her attitudes now are.

This section helps the Seeker to become aware of what is actually going on around her. Often we miss the things we should be paying attention to, because they get lost in the "background noise" of our lives. (I have maintained for years that that's because we don't have background music. If we did, we'd know when important things were happening, and when not to step off the curb, or open the door! If the people on television paid attention to their background music, they wouldn't make half the mistakes they make!) These cards can pull the important things out of the background, and make the Seeker aware of them. At the very least, they can help the Seeker verbalize what is going on, and bring it from the unconscious to the conscious part of her mind.

The final section in most spreads describes the future. When you get to this future, remember that this isn't the "written in stone" kind of future. It's the "if you keep on the way you are going" kind of future, like all futures are.

Think of it as if you, the Reader, were standing on top of a hill, watching the Seeker walk down the street. From where you stand, you can see around a corner that is hidden from the Seeker. You can also see farther down the street in both directions. You may see a storm blowing up, and know it's coming his way. You also see that if he keeps walking the way he is, he'll pass a hardware store, a school, and a young woman with a baby even though he can't see them, because of the hill. You can also see that if he turns the corner that is invisible to him, he'll get caught in a crowd of spectators watching a street performer.

He is probably aware of the storm, although he doesn't know exactly where it is. He may also be aware of the crowd, because he can hear them. But he can't tell exactly where they are, either. He doesn't know if they are directly in his path, or not.

If you both had walkie-talkies, you could let him know what he would find if he goes on the way he is. At that point, he'll know, and the choice will be his. He may decide to turn the corner, because he has always liked street performers, and wants to see the act. He may decide to avoid the crowd, or meet the woman and baby, or drop into the hardware store. But he isn't compelled to pass by the performance, just because you saw that it wasn't on the path he is on now, any more than he is compelled to walk past the woman. He always has the choice. All you are doing is warning him about it slightly sooner than he would have otherwise found out.

And some of the things around him may change before he gets there, because of the free will of the other people involved. The performance may end, and he may be just in time to see the crowd breaking up. Or the young woman may go into the school, and not be on the sidewalk at all by the time that he gets there.

This doesn't mean that they weren't where you saw them when you saw them. It just means that things are constantly changing.

Remember this when you read the cards, and you'll be able to give much more accurate readings. Some things are decided by the free will of the Seeker, or the other people involved. Some things are so large that they are more or less fixed (like the school, or the store.) Some things are hard to avoid, like the rain. Most of the time the fixed things, or those that are hard to avoid, are represented by cards from the Major Arcana. If you can tell the difference, and communicate to the Seeker that he is in control here, and this is just information about the way things are leaning, then you'll be well on your way to doing your job. (Remember, even if there are a lot of Majors, and it looks like the Seeker is just going to have to ride it out, he can still control his attitudes, and how well he learns!)

Some spreads have other parts, that are unique to the spread, such as the influence of the stars in an astrological spread, or the elements in an elemental spread.

Because of space, I'm only going to give you three spreads here. The first is the one I almost always use myself.

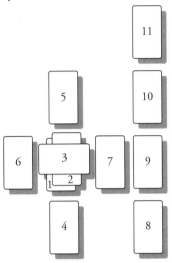

A Modified Celtic Cross

(Don't ask me why it's called that. I know it's not Celtic, and it's hardly even a cross! I think it's because it looked to someone like the stone crosses that dot the Celtic countryside, and the rod up the side was added later; but I'm just making that up.)

The first card to be laid out is the Significator. Some people choose a significator; a card that has special meaning for the Seeker, or just happens to look like her. (Using the Queen of Pentacles for a mature woman with dark hair and eyes, for instance.) I don't do this for three reasons. The first reason is that when used the first way it limits the significator to something you already know about the person, and takes one card out of the deck. That card may be far more appropriate in some other position. The second is that if you choose a card by physical type, then anyone who isn't Caucasian is perforce a member of the court of Pentacles. I think that's silly. And the final reason is that I'm not always able to give a good reading, because of a whole host of factors. I use the Significator as the first check for accuracy.

I let the deck choose the Significator. It's the first card I lay down. As I place it, face up, on the table I say, "This card is you." And most of the time, it's clear that it is showing some aspect of the Seeker. If it's way off base, then I start to wonder.

The second card I lay down is the Question. It shows, in a single card, the main thing the Seeker is concerned about in this reading. As I place it on top of the Significator, so only a bit shows underneath, I say, "This card is the Question." Once again, most of the time it's obvious that it is. If it isn't, and if the Significator appears to be off-base too, then I ask myself if there is something blocking me at this time.

I usually find that there is. I'm tired, or hungry, or distracted by something, or would really like to be doing something else, or have some unfinished business with the Seeker that is in the way of the reading, or I just have a hunch that I really shouldn't be doing this reading at all.

In any case, unless I get a clear feeling that the question asked is not the question the Seeker really needs answered, and what we are going to address here is the real question, I pack up the cards at this point. If I can't give an accurate reading, then there is no point in going through with this, and it's even likely to be counter-productive.

That is one of the reasons I don't accept money for reading the cards. When it becomes clear that I can't do this reading right now, I have no problem apologizing for the disappointment, explaining if I can, and picking all the cards up. If I were being paid, I might feel an obligation to continue; and that, for me, would not always be a good idea.

You have to decide this issue for yourself.

But, assuming that the Significator and the Question make sense, I am ready for the next card.

This is the card I call "The Cross." I put it down perpendicular to the two cards already down, and as I do I say, "This crosses it, a bridge and a block." This card is the one that could stymie further progress, and/or could be used to cross from one part of the pattern to the other; from the past to the future. This may seem contradictory at first, but it depends on how you look at things. (Actually, everything in your life depends on how you look at things.) For example, lets say that when you laid this card down it was the Nine of Swords. This is not generally seen as an auspicious card. It shows a young person, sitting up in bed with her face in her hands, clutching the covers in her fist, obviously in despair. Behind her, nine identical swords hang unsupported against a black background. This is the card I call "Night Terrors." It's a bad case of the "3 A.M.-sies;" the time in the blackest part of the night when you wake up, and doubt that anything will ever turn be alright again.

I don't use reversed cards (I think there are enough cards in the deck to describe anything; and reversed cards are simply unnecessarily confusing.) But even so, there are two ways to look at this. As you will find if you look in the description of this card, all of these swords are the same. It's not an overwhelming number of problems; it's a single problem that has assumed overwhelming magnitude. So in the reading I might say, "Your fear of this situation has led you to blow it all out of proportion, until it looks insurmountable. That's blocking any progress, because you are afraid to try to go forward. But you can use that very fear as a bridge. If you stare it down, you will notice that it is only one problem, like there is really only one sword here. And with that knowledge, and with the magic that is also at your command, which you can see here in the symbols on the quilt, you can face this and use it as a stepping stone to the next point. And once you have, you will never be quite as paralyzed by fear like this again, because you will know you can overcome it!"

You get the idea. Anything, represented by any card, can block your progress along your path. And anything, represented by any card, can serve as a bridge to further progress. It all depends on how you let if affect you.

The next card I lay below the first three. As I do so, I say "Below you, to build on." This card represents the strengths (or weaknesses) a person has in their background, that will prove useful in this situation. It may show a similar problem, successfully overcome in the past, or point to an individual that could help them. Or it may be an attribute of their own character. If it seems to be showing a weakness, instead of a strength, then go with that feeling. (Always go with your feelings when you are reading the cards. That's what they are for!)

The fifth card goes directly above the first three. As I lay it down, I say "Above you." It represents the things that are coming, that have a bearing on this situation. The card shown here will be about as far in the future as the previous card was behind in the past. Remember, it's not a fixed future; it's a tendency, if things continue as they are now.

The sixth card goes to the left of the first three, and as I lay it down I say, "In the recent past." It shows the influences that have just finished bearing on the situation. Things that the Seeker can probably recognize, that had a direct effect on what is going on, although that effect is likely to be waning at this time.

The seventh card goes to the right of the first three, and as I lay it down I say, "In the near future." It shows what is about to happen if things continue unchanged. At this point, it often becomes clear exactly what the third card, the "Bridge or Block" was bridging or blocking. This will also lead into the "Above" card, so the Seeker can use this point as a corner in the path, to turn away from the Above if he doesn't like the look of it.

That completes the cross. The next four cards are laid out in a vertical line to the right of the cross, starting from the bottom. This is called the "rod."

As the eighth card is laid down, I say, "This is you right now." This card represents the Seeker at this moment in time. It may show his emotional state, his perceptions about the situation, or the part he is playing in this drama, whether he is aware of it or not. Normally, the Seeker has no trouble seeing himself in that card.

The ninth card goes directly above the eighth. As I lay it down I say, "This is your environment, your family, and your friends." This card represents the people and influences around the Seeker. It can show support, active opposition, hidden opposition, other plans for him, and so on.

The tenth card goes above the ninth. As I lay it down I say, "This shows your hopes and fears." Once again, the hopes and fears are in the same card, because these two things are often mixed. You hope for something at the same time that you fear that thing will change your life beyond recognition. Familiarity is, at least, comfortable. And any change great enough to hope for carries its own fear of the change with it. You can hope to marry the person you are dating, and yet fear the marriage won't work out; or hope to win the lottery, and yet fear that your family will hate you if you don't share the money equally with them, and so on.

The eleventh card goes directly above the tenth. As I lay it down, I say, "And this is the final outcome." It shows how all the things that have gone before will combine to produce the end result of this situation. Remember, once again, that this is what the end result will be if the Seeker continues exactly as he is going; as if he had never had a reading done at all. If he doesn't like the final outcome shown here, he is free to change it, based on the path that he takes from this point.

As a matter of fact, when I am trying to decide between two courses of action, I frequently lay out the cards one time for the first course, and a second time for the second. For instance, if I were trying to decide whether or not to take a job, I would do one reading asking, "What will happen if I take this job," and a second asking, "What will happen if I don't take this job." Then I choose the outcome I like the best, and go that direction!

I'm sorry that there isn't room for a sample reading here, but I hope the information above makes it clear enough.

Now that you have an idea of how the mechanics of a spread work, I'm going to give you the last two spreads in abbreviated form. I'm sure that you can figure out for yourself what to say as you lay them down!

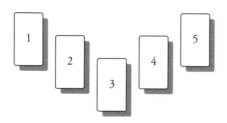

The Short Five Spread

This spread was invented by my husband, Michael Short, to get an answer to a very specific question.

The cards are laid out left to right, in a V shape.

Card 1 - The Question. This card shows the question being asked in symbolic terms. If it makes no sense, it may be best to postpone the reading.

Card 2 - The Background. This card describes the general situation and events leading up to the question.

Card 3 - The Seeker. This card represents the person asking the question. It may show what the Seeker has done to try to answer the question, or it may indicate the character strength (or flaw) which has the most bearing here.

Card 4 - The Environment. This card shows the impact of the world on this situation, including the influence of friends, family, and associates.

Card 5 - The Answer. This card shows the answer to the question. The appropriate action to take is inherent in the interpretation of this card.

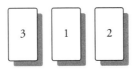

Yes/No Three

This is a simple spread that I developed to give a quick yes or no answer to a question. It's fast and easy, but it lacks depth.

The cards are laid out as shown in the diagram.

Card 1 - Question. This card shows in symbolic form the question that is being asked. If it makes no sense, then the reading is suspect, and should probably be skipped.

Card 2 - If Yes, Then. This card shows what will happen if yes is the answer chosen. It's more or less like skipping directly to the final outcome of a reading where the question was phrased, "If I do this, what will happen?"

Card 3 - If No, Then. This card shows what is likely to happen if "No" is the answer chosen. Like going directly to the final outcome of "If I don't do this, what will happen?"

Then the person asking the question (the Seeker) should choose which outcome they like best!

I don't use this very often, because it doesn't give any background. It tells you what is likely, but not why, or how to change it if you don't like either answer. If you don't like either outcome, by the way, I recommend doing one of the longer readings to determine what is going on, and how to arrive somewhere you want to be.

I hope this gives you enough to get started with. Remember, don't be afraid to make up your own spreads, now that you can get a feeling for the patterns involved. And if you wind up with a particularly great or useful one, share it with others!

Notes:

Appendix A
The Blind Men and the Elephant

Once upon a time, five blind men came upon an elephant.

"What is this?!" asked the first one, who had run headlong into its side.

"It's an Elephant." said the elephant's keeper, who was sitting on a stool, cleaning the elephant's harness.

"An Elephant! You don't say! An elephant is exactly like a large, warm wall!"

"Wall! What do you mean, wall!" exclaimed the second, who had hold of the elephant's tail, "It's nothing like a wall! An Elephant clearly has the same nature as a rope!"

"Well, if it's a rope, it's the thickest rope that ever was!" said the third, with his arms wrapped around one of the elephant's legs. "Thicker than my entire body! More like a pillar, I'd say."

"Strange pillar! No thicker than my arm, whatever you say," declared the fourth man, stoking the elephant's trunk. "And flexible as all get out to boot. Any fool can tell an Elephant is exactly like a Snake."

"You are all completely crazy!!" the fifth man cried, waving the elephant's ear back and forth. "It's large, all right, but thin as a leaf, and no more flexible than any piece of cloth this size should be. I don't know what's wrong with all of you, but no one except a complete idiot could mistake an Elephant for anything except a sail!!!"

And they tramped off down the road, arguing more loudly and violently as they went, each sure that he, and he alone, was right; and all the others were wrong.

The Elephant keeper sighed, and went back to polishing the harness, while the elephant winked solemnly at him.

Persephone was the daughter of Demeter and Zeus, and with her mother she was the Goddess of Vegetation and Growth.

Bright she was, and beautiful, as lovely as the flowers she tended so carefully, and the apple of her mother's eye. Young and supple, she delighted in play, and in the sunshine, and in all growing things.

Now one day when she was dancing among the flowers, she was seen by Hades, the God of the Underworld. He no sooner saw her, than he fell in love with her. And he no sooner loved her than he wanted her for his own. Now what he wanted, he was accustomed to take.

And so he took Persephone; grabbing her and holding her fast as his chariot thundered across her beloved fields. All of her screaming didn't help her, and all of her cries were in vain. Off they galloped to the River Cyane, but the River had no mind to let Persephone be carried off like that, and wouldn't let him pass.

This made Hades very angry, because he wasn't used to being opposed, and he struck the river bank with his trident, so that a great crack opened in it. And into this crack he rode with the sobbing Persephone; chariot, steeds, iron-colored reins and all. And the bank closed over them.

Now when evening came, and it was time for Persephone to return to her mother, she was nowhere to be found. Demeter, of course, became very anxious and worried, and began to search for her daughter.

All the world over she sought, day and night she sought, rain or fair weather she sought. But she found nothing.

Finally, in her seeking, she returned to the land where she had started, and sank down on the banks of the River Cyane to rest. Now the River Nymph knew what had happened, and she would gladly have told Demeter; but she was afraid of Hades, for he was terrible when he was angry.

But there was one thing she could do, and that she did. She picked up the girdle which Persephone had dropped while Hades was abducting her, and waved it at Demeter's feet.

Of course, Demeter recognized it immediately, and noticed where the Earth had opened and swallowed her daughter. But she still didn't know what had really happened. So, in her grief and loss, she blamed the Earth.

"Oh, ungrateful Earth!" she cried, "I've loved you and blessed you with fertility! I've clothed you with flowers, and covered you with grain, and shaded you with trees! But no more! You have stolen my daughter, and taken her from me, and now you shall be barren forevermore!!"

And as she spoke, it was so. All green and growing things withered, the rich soil turned to dust, and a desolate wind blew upon the land. And Demeter wept.

But there was a fountain there, named Arethusa, and when she realized what was happening, she decided that Hades couldn't be worse than this! So she called out, and said, "Oh Goddess, Great Demeter! Don't blame the innocent land. It opened unwillingly to give passage to your daughter. It had no choice, for Hades forced it. He it is who has stolen your daughter from you. He has taken her to his shadowy realms, to make her his Queen."

Now when she heard this, Demeter stopped her weeping, and stood silent and amazed. But as soon as she recovered from the shock, she sprang into her chariot, and rode as quickly as she could to Zeus.

There she pleaded with him to intervene, and to recover her daughter from Hades, through force or persuasion, it mattered not to her. Zeus looked at her; and she was distraught, and all the Earth with her. And he consented, on one condition; that Persephone had neither eaten nor drunk of anything during her stay in the Underworld. If she had, the Fates would not allow her to return.

So Hermes made the journey, and presented himself in Hades' realm, and demanded the return of Persephone, explaining the condition to him.

And when he heard, Hades consented. But he left Hermes waiting in his outer court, and went by himself into the room where Persephone was.

She was very beautiful, and she was dressed as a Queen; and at the sight of her, Hades realized that he could not simply give her up. So he picked up a pomegranate, and opened it, and held one half out to her, and said, "My dearest love. Long days have you spent here, with neither food nor drink, although I have offered you feasts and wine, and such dancing and song as there is in my realm. Please, for my sake, taste just a bit of this pomegranate. It's ripe, and sweet, and will ease my heart if you try it."

Then Persephone looked at it, and it did look very good. And she was very hungry. And Hades wasn't a bad sort, once you got used to him. And so she reached out, plucked a few seeds from the fruit, and sucked the pulp off of them.

Then Hades returned to Hermes, and said, "She is mine! She has eaten some seeds from a pomegranate, and now you cannot take her!"

But when he heard the news, Hermes' heart sank within him, for he realized that it spelled doom for all the world above. And he reasoned most sweetly with Hades, and finally they reached an agreement.

Persephone would spend one month with Hades for each seed she had eaten. For the rest of the year, she would return to her mother and the upper lands.

And so it was.

But Demeter still mourns for her daughter when she is away, and during that time, nothing grows upon the Earth. We call that Winter.

The rest of the year, Persephone dances among the flowers, and Demeter blesses the Earth with an abundance of fruit and grain, and that's Summer.

And for all we know, Hades also mourns Persephone when she is gone, and the Dead have a very hard time of it. But if that is so, none of them have ever told us.

Appendix C
The Wheel of the Year

The Wiccan year is divided into 8 parts, the Quarters and the Cross Quarters.

The Quarter celebrations are held at the two solstices and the two equinoxes; the longest and shortest days of the year, and the two days when night and day are equal in length.

The Cross-Quarter days are roughly midway between these days; on Feb. 2, May 1, August 1, and October 31.

We call all these days Sabbats, Feast Days, the Days of Festival.

Since we see the Wheel as round, and ever continuing, it really doesn't matter where one starts to count it; but traditionally the Wiccan year starts at Samhain, after dark on October 31.

The days themselves are as follows;

October 31 – Samhain (SEW-in or SOW-in (where sow is a female pig.))
This is the festival of the dead, All-Hallows-eve, when the Goddess gives the reins of government to the God. Here He presides, and the gates between the worlds are very thin. Now is the time to remember those we love who have died in the past year; for now they can join us in our celebration. The year is dying. We look forward to its rebirth. Colors for Samhain are black, red and orange. Plants associated with it are Indian corn, pumpkins, gourds, apples and corn stalks.

Winter Solstice (December 20 - 23) **– Yule** (Yule)
This is the festival of the return of the Sun, when the Great Mother brings him forth new-born. The colors associated with Yule are red and green; plants are the Yule Log, mistletoe, holly, pine and pine cones, and all sorts of nuts. Traditionally, a candle (or other flame) is left burning all night on this longest of nights, to teach the new Sun how to shine.

February 2 – Imbolc (IM-bolk) or **Candlemas** (CAN-dl-miss)
This is the feast of the torches, also known as Bridget's Day. We bid our Lady return from the darkness, and light the flames so She may see the way. The colors of Candlemas are red and white; plants are roses, cherries, and apples. This is the night that we light all the candles in the house!

Spring Equinox (March 20-23) **– Eostar** (Easter or e-O-star) or **Ostara** (o-STAR-a)
This is the festival of spring, when we welcome the Goddess back from her place of rest and ask Her blessings for new growth in the coming year. The colors of Eostar are green, white, and silver; plants are all spring flowers and seeds. Colored eggs are exchanged now, to wish each other the joy and continuance of life that are inherent in an egg.

May 1 – Beltane (BELL-tane)

This is May Eve, the festival of fertility, when invocations and dances are performed to ensure bountiful crops and the continued fertility of all nature (including humans!). This is the time when the God and the Goddess meet as lovers, and He gives the governing of the year to Her until Samhain. The entire rainbow is associated with Beltane, as are all flowers, garlands, trees, and fresh leaves. This is when we dance together around the Maypole.

Summer Solstice (June 20-23) – **Litha** (LITH-a)

This is the festival of summer, when we dance and make merry magic in thanks for the crops growing, and the abundance of nature. This is when light is at its peak, when the day is longest. The color of Litha is green, and plants associated with this day are roses, vines, and leaves. Traditionally, this celebration begins at sunup, and continues throughout the short night. It is also traditional to invite the Fay to this celebration.

August 1 – Lughnassad (LOU-na-saad) or **Lammas** (LA-miss)

This is the festival of the corn, when the first fruits of the harvest are brought in, and in the fields the grain is ripe but not yet harvested. We rejoice in the gifts of the Great Mother. Colors for Lammas are green, yellow, and red. Plants are corn, grains, tomatoes, berries, and flowers. Since this is the first harvest, this is day is given to thanking the Corn God, and eating all the corn that we possibly can!

Fall Equinox (September 20-23) – **Mabon** (MAY-bon)

This is harvest-home, when the crops have been gathered. We give thanks for the Lady's abundance, and feast on the plentiful food. The colors of Mabon are orange, brown, yellow, and red. All crops are associated with this festival, as are the brilliant fall leaves. Traditionally, this is a day of feasting. In our tradition, we sometimes have to put Tums in the libation bowl after this one, so the Gods won't get indigestion!

With these festivals, we celebrate the turning of the Wheel of the Year, the continuance of life and the dance of the Earth around the Sun.

Traditionally, the colors and plants attributed to the holiday are used in the decorations; legends that mark the turning are told, and seasonal foods are eaten. This is also the time to do magic that helps the Wheel to turn, and to take advantage of the turning to plant or harvest things in our own lives, and thank the Gods for the things that they have done for us.

Tarrochi, or Trionfi, or Tarrock, or Tarot is a trick-taking game, like bridge or whist, played with the 78 card Tarot deck. (*Tricks*, by the way, are all the cards played in one round; one per player. The player with the highest card gets to put all of the cards into his *Trick Pile*.)

Originally the Trumps, known in occult circles as The Major Arcana, had no numbers. The order had to be memorized by the players.

The numbered cards from the four suits, which formed the original ordinary card deck, are played numerically, with 10 being highest and Ace lowest in the suits of Swords and Batons, and Ace being highest and 10 lowest in the suits of Cups and Coins. (You can ignore this rule if you want to; but it's historic.)

The court cards are played with King highest and Page lowest in all suits.

The Trumps are played with 21 highest and 1 lowest, except that Judgement (20) outranks the World (21.) The Fool has no number, doesn't take tricks. We'll get more into that later.

Three of the Trumps are worth card points. These are the Magician (#1, also called *The Petite*) the World (#21) and the Fool. They are called *Oulders*, perhaps because they are at both ends of the Trump cards. They are worth 5 points, and having them changes how many points you need to win.

The game is played with four players. One deals, and then there is *Bidding* to determine who is the *Declarer*. Everyone else teams up as *Defenders* to try to beat that one, so it's always three against one.

Everyone cuts the deck, and the low card deals. The dealer deals three cards at a time, face down, to the players. At some point he deals six cards to the table. (He has to, because 4 doesn't go evenly into 78.) These cards are known as the *Chein*. We would call it a "kitty," but the French call it a "Dog."

Players then organize the cards in their hands, and decide if they have a strong enough hand to win a lot of tricks. Based on this, they either bid or pass, starting at the Dealer's right. They may only bid once, and the one with the highest bid becomes the Declarer.

If anyone holds The Petite and no other Trump, he says so now, the cards are thrown in, and the player to the Dealer's right becomes the Dealer, and starts again.

The lowest possible bid is *Prise*, in which the player picks up the Chein, integrates it into his hand, and discards six cards face down. They begin his trick pile. He cannot discard any Trump cards if he has any other cards at all. In any case, he may never discard Oudlers or Kings. If he wins, he multiplies his card points by 1.

The next is *Garde*, just like Prise, but worth more. If he wins, he multiplies his card points by 2.

Then *Garde without Chien*, in which the player picks up the Chein, but doesn't use (or even look at) it. It goes straight into his trick pile. He multiplies by 4.

Highest is *Garde against Chien*, in which the Chien goes to the Defender's trick pile. (They don't look at them.) This one is multiplied by six, and cannot be out-bid.

If everyone passes, the cards are thrown in, and the deal goes to the next guy.

Before play starts, there are declarations that can be made. Anyone who has 10, 13, or 15 Trump cards in their hand can say so, and declare a *Bonus*. 10 Trump are a *Single Fist*, and are worth 20 points. 13 are a *Double Fist* and worth 30. 15 are a *Triple Fist* and worth 40. To declare a bonus, the player states which fist, and shows the cards. He doesn't have to do this, and he doesn't have to declare all the Trump he has; but if he shows the Fool, it implies that he has no other Trumps. To do this with other Trumps in the hand is dishonorable. Don't do it.

If the Declarer thinks she can win all the tricks, she may state this now. This is known as a *Chelem*. (Call it Slam.) If she declares it, and pulls it off, she gets 400 bonus points. If she declares and fails, she loses 200 points. If she doesn't declare, but still gets all the tricks, she gets 200 bonus points.

After declaring a Slam, she gets to lead the first card. Otherwise, the player to the dealer's right leads. Play proceeds counterclockwise.

The leading player places a card on the table. The next player must *Follow Suit*, that is play a card from the same suit, unless he doesn't have any. In that case, he must Trump if he can. The highest card takes the Trick. Trumps are higher than any of the other cards. (Non-Trump cards that don't follow suit are worthless.)

The only exception to this is the Fool. It can be played at any time, regardless of suit. It can't take any tricks, but the next player can play any suit he likes, and everyone else has to follow *his* suit! After the Trick is taken, the guy who played The Fool gives the winner a 1 point card from his Trick Pile, and gets the Fool back. Unless, that is, he waited too long, and has to play it on the last Trick. In that case, he loses it, and it's picked up with the other cards from the Trick.

The exception to *that* rule is if the Fool is held by the Declarer, and she called a Slam. Then, if she wins all the others, she keeps the Fool until the last trick, and it takes that one.

If Trump is led, then all subsequent players must play a higher Trump if they can, even if it means they are overtrumping someone on their own side.

Whoever wins the Trick leads the next Trick.

If the Petite (The Magician) is played on the last trick it's worth a bonus of 10 points to whoever wins that trick. This bonus is multiplied if the winner is the Declarer, and she keeps that bonus even if she doesn't win the hand. If she declared a Slam in the beginning, she can play the Petite on the next-to-last trick for the bonus.

Play continues until all the cards have been used. Then comes scoring. That's the hard part. If you want to make it even more challenging, the dealer can add an agreed-upon stake to the pot before he deals. If the Declarer wins the hand, she wins the pot. If she doesn't, she adds an equal stake to the pot, and it's carried over to the next hand.

The Declarer is the only one who totals the score in her trick pile. If she makes her *Contract*, the points she needed for the bid, then she is paid the value of the tricks from each Defender. If she doesn't, she pays the value to each of them.

So. She takes her Trick pile, including the Chien (if she has it.) Then she pairs off all the cards, with one scoring and one non-scoring card in each pair. If she runs out of scoring cards, she pairs non-scoring ones with each other. The scoring cards are; Kings and Oudlers, 5 points. Queens, 4 points. Knights, 3 points. Pages, 2 points. Non-scoring cards are worth one point per pair. So a Knight (3 points) and Death (non-scoring) are worth 3 points. But Death (non-scoring) and a 10 (non-scoring) are worth one point.

The number of points she needs is determined by the number of Oudlers that she has in her Trick Pile. If she has none, she needs to make 56 points. If one, 51 points. If 2, 41 points. If all 3, 36 points.

If the value of the cards in her Trick Pile exceeds the amount she needs, she wins the hand. If not, she loses it, and her final score will be a negative number.

Each hand is worth 25 base points. To determine the value of the hand, the Declarer adds the base points to the number above *or* below what was needed to win. The total is then multiplied by the multiplier for her bid.

For example, say she bid Guard against Chien, which has a multiplier of 6. She took 9 tricks, and got The Magician, The World, 2 Kings, 2 Queens, 3 Knights, a Page, and 26 non-scoring cards. Pairing them off, she has The Magician (5) + the World (5) + 2 Kings (5X2=10) + 2 Queens (4X2=8) + 3 Knights (3X3=9) + 1 Page (2) + 8 pairs of non-scoring cards (8) for a grand total of 47 card points. With two Oudlers (The Magician and the World) she needed to make 41 points. She made it, with 6 to spare, so she wins! The base hand is worth 25 points, and she had 6 more than she needed, so the value of this hand is 31 points. (25+6.) Since she bid Guard against Chien, which has a multiplier of 6, she multiplies 31 by 6 to get 186. The total value is 186 points.

So each Defender must give her 186 points, subtracting this from their game total. Their scores all go down by 186 points, and hers goes up by 558 points. (186X3.)

If she been 6 points short, instead of six points over, the math would have been the same; but she would be losing 558 points, and each Defender would gain 186.

Bonuses (except the one for the Petite in the last trick) are added to the score after the multiplication. So if she declared a single fist bonus (20 points) at the beginning, the Defenders would each pay her 206 points (186+20) and her total score for that hand would be 618 points (206X3.)

Play continues until the players agree to stop. The one with the highest score at the end wins the game.

I'm grateful to Han Morrow Scott, who generously gave me much of the material used to prepare this chapter. Thanks!

This is the history of my deck, in pictures, for anyone who is interested. I'll warn you before we begin, though, that I draw *much* better now than I did when I started! By the same token, these should give heart to any aspiring artists. If I can get where I am now from where I was then, there is hope for anyone!

I mention in the text that I began by sending three pictures to Llewellyn. Here they are. Bear in mind that when I drew these, I hadn't even begun to study the Tarot itself. I'm no longer sure why I did these, but it must have seemed like a good idea at the time!

When I actually began to draw the cards in earnest, I started with the Fool, as I've mentioned before. Here is that first sketch, and the painting on the blank card that came from it. As you can see, the design never changed much; what I wanted on the card at this point remained what I thought should be on it. But the drawing improved!

The Lovers, on the other hand, changed quite a bit!

If you look at the previous page, that was the first incarnation, when I had only seen the Rider-Waite deck, and before I really understood what the card meant. By the time I was painting the little cards, it had developed into the design below. And by the time I did the Tarot Coloring Book, it looked like the one on the right.

It was after that that I did the following illustration for a magazine article. And I liked the image of balance so well that I decided to modify it a bit, and use it in the Lovers card.

And that's how I came up with the card that is in the deck now.

In the text I also mentioned other cards that changed. There isn't room to show you all of them here, but I thought you might be interested in seeing some of them!

The Empress, for example, went from an almost completely passive card where the Empress was just sitting there with her hands folded, to the current one, where she is pregnant and spinning. This is what she looked like in the first card, which showed up in the Tarot Coloring Book. (By this time, of course, she had already been drawn and re-drawn several times. But I think you've seen enough of the very bad early drawings!)

Along with her, I'm showing you The Devil from the same era. If you look closely, you'll notice that I hadn't yet put an actual drawing of the Monkey Trap on the chest, although the idea was already there. I also hadn't yet decided to put the two figures facing in opposite directions. They were pulling at odds with each other, but that wasn't as obvious as it would become. I also hadn't made the things in the chest as clear as I later would.

The court cards all changed. I started with all of the Kings and Queens seated, and then decided to have them stand in the suits of wands and swords, since those correspond to fire and air, and they are active elements. Having the Rulers on their feet just seemed to me to emphasize that more; and since I was still having problems figuring out where the Court Cards fit in, I needed all the help I could get! So here are the three Queens who really changed as the deck evolved.

The Queen of Pentacles didn't change much. The others really got a boost when Animal X posed for them!

Another card that got help from Animal was the World. Although Animal herself didn't pose for that one, it was at a party at her home that I met a young woman who was a dancer. I was struggling with the leaping figure for the World at that point, and when I found that she knew dance, I said, "You can dance! Take your clothes off! Put this leotard on! Now hold these two candles, and do leaps down the driveway please ..." And she did, and the World got a facelift!

Here is the first sketch for the World, when I was still going to use symbols instead of just using the wreath with scenes featuring the elements in the corners. And, again, the card that eventually made it into the Tarot Coloring Book.

And, finally, here are two back designs that Llewellyn rejected. The one on the left is the spiral that I liked so well. The one on the right is the original knotwork that changed when the size of the card changed by a sixteenth of an inch!

Abraham, Sylvia *How to Read the Tarot* ©1994 by Sylvia Abraham. Llewellyn Publications, St. Paul, MN. ISBN 1-56718-001-9

Arnold, Peter *The Book of Games* ©1985 by Peter Arnold. Exter Books, NY, NY

Bullfinch, Thomas *Bullfinch's Mythology* (with Introduction, Notes and Bibliography by Richard P. Martin) ©1991 by HarperCollins Publishers. HarperCollins Publishers, New York. ISBN 0-06-270189-4

Clayton, Peter *Great Figures of Mythology* ©1990 by Brompton Books Corp. Brompton Books Corp. Greenwich, CT. ISBN 0-517-00538-7

Connolly, Eileen *Tarot; a Workbook for the Apprentice* ©1979 by Eileen Connolly. Newcastle Books, North Hollywood, CA ISBN 0-87877-045-3

Crossley-Holland, Kevin *The Norse Myths* ©1980 by Kevin Crossley-Holland. Pantheon Books, Random House, Inc. New York, NY. ISBN 0-394-74846-8

Decker, Ronald, Depaulis, Thierry, & Dummett, Michael *A Wicked Pack of Cards - The Origins of the Occult Tarot* ©1996 by Ronald Decker, Thierry Depaulis, & Michael Dummett. St. Martin's Press, Scholarly and Reference Division New York, NY. ISBN: 0-312-16294-4

Doane, Doris Chase and Keyes, King *How to Read Tarot Cards* ©1967 by Doris Chase Doane. Harper & Row, New York, NY. ISBN 0-06-463481-7

Erdoes, Richard and Ortiz, Alfonso *American Indian Myths and Legends* ©1984 by Richard Erdoes and Alfonso Ortiz. Pantheon Books, Random House, Inc. New York, NY. ISBN 0-394-74018-1

Fenton, Sasha *Fortune-Telling by Tarot Cards – A Beginner's Guide to Understanding the Future Using Tarot Cards.* ©1985 by Sasha Fenton. Aquarian Press, Wellingborough, Northamptonshire, England. ISBN 0-85030-445-8

Gearhart, Sally and Rennie, Susan *A Feminist Tarot* ©1981 by Sally Gearhart and Susan Rennie, Alyson Publications, Inc., Boston, MA first published by Persephone Press ISBN 0-932870-56-2

Gerulskis-Estes, Susan *The Book of Tarot* ©1981 by Morgan & Morgan, Inc. Morgan & Morgan Inc., Dobbs Ferry, NY. ISBN 0-87100-172-1

Giles, Cynthia *The Tarot: History, Mystery and Lore* ©1992 by Cynthia Giles. Paragon House, New York, NY. ISBN 1-557788-312-8

Gray, Eden *Mastering the Tarot, Basic Lessons in an Ancient, Mystic Art* ©1971 by Eden Gray. Signet Books, New York, NY.

Grolier *The New Grolier Multimedia Encyclopedia Release 6* ©1993 by Grolier Inc., Danbury, CT ISBN 07172-3966-7

Kaplan, Stuart *The Encyclopedia of Tarot, Vol. I* ©1978 by Stuart R. Kaplan. US Games Systems, New York, NY. ISBN 0-91386-611-3

Louis, Anthony *Tarot Plain and Simple* ©1996 by Anthony Lewis. Llewellyn Publications, St. Paul, MN ISBN 1-56718-400-6

MacDonald, George *The Princess and Curdie* First published in 1882. Published by Penguin Books, Ltd. Middlesex, England 1971. Now available in Puffin edition, ISBN 0140367624

Matthews, Caitlín *The Elements of the Celtic Tradition* ©1989 by Caitlín Matthews. Element Books, Ltd. Longmead, Shaftesbury, Dorset, England ISBN 1-85230-075-2

Mohr, Merilyn Simonds *The New Games Treasury* ©1993, 1997 by Merilyn Simonds Mohr. Houghton Mifflin Co. New York, NY ISBN 1-57630-058-7

Murry, Liz and Colin *The Celtic Tree Oracle, A System of Divination* ©1988 by Liz and Colin Murray. St. Martin's Press, New York. ISBN 0-312-02032-5

Roberts, Richard *The Original Tarot & You* ©1971, 1987 by Richard Roberts. Vernal Equinox Press, San Anselmo CA. ISBN 0-942380-06-1

Walker, Barbara G. *The Secrets of the Tarot Origins, History and Symbolism* ©1994 by Barbara G. Walker. Harper & Row, New York, NY. ISBN: 0-06-250927-6

I am also indebted to the hundreds of Seekers and Readers who, through thousands of discussions at Festivals, Conventions, and Gatherings, have taught me so much.

I am currently writing the Workbook that will be the companion for this volume. In it, I plan to have a detailed discussion of how to read the Tarot, including a number of spreads that I have developed, or collected, over the years, and a section about how to design your own spreads!

In order to have as wide a variety of spreads as possible, however, I'm currently soliciting original spreads. If you have a spread that you have invented, and you would like to share it, please send it to me by the end of February 1999, at:

Robin Wood   3319 Greenfield Rd. #102   Dearborn, MI 48120

or e-mail me at:

spreads@robinwood.com

In return for your generosity, I will credit you, and send you a copy of the Workbook when it comes out. And you will retain the rights to your own spread, of course.

Thank you!

Robin Wood began studying the Craft in 1979, and was initiated in 1980. As she learned more, she began to realize just how much there was to learn; and she became fascinated with the Tarot, and the symbolic language that it represents, as well as the patterns that it reveals.

Since none of the decks that she could find suited her, she started to design her own in 1981. At first it was just for herself.

She began illustrating books for Llewellyn in 1983, doing dozens before she wandered off to do other things. It was during that time that she mentioned to the Art Director at Llewellyn that she had drawn part of a Tarot Deck, and they decided to publish it. But that story is told in this book.

In 1993 she contracted Fibromyalgia, an interesting little syndrome that makes you feel as if you have the flu for the rest of your life. Since the FMS and its attendant muscle aches and cramps made it difficult to continue drawing, Robin turned her attention to other things. She felt compelled to write anyway, so that's what she did.

Her first book, *When, Why ...If, an Ethics Workbook*, was published in 1997, and was a success. (A number of places have made it required reading.)

After that, Robin found it difficult to maintain the fiction that she can't do anything but draw; honest. So she gave in to a decade of pressure, and wrote this book too. But all of that is in the Foreword.

Now she plans to sit around, and play with the 3-D programs on her trusty Macintosh. I mean, she plans to continue her writing. Next in line is a workbook that will be a companion to this one, concentrating on how to actually read the cards, and exploring spreads and how to invent them. After that, she plans a book on either Pagan Philosophy or Pagan Etiquette. (Most of the people she meets are rooting for the etiquette book!) She also plans to continue going to shows and festivals, of course, with her wonderful husband, Michael Short.

Robin Wood Online!

Robin has a webpage!

http://www.robinwood.com

If you enjoyed this book, and are interested in more of Robin's work, she has a whole catalog of stuff posted on the Net!

Prints of her artwork, disks full of fonts and clipart, all the books she has written, The Robin Wood Tarot; an abundant and wonderful selection of beautiful things! All for sale, there at **robinwood.com**

Or, if you like, you are invited to visit her on-line Pagan Grove! There she posts answers to Frequently Asked Questions about the Craft, the Tarot, Ethics, and many other topics of interest to Pagans (or you can write and ask her your own questions!)

She also has free GIFs and JPEGs for you to use in making your own site (with permission) and a visual treat of things to enjoy, words to comfort, rites to celebrate the turning of the Wheel, and much, much more.

So Visit the Grove at **http://www.robinwood.com/Livingtree.html**

Meet Robin in Person!

Her schedule is posted on her webpage.

http://www.robinwood.com/Schedule.html

The Robin Wood Tarot

78 card Tarot Deck

A colorful Tarot designed from a Wiccan viewpoint. Every card in both the Major and Minor Arcana thoughtfully and carefully drawn.

It's the deck this book was written about. So if you enjoyed the book, but don't have a copy of the deck, you might want to get one!

I have not met a Pagan who didn't like this deck ...a lot!

Shahara LeFay

A wonderful Tarot deck. *The Robin Wood Tarot* deck is one of the easiest for beginners to use. Its vivid natural imagery fosters an intuitive awareness that aids with interpreting the cards. It is one of my favorite decks and the one I chose to illustrate my book *Tarot Plain and Simple*. (Llewellyn, 1996)

Anthony Louis, Tarot Plain and Simple

The Robin Wood Tarot is a singularly beautiful deck. Because of its clarity in illustration, this is the deck I use for examples in my classes.

Katherine Keene, Body Mind and Soul Books

...psychically one of the easiest decks to attune to I've ever used. The vivid colors and subtle shading enhance the Reader's ability to pick up on things, as does the use of symbolism as mnemonic devices. It's my favorite deck.

Carey Hall, Reader

78 Full color cards in a clamshell box, with instruction booklet. 2³/₄" x 4⁵/₈"

To get your copy, send $19.95 + $5.00 shipping and handling to
Robin Wood   3319 Greenfield Rd. #102   Dearborn Hts., MI   48120
We take Visa, MasterCard, American Express, Discover, Checks and MOs.

When, Why ...If

An Ethics Workbook

Explores the question of Ethics from a Pagan/Wiccan perspective, and leads the reader on a quest to define their own personal ethical system.

This book has been made required reading by dozens of groups across the country.

...One of the most important books ever written for the benefit of the Pagan and Wiccan community...
Cate Dalton, CraftWise

...Begins where Starhawk leaves off.
Pete Pathfinder, ATC

...A thoughtful exploration of ethics for those not fortunate enough to find a mentor to explain such things in person...this book offers guidance from an experienced viewpoint in a confident yet gentle tone.
Elizabeth Barrette, in PanGaia Magazine

SIX thumbs up – *Vishnu, in Jules Magazine*

This book should be required reading for everyone who is starting magickal study. It also is perfect as an occasional refresher for everyone already practicing.
Morning Wren, in Jules Magazine

Robin's writing is clear, concise, and quite entertaining.
Magdalene O'Brien in the Wiccan Read

Paperback, 208 pages. 5¹/₂" x 8¹/₂" Full color cover.

To get your copy, send $12.95 + $5.00 shipping and handling to
Robin Wood   3319 Greenfield Rd. #102   Dearborn Hts., MI   48120
We take Visa, MasterCard, American Express, Discover, Checks and MOs.